AMERICAN INDIAN QUOTATIONS

Compiled and Edited by Howard J. Langer

Greenwood Press
Westport, Connecticut • London

Library of Congress Cataloging-in-Publication Data

American Indian quotations / compiled and edited by Howard J. Langer.
    p. cm.
    Includes index.
    ISBN 0–313–29121–7 (alk. paper)
    1. Indians of North America—Quotations. 2. Indians of North
America—History. I. Langer, Howard.
    PN6081.4.A43   1996
    973'.0497—dc20   95–33151

British Library Cataloguing in Publication Data is available.

Library of Congress Catalog Card Number: 95–33151
ISBN: 0–313–29121–7

First published in 1996

Greenwood Press, 88 Post Road West, Westport, CT 06881
An imprint of Greenwood Publishing Group, Inc.

Printed in the United States of America

The paper used in this book complies with the
Permanent Paper Standard issued by the National
Information Standards Organization (Z39.48–1984).

10 9 8 7 6 5 4 3 2 1

AMERICAN INDIAN QUOTATIONS

For my grandsons, Alexander and Matthew

Contents

Illustrations   xi

Acknowledgments   xiii

Introduction   xvii

American Indian Quotations   1

Anonymous Quotations, Prayers, and Proverbs   199

Author Index   221

Subject and Key Word Index   225

Tribe Index   259

Illustrations

Cornplanter 12

Black Hawk 18

John Ross 28

The Four Bears 35

Osceola 39

Washakie 42

Dull Knife 48

Ouray the Arrow 54

Red Cloud 57

Spotted Tail 59

Ely Parker 63

Ponca Indians skinning a buffalo 66

Sitting Bull 73

Kicking Bird 75

Captain Jack 80

Quanah Parker 87

Medicine man killed at Wounded Knee   *95*

Jim Thorpe   *120*

Ira Hayes   *139*

Ben Nighthorse Campbell   *156*

W. Richard West, Jr.   *175*

Wilma Mankiller   *180*

Acknowledgments

First of all, I would like to acknowledge the assistance of my wife, Florence. It is a cliche to use the phrase, "without whose help this book would not have been possible." It is certainly no exaggeration in this case. She has been not only my chief researcher, but also my driver, critic, cheerleader, and best friend.

At Greenwood, I want to thank Bob Hagelstein, Jim Sabin, and especially my editor, Cynthia Harris.

The Ramapo Catskill Library System enabled me to obtain books and documents from many sources. I am most grateful to the staff of the New City (Rockland County, N.Y.) Public Library, as well as the Huntington Library in the Bronx, New York. In addition, I worked with the Spring Valley (N.Y.) Public Library, the West Point Library, and the Seneca Nation Library.

I am grateful to the following organizations: the National Museum of the American Indian (New York City), the Bureau of Indian Affairs, the Federal Bureau of Investigation, the Oklahoma Historical Society, and the National Indian Health Board.

Also, I am grateful to the following individuals: U.S. Senator Ben Campbell, Dr. Duane King, Gaetana DeGennaro, Laurance D. Linford of the Inter-Tribal Indian Ceremonial Association, Ruth Ziolkowski of the Crazy Horse Memorial Foundation, Dr. Wil Rose of the American Indian Heritage Foundation, Hap Gilliland of the Montana Council for Indian Education, Marilyn Roberts, Wilma Mankiller, Peter Matthiessen, Harvey Arden, Delores McAuliffe, Robert Robideau, Daniel Peaches, and Harold Foster.

Authors who had the greatest influence on me were Vine Deloria, Jr., Dee Brown, Peter Matthiessen, and Alexander Posey.

In addition to the usual encyclopedia sources, dates, places, and tribal names were checked out with such sources as *Who Was Who in Native American History,* by Carl Waldman (Facts on File, 1990), *The Native North American Almanac,* by Duane Champagne (Gale Research, 1994), *Great North American Indians: Profiles in Life and Leadership,* by Frederick J. Dockstader (Van Nostrand Reinhold, 1977), and *Reference Encyclopedia of the American Indian,* by Barry T. Klein (Todd Publications, 1993).

I want to thank all those who sent along newspaper and magazine clippings, books, and video cassettes on Native American history.

Finally, a special note of thanks to Tom Maguire.

They will be powerful people, strong, tough. They will fly up into the sky, they will dig under the earth, they will drain the earth and kill it. All over the earth they will kill the trees and the grass, they will put their own grass and their own hay, but the earth will be dead—all the old trees and grass and animals.

Fred Last Bull
(Cheyenne, undated)

(*Cheyenne Memories*, by John Stands in Timber and Margot Liberty, Yale University Press, 1967.)

So tractable, so peaceable, are these people that I swear to your Majesties there is not in the world a better nation. They love their neighbors as themselves, and their discourse is ever sweet and gentle, and accompanied with a smile, and though it is true that they are naked, yet their manners are decorous and praiseworthy.

Christopher Columbus
(Letter to Ferdinand and Isabella, 1493)

You will do well to try to inoculate the Indians by means of blankets in which smallpox patients have slept, as well as by every other method that can serve to extirpate this execrable race. I should be very glad if your scheme of hunting them down by dogs could take effect.

General Jeffrey Amherst
(Letter to a subordinate, 1732)

(*Great Documents in American Indian History*, edited by Wayne Moquin with Charles Van Doren, Praeger, 1973.)

Introduction

It is a common complaint that we do not know very much about "American" history. When this is said, it usually refers to the history of Europeans in America.

If that criticism is valid, what can be said about our knowledge of the history of Native American Indians—millions of whom lived here many centuries before Columbus outfitted the *Niña,* the *Pinta,* and the *Santa María?*

For years, Americans learned about Indians from stereotyped images: so-called Wild West Shows, lurid newspaper accounts, and Western movies. Invariably, the Indian was the bad guy. That image has slowly been changing. Movies such as *Dances with Wolves,* television series on Indian history, and the opening of new national Indian museums have created a greater interest and awareness of Native American culture, ideas, and values.

There is certainly a greater sensitivity to the major trends in Native American history: the massive invasion from Europe, the stolen lands, and the violated treaties.

What has been missing from our newly acquired knowledge is the human element: men and women fighting for their values, their culture, their religion—indeed, their very civilization.

In looking back at our past, we often think of history in terms of individuals. We remember Patrick Henry choosing "liberty or death," Abraham Lincoln promising "a new birth of freedom," Franklin Roosevelt challenging that "this generation of Americans has a rendezvous with destiny."

Quotations are powerful. They are the building blocks of popular history: "Don't shoot until you see the whites of their eyes," "this nation cannot endure half-slave and half-free," "ask not what your country can do for you." The words breathe life into past history, giving it a relevance and dignity we cannot get from names, dates, and places. There are loads of books of American quotations: historical, social, political, literary, humorous, cynical, and satirical. Few American Indians, with such rare exceptions as Chief Joseph and Will Rogers, ever make it into *Bartlett's*. This volume is an attempt to fill that void.

There is much worth quoting. American Indians also have their leaders and orators, their writers and doctors, their poets and warriors, their historians and satirists.

This book is a compilation of some 800 quotations, going back to the mid-sixteenth century. The quotes appear in chronological sequence, giving the reader the opportunity to follow Native American history from the appearance of the white man in the New World. Because there was no written Indian language until the nineteenth century, most of the early quotations are based on the translations of white interpreters. How do we know they are reasonably accurate? We know because certain themes and viewpoints emerge time and again over several centuries, among different tribes, in different regions of the country.

An extensive index—broken down by author, tribe, and subject/key word—will enable the reader to locate quotations by specific individuals about specific topics.

The quotations in this book represent only a tiny fraction of Indian history—only 450 of at least 10,000 and possibly 50,000 years in America. Several hundred Native Americans are quoted, many famous, others less well-known.

Anonymous quotations, including prayers and proverbs, appear in a separate section. A few anonymous quotes do appear in the main section in their chronological sequence. These quotes came from organized groups of Native Americans that issued statements as organization viewpoints. For example, "Indians of All Tribes" was the group that occupied Alcatraz Island, giving specific reasons for its action.

The sources do not always agree on such facts as dates, places of birth, spellings of names, and tribal identifications. For example, the Lakota and the Apache nations have different tribes. The tribe most commonly identified with the individual is the one given here. The dates and places are the ones most historians seem to agree on.

On the matter of quotation source, the original source is given wherever possible, rather than the secondary source. The most serious problem is one of historical interpretation: good guy versus bad guy, sellout versus recognition of inevitability, battle victory versus massacre. I have attempted to play this as straight as possible, most often just letting the facts speak for themselves.

Although every effort has been made to track down factual information, some information was not available as this book went to press. Additions and corrections are welcomed for subsequent editions.

Please Note: Following the name of an individual, the letters *q.v.* (*quod vide*) refer the reader to a separate entry for that individual elsewhere in the book. This entry can be found using the author index.

American Indian Quotations

SWEET MEDICINE

(Undated)

Cheyenne

Sweet Medicine has been described as a cultural hero of the Cheyenne, who may have been based on a real person.

1. There is a time coming ... when many things will change. Strangers called Earth Men will appear among you. Their skins are light-colored, and their ways are powerful. They speak no Indian tongue. Follow nothing that these Earth Men do, but keep your own ways that I have taught you as long as you can. (*Cheyenne Memories,* by John Stands in Timber and Margot Liberty, Yale University Press, 1967.)

2. The buffalo will disappear, at last, and another animal will take its place, a slick animal with a long tail and split hoofs, whose flesh you will learn to eat. But first there will be another animal you must learn to use. It has a shaggy neck and a tail almost touching the ground. Its hoofs are round. This animal will carry you on his back and help you in many ways. Those far hills that seem only a blue vision in the distance take many days to reach now, but with this animal you can get there in a short time, so fear him not. (Ibid.)

3. Those people will wander this way ... they will be looking for a certain stone. ... These people will not listen to what you say; what they are going to do they will do. You people will change: ... They will tear up the earth, and at last you will do it with them. When you do, you will become crazy, and will forget all that I am teaching you. (*In the Spirit of Crazy Horse,* by Peter Matthiessen, Viking, 1983.)

POWHATAN

(1547–1618)

Powhatan, Virginia

Powhatan was the leader of the Powhatan Confederacy at the time of the first English settlement in America at Jamestown, Virginia.

4. Why should you take by force that from us which you can have by love? Why should you destroy us, who have provided you with food? What can you get by war? We can hide our provisions, and fly into the woods; and then you must consequently famish by wronging your friends. What is the cause of your jealousy? You see us unarmed, and willing to supply your wants, if you will come in a friendly manner, and not with swords and guns, as to invade an enemy. (Address to John Smith, ca. 1609, *Biography and History of the Indians of North America*, by Samuel G. Drake, 11th ed., Boston, 1841.)

5. I, therefore, exhort you to peaceable counsels, and, above all, I insist the guns and swords, the cause of all our jealousy and uneasiness, be removed and sent away. (Ibid.)

6. I am not so simple as not to know that it is better to eat good meat, be well, and sleep quietly with my women and children, to laugh and be merry with the English, and, being their friend, to have copper hatchets and whatever else I want, than to fly from all, to lie cold in the woods, feed upon acorns and roots . . . and to be so hunted that I cannot rest, eat, or sleep, and so, in this miserable manner, to end my miserable life; and, Captain Smith, this might soon be your fate too, through your rashness. (*Our Indian Wards*, by George W. Manypenny, Clarke & Co., 1880.)

KING PHILIP

(1620–1676)

Wampanoag, Massachusetts?

King Philip was the son of Massasoit, who had helped the Pilgrims when they arrived in the New World. In 1671 the English colonists in Massachusetts asked King Philip for a new peace treaty, one in which the Indians would have to turn over their guns. In 1675 King Philip called on other tribes in the area to join in a war against the whites. King Philip's War began in January 1675. Many towns were attacked by the Indians, and King Philip was killed in battle.

7. Your governor is but a subject of King Charles of England. I shall not treat with a subject. I shall treat of peace only with the King, my brother. When he comes, I am ready. (ca. 1674, spoken to a messenger sent by Governor Winslow to discuss a peace treaty.)

TAHAJADORIS

(Seventeenth century)

Mohawk

Tahajadoris was a Mohawk leader. In 1689 he was urged by English colonists in Massachusetts and Connecticut to go to war against the Abenakis. The colonists argued that the Abenakis would ally themselves with the French, whom the Mohawks despised. This was his response.

8. We patiently bore many injuries from the French, from one year to another, before we took up the axe against them. Our patience made the governor of Canada think that we were afraid of him, and dared not resent the injuries we have so long suffered, but now he is undeceived. We assure you that we are resolved never to drop the axe; the French

shall never see our faces in peace, we shall never be reconciled as long as one Frenchman is alive. We shall never make peace, though our nation should be ruined by it, and every one of us cut in pieces. (*Red & White: Indian Views of the White Man,* by Annette Rosenstiel, Universe Books, 1983.)

9. As to what you told us of the Owenagungas [Abenakis] and Uragees [Mahicans], we answer that we were never so proud and haughty, as to begin a war without just provocation. You tell us that they are treacherous rogues—we believe it—and that they will undoubtedly assist the French. If they shall do this, or shall join with any of our enemies, either French or Indians, then we shall kill and destroy them. (Ibid.)

TEEDYUSCUNG

(1700?–1763)

Delaware, New Jersey

Teedyuscung was a Delaware chieftain who, at various times, fought against or negotiated with Indians and whites. He finally supported the British during the French and Indian War.

10. All their chiefs and all their warriors have made themselves as one man, and formed their hands to our peace, and promise never to break it, but to hold the peace belt fast. (Report of his trip to speak to other Delaware tribes; remarks were made to members of the Governor's Council in Philadelphia, 1760. *Colonial Records of Pennsylvania,* vol. 8.)

CONASSATEGO

(Early to mid-eighteenth century)

Iroquois

Conassatego gave this response to a 1744 invitation from Maryland and Virginia commissioners. They asked him to send a dozen Indian boys to the College of William and Mary for formal education.

11. We know that you highly esteem the kind of learning taught in those Colleges, and that the Maintenance of our young Men, while with you, would be very expensive to you. We are convinced that you mean to do us Good by your Proposal, and we thank you heartily. But you, who are wise must know that different Nations have different Conceptions of things and you will therefore not take it amiss, if our ideas of this kind of Education happen not to be the same as yours. (*Biography and History of the Indians of North America,* 3d ed., by Samuel G. Drake, Perkins and Hillard, Gray & Co., 1834.)

12. We have had some experience of it. Several of our young People were formerly brought up at the Colleges of the Northern Provinces, where they were instructed in all your Sciences; but, when they came back they were bad Runners, ignorant of every means of living in the woods . . . neither fit for Hunters, Warriors, nor Counsellors, they were totally good for nothing. (Ibid.)

13. We are, however, not the less obliged by your kind offer, tho' we decline accepting it; and, to show our grateful Sense of it, if the Gentlemen of Virginia will send us a dozen of their sons, we will take Care of their Education, instruct them in all we know, and make Men of them. (Ibid.)

OLD TASSEL

(?–1788)

Cherokee

Old Tassel, also known as Corn Tassel, was a Cherokee chief.

14. It is surprising that when we enter into treaties with our fathers the white people, their whole cry is more land. Indeed it has seemed a formality with them to demand what they know we dare not refuse. (1780s; *Old Frontiers,* by John P. Brown, Kingsport, Tenn., 1938.)

15. Much has been said of . . . what you term "civilization" among the Indians. Many proposals have been made to us to adopt your laws, your religions, your manners, and your customs. . . . You say, "Why do not the Indians till the ground and live as we do?" May we not ask . . . , "Why do not the white people hunt and live as we do?" (Ibid.)

16. We do not quarrel with you for the killing of an occasional buffalo or deer in our lands, but . . . it is very criminal in our young men if they chance to kill a cow or a hog for their sustenance when they happen to be in your lands. (Ibid.)

17. The Great Spirit has given you many advantages, but he has not created us to be your slaves. . . . He has stocked your lands with cows, ours with buffalo; yours with hogs, ours with bears; yours with sheep, ours with deer. He has given you the advantage that your animals are tame, while ours are wild and demand not only a larger space for range, but art to hunt and kill them. They are, nevertheless, as much our property as other animals are yours, and ought not to be taken from us without our consent. (Ibid.)

PONTIAC

(1720–1769)

Ottawa, Ohio

Pontiac and his people lived peacefully in the Great Lakes area when it was largely controlled by the French. During the French and Indian War, Pontiac led an Algonquin force against the British. In 1763 France made peace with Britain. Pontiac later tried to get help from the British so his people could hunt for food. In 1769 he either died in a fight or was murdered by a hired assassin.

18. I mean to destroy the English and leave not one upon our lands. (1763; *The Conspiracy of Pontiac and the Indian War after the Conquest of Canada*, by Francis Parkman, 1851.)

19. Father, be strong and take pity on us, your children, as our former Father did. 'Tis the hunting season of your children. Our Fathers, the French, formerly used to credit his children for powder and lead to hunt with. I request in behalf of all the nations present that you will speak to the traders now here to do the same. My Father, once more I request you will take pity on us, and tell your traders to give your children credit for a little powder and lead, as the support of our families depend upon it. (A meeting with British representatives at Fort Detroit, 1765; *Collections of the Illinois State Historical Society*, vol. 11.)

LOGAN

(1725–1780)

Mingo, Pennsylvania

Logan was a Mingo leader during Lord Dunmore's War.

20. I appeal to any white man to say if ever he entered Logan's cabin hungry and I gave him not meat, if ever he came cold or naked and I gave him not clothing. (Message to Lord Dunmore, 1774; "Tah-Gah-Jute or Logan and Captain Cresap," by Brentz Mayer, Maryland Historical Society, 1851.)

21. During the course of the last long and bloody war Logan remained in his hut an advocate for peace; nay, such was my love for the whites, that those of my own country pointed at me as they passed by, and said, "Logan is the friend of white men"; I have even thought to live with you, but for the injuries of one man, Colonel [Captain Michael] Cresap, the last spring, in cool blood and unprovoked cut off all the relations of Logan not even sparing my women and children. (Ibid.)

22. There runs not a drop of my blood in the veins of any human creature. This called on me for revenge. I have sought it. I have killed many. I have fully glutted my vengeance. (Ibid.)

23. For my country I rejoice in the beams of peace; but do not harbor the thought that mine is the joy of fear. Logan never felt fear. He will not turn on his heel to save his life. (Ibid.)

24. Who is there to mourn for Logan? Not one. (Ibid.)

DRAGGING-CANOE

(1730?–1792)

Cherokee, Tennessee

Dragging-Canoe was a Cherokee chief who fought attempts of the whites to buy tribal lands. In 1775 he spoke out against a treaty to sell such lands. He sided with the British during the American Revolution.

25. Whole nations have melted away like balls of snow before the sun. (Address to the Cherokee council, 1775; *The Wilderness Road*, by Robert L. Kincaid, Bobbs-Merrill, 1947.)

26. The whites have passed the mountains and settled upon Cherokee lands, and now wish to have their usurpation sanctioned by the confirmation of a treaty. New cessions will be required, and the small remnant of my people will be compelled to seek a new retreat in some far distant wilderness. There they will be permitted to stay only a short while, until they again behold the advancing banners of the same greedy host. (Ibid.)

27. When the whites are unable to point out any farther retreat for the miserable Cherokees, they will proclaim the extinction of the whole race. (Ibid.)

28. Should we not therefore run all risks, and incur all consequences, rather than submit to further laceration of our country? Such treaties may be all right for men too old to hunt or fight. As for me, I have my young warriors about me. We will have our lands. (Ibid.)

29. You will find the settlement of this land dark and bloody. (Speech, 1775; *Great North American Indians: Profiles in Life and Leadership,* by Frederick J. Dockstader, Van Nostrand and Reinhold, 1977.)

CORNPLANTER

(1736?–1836)

Seneca, New York

Cornplanter, a Seneca chief, fought on the French side during the French and Indian War and on the British side during the American Revolution. He later signed a number of treaties with the white man. On numerous occasions he appeared before the white man's councils to protest mistreatment of Indians.

30. In former days when you were young and weak, I used to call you brother, but now I call you father. (*Colonial Records of Pennsylvania,* vol. 16.)

31. I hope that you, the Fathers of the Quaker State, will fix some person at Fort Pitt to take care of me and my people. I wish, and it is the wish of my people if agreeable to you, that my present interpreter, Joseph Nicholson, may be the person, as I and my people have a confidence in him, and are satisfied that he will always exert himself to preserve peace and harmony between you and us. My reasons for

"In former days when you were young and weak I used to call you brother, but now I call you father."

—CORNPLANTER, SENECA

wishing an interpreter there, are that often times when my hunters and people come there, their canoes and other things are stolen, and they can obtain no redress, not having any person there on whom they can rely to interpret for them and see justice done to them. (Ibid.)

LITTLE TURTLE

(1747?–1812)

Miami, Indiana

Little Turtle, a war chief of the Miamis in the early 1790s, led the Miamis, the Shawnees, and the Chippewas to several major victories over the white man. Later, he made peace and signed several treaties.

32. We have beaten the enemy twice under separate commanders. We cannot expect the same good fortune always to attend us. (To the tribal council, 1794. Soon after, the Indians were decisively defeated in the battle of Fallen Timbers, Ohio. *Chronology of Native North American History*, by Duane Champagne, Gale, 1994.)

33. The Americans are now led by a chief who never sleeps [Anthony Wayne]; the day and the night are alike to him. And, during all the time that he has been marching upon our villages, notwithstanding the watchfulness of our young men, we have never been able to surprise him. (Ibid.)

34. Think well of it. There is something that whispers to me, it would be prudent to listen to his [Anthony Wayne's] offers of peace. (Ibid.)

35. Elder Brother: . . . You have told your younger brothers [the Indians] that the British imposed falsehoods on us when they said the United States wished to take our lands from us, and that the United States had no such designs. You pointed out to us the boundary line [of the proposed treaty]. . . . This line takes in the greater and best part of your brothers' hunting ground. Therefore, your younger brothers are of opinion you take too much of their land away and confine the hunting of our young men within the limits too contracted. (Discussion with American officials on the proposed Treaty of Greenville (1795); *American State Papers*, vol. 7.)

36. When I walk through the streets I see every person in his shop employed about something. One makes shoes, another hats, a third sells cloth, and everyone lives by his labor. I say to myself, which of all these things can you do? Not one. I can make a bow or an arrow, catch fish, kill game, and go to war; but none of these is of any use here. . . . I should be a piece of furniture, useless to my nation, useless to the whites, and useless to myself. (After a visit to Philadelphia, 1797; *Little Turtle, the Great Chief of the Miami Indian Nation,* by Calvin M. Young, Sentinel Printing, 1917.)

RED JACKET

(1758?–1830)

Seneca, New York

Red Jacket was so named because of the red coat he wore when he fought on the side of the British during the Revolutionary War. He was an outstanding orator.

37. We first knew you a feeble plant which wanted a little earth whereon to grow. We gave it to you and afterward, when we could have trod you under our feet, we watered and protected you, and now you have grown to be a mighty tree, whose top reaches the clouds, and whose branches overspread the whole land, whilst we, who were the tall pine of the forest, have become a feeble plant and need your protection. (Statement, ca. 1792; *Life and Times of Sa-Go-Ye-Wat-Ha, or Red Jacket,* by William L. Stone, Wiley & Putnam, 1841.)

38. We stand a small island in the bosom of the great waters. We are encircled—we are encompassed. The evil spirit rides upon the [wind], and the waters are disturbed. They rise, they press upon us, and the waves will settle over us, and we shall disappear forever. Who then lives to mourn us? None. What marks our extermination? Nothing. We are mingled with the common elements. (1797; *Extraordinary American Indians,* by Susan Avery and Linda Skinner, Children's Press, 1992.)

39. Brother! . . . Your forefathers crossed the great waters, and landed on this island. Their numbers were small. They found friends and not enemies. They told us they had fled from their own country for fear of wicked men, and come here to enjoy their religion. They asked for a small seat. We took pity on them, granted their request, and they sat down amongst us. We gave them corn and meat. They gave us poison in return. The white people had now found our country. Tidings were carried back, and more came amongst us. Yet we did not fear them. We took them to be friends. They called us brothers. We believed them, and gave them a larger seat. At length their numbers have greatly increased. They wanted more land. They wanted our country. (Response to missionary, 1805; *Indian Biography*, by B. B. Thatcher, New York, 1845.)

40. Brother! You have got our country, but are not satisfied. You want to force your religion upon us. (Ibid.)

41. Brother! We understand that your religion is written in a book. If it was intended for us as well as for you, why has not the Great Spirit given it to us? (Ibid.)

42. I am an aged tree, and can stand no longer. My leaves are fallen, my branches are withered, and I am shaken by every breeze. Soon my aged trunk will fall. (1830; Avery and Skinner, *Extraordinary American Indians*.)

MINAVAVANA

(Mid to late eighteenth century)

Chippewa

43. Englishman! Although you have conquered the French, you have not yet conquered us! We are not your slaves. These lakes, these woods and mountains, were left to us by our ancestors. They are our inheritance, and we will part with them to none. Your nation supposes that we, like the white people, cannot live without bread, and pork, and beef! But, you ought to know, that He—the Great Spirit—and Master of Life— has provided food for us, in these broad lakes, and upon these mountains. (*Indian Biography*, by B. B. Thatcher, vol. 2, New York, 1841.)

PUSHMATAHA

(1764–1824)

Choctaw, Mississippi

Pushmataha, a Choctaw leader, was regarded as a friend of the white man who often defended him against other warlike tribes. He made a number of trips to Washington to confer on Indian matters. He took part in President Andrew Jackson's inaugural parade.

44. If Tecumseh's [q.v.] words be true, and we doubt them not, then the Shawnee's experience with the whites has not been the same as that of the Choctaws. These white Americans buy our skins, our corn, our cotton, our surplus game, our baskets, and other wares, and they give us in fair exchange their cloth, their guns, their tools, implements, and other things which the Choctaws need but do not make. It is true we have befriended them, but who will deny that these acts of friendship have been abundantly reciprocated? (Arguing against Tecumseh's efforts to have the Choctaws fight the white men, 1811; *Congressional Record*, June 13, 1921.)

45. During its darkest hours, these neighbors whom we are now urged to attack responded generously to our needs. They doctored our sick, they clothed our suffering, they fed our hungry. (Ibid.)

46. Forget not, O Choctaws and Chickasaws, that we are bound in peace to the Great White Father at Washington by sacred word. The Great White Father has never violated that treaty and the Choctaws have never been driven to the necessity of taking up the tomahawk against him or his children. . . . We do not take up the warpath without a just cause and honest purpose. (Ibid.)

47. None of my fathers, or grandfathers, nor any Choctaw ever drew bow against the United States. They have always been friendly. (Statement to the Secretary of War, 1824; *Chronology of Native North American History*, by Duane Champagne, Gale, 1994.)

48. I shall die, but you will return to our brethren. . . . They will ask you, "Where is Pushmataha?" and you will say to them "He is no more." They will hear the tidings like the sound of the fall of a mighty oak in the stillness of the woods. (Statement to friends, 1824; Ibid.)

BLACK HAWK

(1767–1838)

Sac, Illinois

Black Hawk and his people lived in the rich lands of Illinois and Wisconsin. In the 1820s, whites began occupying Indian lands. Under an old treaty, the Indians were supposed to move and allow the whites to move in, but Black Hawk decided to fight. The Black Hawk War, which began in 1831, ended in the defeat of the Indians.

49. We always had plenty; our children never cried from hunger.... The rapids of Rock River furnished us with an abundance of excellent fish, and the land being very fertile, never failed to produce good crops. ... Here our village stood for more than a hundred years, during all of which time we were the undisputed possessors of the Mississippi Valley. ... Our village was healthy and there was no place in the country possessing such advantages, nor hunting grounds better than those we had in possession. If a prophet had come to our village in those days and told us that the things were to take place which have since come to pass, none of our people would have believed him. (*Autobiography of Black Hawk as Dictated by Himself to Antoine LeClair*, Historical Society of Iowa, 1833.)

50. How smooth must be the language of the whites, when they can make right look like wrong, and wrong like right. (*Native American Wisdom*, edited by Kent Nerburn and Louise Mengleboch, New World Library, 1991.)

51. The changes of many summers have brought old age upon me and I cannot expect to survive many moons. Before I set out on my journey to the land of my fathers, I have determined to give my motives and reasons for my former hostilities to the whites and to vindicate my character from misrepresentation. I am now an obscure member of a nation, that formerly honored and respected my opinions. (1833; *Pathway to Glory*, by Robert W. Wheeler, Carlton Press, 1975.)

52. The path to glory is rough, and many gloomy hours obscure it. May the Great Spirit shed light on yours and that you may never experience the humility that the power of the American government has

"How smooth must be the language of the whites, when they can make right look like wrong, and wrong like right."
—BLACK HAWK, SAC

reduced me to, is the wish of him, who, in his native forests, was once as proud and bold as yourself. (Ibid.)

53. An Indian who is as bad as the white men could not live in our nation; he would be put to death and eat up by the wolves. (Statement of surrender, August 1835; *Biography and History of the Indians of North America* 11th ed., by Samuel G. Drake, Boston, 1841.)

54. The white men are bad schoolmasters . . . they smile in the face of the poor Indian to cheat him; they shake them by the hand to gain their confidence, to make them drunk, to deceive them, and ruin our wives. (Ibid.)

55. We told them [the white men] to let us alone and keep away from us: but they followed like the snake. They poisoned us by their touch. We were not safe. We lived in danger. We were becoming like them, hypocrites and liars, adulterers, lazy drones, all talkers, and no workers. (Ibid.)

56. We went to our great father. We were encouraged. His great council gave us fair words and big promises; but we got no satisfaction. There were no deer in the forest. The opossum and beaver fled; the springs were drying up, and our squaws and papooses [were] without victuals to keep them from starving . . . we called a great council, and built a large fire. The spirit of our fathers arose and dug up the tomahawk; our knives were ready, and the heart of Black Hawk welled high in his bosom when he led his warriors to battle. He is satisfied. He will go to the world of spirits contented. (Ibid.)

57. Black Hawk is a true Indian and disdains to cry like a woman. He feels for his wife, his children and friends. But he does not care for himself. He cares for his nation and the Indians. They will suffer. He laments their fate. The white men do not scalp the head, but they do worse—they poison—they poison the heart; it is not pure with them. His [Black Hawk's] countrymen will not be scalped, but they will, in a few years, become like the white men, so that you can't trust them. (Ibid.)

58. Farewell, my nation: Black Hawk tried to save you and avenge your wrongs. He drank the blood of some of the whites. He has been taken prisoner and his plans are stopped. He can do no more. He is near his end. His sun is setting and he will rise no more. Farewell to Black Hawk. (Ibid.)

TECUMSEH

(1768–1813)

Shawnee, Ohio

Tecumseh united many tribes in the Ohio Valley. He dreamed of one huge area for Indians from the Great Lakes to Florida. He tried to negotiate land claims in the Northwest Territory with Governor William Henry Harrison, but the talks failed. During the War of 1812, Tecumseh fought on the side of the British, who made him a brigadier general, and he died fighting the Americans.

59. Brothers—the white people are like poisonous serpents: when chilled, they are feeble and harmless, but invigorate them with warmth, and they sting their benefactors to death. (Tecumseh to the Osage tribe

while lining up support to fight the white man, 1811; *Memoirs of a Captivity among the Indians of North America*, by John D. Hunter, London, 1924.)

60. Brothers—who are the white people that we should fear them? They cannot run fast, and are good marks to shoot at: they are only men; our fathers have killed many of them; we are not squaws, and we will stain the earth red with their blood. (Ibid.)

61. Brothers—we must be united; we must smoke the same pipe; we must fight each other's battles; and more than all, we must love the Great Spirit; he is for us; he will destroy our enemies, and make his red children happy. (Ibid.)

62. Accursed be the race that has seized on our country and made women of our warriors. Our fathers from their tombs reproach us as slaves and cowards. I hear them now in the wailing winds . . . the spirits of the mighty dead complain. Their tears drop from the wailing skies. Let the white race perish. They seize your land, they corrupt your women, they trample on the ashes of your dead! Back whence they came, upon a trail of blood, they must be driven. (Indian council meeting in Alabama, 1811; *The American Indian*, vol. 3, no. 11, August 1929.)

63. It is my determination, nor will I give rest to my body feet until I have united all the red men. (Statement to William Henry Harrison.)

64. Where today are the Pequot? Where are the Narragansett, the Mohican, the Pokanoket, and many other once powerful tribes of our people? They have vanished before the advance and the oppression of the White Man, as snow before a summer sun. (*Bury My Heart at Wounded Knee*, by Dee Brown, Holt, Rinehart & Winston, 1971.)

65. Will we let ourselves be destroyed in our turn without a struggle, give up our homes, our country bequeathed to us by the Great Spirit, the graves of our dead and everything that is dear and sacred to us? I know you will cry with me, "Never! Never!" (Ibid.)

66. So live your life that the fear of death can never enter your heart. (*As Long as the Rivers Shall Flow*, War Resisters League, 1974.)

67. Show respect to all men, but grovel to none. (Ibid.)

68. Touch not the poisonous firewater that makes wise men turn to fools and robs the spirit of its vision. (Ibid.)

SEQUOYA

(1770?–1843)

Cherokee, Tennessee

Sequoya developed a system of writing for the Cherokees. Originally a hunter and fur trader, he was crippled in a hunting accident. In 1809 he began to set forth a Cherokee alphabet. By 1821 the system was completed. He died while on a search for a missing tribe of Cherokees who were reported to be living in Mexico. The giant redwood sequoya trees were named in his honor. Sequoya was also known as George Gist.

69. [I] thought that if [I] could make certain things fast on paper, it would be like catching a wild animal and taming it. (Reported in indirect discourse in an interview with Jeremiah Evans; *The People's Almanac*, by David Wallechinsky and Irving Wallace, Doubleday, 1975.)

70. "Talking Leaves." (The name given by Sequoya to his Cherokee syllabary, a kind of alphabet.)

MAJOR RIDGE

(1771–1839)

Cherokee, Tennessee

Major Ridge, a Cherokee chief, led the group that negotiated the treaty that gave up Cherokee territory east of the Mississippi to the United States. After the Cherokee removal, he was assassinated.

71. I am one of the native sons of these wild woods. I have hunted the deer and turkey here, more than fifty years. I have fought your battles, have defended your truth and honesty, and fair trading. (Speech before

Cherokee group considering the treaty of cession, December 24, 1835; *Cartersville [Ga.] Courant*, March 20, 1885.)

72. The Georgians have shown a grasping spirit lately; they have extended their laws, to which we are unaccustomed, which harass our braves and make the children suffer and cry; but I can do them justice in my heart. They think the Great Father, the President, is bound by the compact of 1802 to purchase this country for them, and they justify their conduct by the end in view. They are willing to buy these lands on which to build houses and clear fields. I know the Indians have an older title than theirs. We obtained the land from the living God above. They got their title from the British. Yet they are strong and we are weak. They are many. We cannot remain here in safety and comfort. . . . I know we love the graves of our fathers, who have gone before to the happy hunting grounds of the Great Spirit—the eternal land, where the deer, the turkey and the buffalo will never give out. (Ibid.)

73. We can never forget these homes, I know, but an unbending, iron necessity tells us we must leave them. I would willingly die to preserve them, but any forcible effort to keep them will cost us our lands, our lives, and the lives of our children. (Ibid.)

74. There is but one path left, one road to future existence as a Nation. That path is open before you. Make a treaty of cession. Give up these lands and go over beyond the great Father of Waters [the Mississippi]. (Ibid.)

75. I have signed my death warrant. (Upon signing the Treaty of New Echota, December 29, 1835; Ibid.)

BIG ELK

(1772?–1846)

Omaha

Big Elk, an Omaha chief, advocated peace with the whites. He also led attacks against the Pawnee.

76. Death will come, always out of season. It is the command of the Great Spirit, and all nations and people must obey. (*Native American Wis-*

dom, edited by Kent Nerburn and Louise Menglehoch, New World Library, 1991.)

SHABONEE
(1775–1859)
Potawatomi, Ohio

Shabonee refused to war against the whites, despite the efforts of other Indian leaders.

77. The armies of the whites are without number, like the sands of the sea, and ruin will follow all tribes that go to war with them. (*The American Indian,* vol. 2, No. 8, May 1928.)

WILLIAM McINTOSH
(1775?–1825)
Creek, Georgia

William McIntosh's mother was a Creek; his father, a British army officer. As a Creek chief, he fought on the side of the Americans in the War of 1812. Later, he signed the peace treaty granting Creek land to the United States and was assassinated.

78. The country which you now possess, and that which we now remain on, was by the Great Spirit originally given to his red children. Our brothers, the white men, visited us when we were like the trees of the forest. Our forefathers smoked the pipe of peace and friendship with the forefathers of the white man, and when the white man said, we wish to live with the red man and inhabit the same country, we received their presents, and said, welcome, we will give you land for yourselves and for your children. (Speech to the Georgia legislature, 1825; *McIntosh and Weatherford, Creek Indian Leaders,* by Benjamin W. Griffith, Jr., University of Alabama Press, 1988.)

79. We took the white man by the hand, and held fast to it. We became neighbors, and the children of the white man grew up, and the children of the red man grew up in the same country, and we were brothers. (Ibid.)

80. The white men became numerous as the trees of the forest, and the red men became like the buffalo. (Ibid.)

81. Friends and Brothers: You are like the mighty storm, we are like the tender and bending tree; we must bow before you, you have torn us up by the roots, but still you are our brothers and friends. You have promised to replant us in a better soil, and to watch over us and nurse us. (Ibid.)

WILLIAM WEATHERFORD

(1780–1822)

Creek, Alabama

William Weatherford, a Creek chief, fought a bloody series of battles against the whites from 1812 to 1814. The Creeks were defeated at the battle of Horseshoe Bend against forces under Andrew Jackson.

82. I am in your power: do with me what you please. I am a soldier. I have done the white people all the harm I could. I have fought them, and fought them bravely. If I had an army, I would yet fight, and contend to the last. But I have done—my people are all gone—I can do no more than weep over the misfortunes of my nation. (Surrender to General Andrew Jackson, ca. 1814; *Adventures among the Indians,* by W.H.G. Kingston, Chicago, n.d.; cited in *Cry of the Thunderbird,* by Charles Hamilton, University of Oklahoma Press, 1972.)

83. Once I could animate my warriors to battle: but I cannot animate the dead. My warriors can no longer hear my voice—their bones are at Talladega, Tallaschatchee, Emuckfaw, and Tohopeka. (Ibid.)

84. I have not surrendered myself thoughtlessly. Whilst there were chances of success, I never left my post, nor supplicated peace. But my people are gone, and now I ask it for my nation, and for myself. (Ibid.)

85. On the miseries and misfortunes brought upon my country, I look back with the deepest sorrow and wish to avert still greater calamities. If I had been left to contend with the Georgian army [state militia], I would have raised my corn on one bank of the river, and have fought them on the other. But your people have destroyed my nation. (Ibid.)

86. You [Andrew Jackson] are a brave man. I rely upon your generosity. You will exact no terms of a conquered people, but such as they should accede to. Whatever they may be, it would now be madness and folly to oppose them. If they are opposed, you shall find me among the sternest enforcers of obedience. Those who would still hold out, can be influenced only by a mean spirit of revenge, and, to this, they must not and shall not, sacrifice the last remnant of their country. (Ibid.)

SEATTLE

(1786?–1866)

Suquamish, Washington

Seattle was chief of the Suquamish tribe throughout what is now the state of Washington. In 1855 he signed a treaty ceding lands to the white settlers. He was converted by missionaries and later took the name of Noah. When the governor of Washington told Seattle and other chiefs that they would have to move off their lands and onto a reservation, some chiefs chose to fight. Seattle, however, reluctantly agreed and lived out his life on a reservation.

87. My words are like stars that never set. What Seattle says, the great chief . . . can rely upon, with as much certainty as . . . the return of the seasons. (Statement, 1854; *Chronology of Native North American History*, by Duane Champagne, Gale, 1994.)

88. The son of the white chief says his father sends us greetings of friendship and goodwill. This is kind, for we know he has little need of our friendship in return, because his people are many. They are like the grass that covers the vast prairies, while my people are few, and resemble the scattering trees of a storm-swept plain. (Ibid.)

89. The great, and I presume also good, white chief sends us word that he wants to buy our land but is willing to allow us to receive enough to live on comfortably. This indeed appears generous, for the red man no longer has rights that he need respect, and the offer may be wise, also, for we are no longer in need of a great country. (Ibid.)

90. There was a time when our people covered the whole land. . . . But that time has long since passed away with the greatness of tribes now almost forgotten. (Ibid.)

91. I will not mouth over our untimely decay, nor reproach my paleface brothers for hastening it, for we, too, may have been somewhat to blame. When our young men grow angry at some real or imaginary wrong, and disfigure their faces with black paint, their hearts, also, are disfigured and turn black, and then their cruelty is relentless and knows no bounds, and our old men are not able to restrain them. (Ibid.)

92. But let us hope that hostilities between the red man and his paleface brothers may never return. We would have everything to lose and nothing to gain. (Ibid.)

93. We are two distinct races and must ever remain so. There is little in common between us. . . . Your religion was written on tablets of stone by the iron finger of an angry God, lest you might forget it. The red man could never remember nor comprehend it. Our religion is the traditions of our ancestors, the dreams of our old men, given them by the Great Spirit, and the visions of our sachems, and is written in the hearts of our people. (Ibid.)

94. Our great and good Father [the President] sends us word that if we do as he desires he will buy our lands . . . allow us to live comfortably . . . protect us with his brave warriors; his wonderful ships of war will fill our harbors. Then our ancient northern enemies will cease to frighten. (Statement to Territorial Governor Isaac Stevens, when asked to sign a treaty to remove his tribe to a reservation, 1855; Seattle Historical Society.)

95. But day and night cannot dwell together. The red man has ever fled the approach of the white man as morning must flee the rising sun. (Ibid.)

96. It matters little where we pass the remnant of our days. They will not be many. The Indian's night promises to be dark . . . a few more moments . . . a few more winters. (Ibid.)

97. When the last red man shall have perished, and the memory of my tribe shall have become a myth among the white man, these shores will swarm with the invisible dead of my tribe, and when your children's children think themselves alone in the field, the store, the ship, upon the highway, or in the silence of the pathless woods, they will not be alone. . . . At night when the streets of your cities and villages are silent and you think them deserted, they will throng with the returning hosts that once filled them and still love this beautiful land. The white man will never be alone. (Statement to Governor Stevens, 1855; *Now That the Buffalo's Gone,* by Alvin M. Josephy, Jr., Knopf, 1982.)

98. There is no death, only a change of worlds. (*Native American Wisdom,* edited by Kent Nerburn and Louise Menglehoch, New World Library, 1991.)

JOHN ROSS

(1790–1866)

Cherokee, Tennessee

John Ross was an ally of Andrew Jackson against the British during the War of 1812. When Jackson became President, however, Ross could not prevent the removal of the Cherokee Nation from Georgia. The treaty providing for removal was ratified by the U.S. Senate by a single vote. Ross led his people on the "Trail of Tears" (1838–1839) to "Indian Territory" (Oklahoma). During the Civil War, Ross originally tried to keep the Cherokee Nation neutral. He first supported the Confederacy, but later met with Abraham Lincoln and affirmed his loyalty to the Union. He remained chief of the Cherokees until his death.

99. We are told that the President [Andrew Jackson] looks with great anxiety and solicitation in our situation; that he knows our position is an embarrassing one, and that a change is called for by every consideration of present convenience and future security; and that the Government is desirous of entering into a satisfactory arrangement, by which all our difficulties will be terminated, and the prosperity of our people fixed upon a permanent basis. (Letter to Secretary of War Lewis Cass,

"[O]ur removal to the country west of the Mississippi . . . will be injurious, either in its immediate or remote consequences."

—JOHN ROSS, CHEROKEE

1833; *Correspondence on Removal of Indians West of the Mississippi River, 1831–1833,* U.S. Senate Document 512, 1833.)

100. Yet we are assured that you are well convinced that these objects can only be attained by a cession of our possessory rights in Georgia, and by our removal to the country west of the Mississippi; that you can see no cause of apprehension, as we do, that such removal will be injurious, either in its immediate or remote consequences. (Ibid.)

101. I have deemed it proper to send you the enclosed papers [see following quotation] from which you will see that the subjects on which they treat are well calculated, if agitated under the influence of political demagogues and through the prejudices of sectarianism on religious-doctrinal points, to create excitement and strife among the Cherokee people. (Letter to Evan Jones, May 5, 1855; *American Baptist Mission Union Papers*, American Baptist Historical Society.)

102. [One enclosure by Ross, alluded to in the previous quotation.] You do solemnly swear that you will answer such questions as may be put to you: Are you in favor of supporting slavery in Kansas, in the Cherokee Nation and in other countries? You do solemnly swear you will, for the support of Slavery, support any person that you may be instructed to by the Mother Lodge for any office in the Cherokee Nation or anywhere else, and to assist any member that may get into difficulty on account of being a Brother of the Secret Society and to keep secret the names of all the Brothers of the Society and other secrets of the Society? (Oath of allegiance of a secret society, 1855; Ibid.)

103. Your demand that those people of the [Cherokee] nation who are in favor of joining the Confederacy be allowed to organize into military companies as home guards for the purpose of defending themselves in case of invasion from the North is most respectfully declined. (Letter to Confederate official, June 17, 1861; *Papers of Chief John Ross*, University of Oklahoma Press, 1984.)

104. I cannot give my consent to any such organization. . . . It would be a palpable violation of my position as a neutral. . . . It will place in our midst organized companies not authorized by our laws who would soon become efficient instruments in stirring up domestic strife and creating internal difficulties among the Cherokee people. (Ibid.)

105. At the beginning of the conflict [the Civil War], I felt that the interests of the Cherokee people would be best maintained by remaining quiet and not involving themselves in it prematurely. Our relations had long existed with the United States Government and bound us to observe amity and peace alike with all the States. Neutrality was proper and wise so long as there remained a reasonable probability that the difficulty between the two sections of the Union would be settled, as a different course would have placed all our rights in jeopardy and might have led to the sacrifice of the people. But when there was no longer any reason to believe that the Union of the States would be continued, there was no cause to hesitate as to the course the Cherokee Nation should pursue. Our geographical position and domestic institutions allied us to the South. (Speech to the Cherokee National Assembly, Tahlequah, Oklahoma, October 9, 1861.)

106. In consequence of the want of protection [from the Union] . . . and of the overwhelming pressure brought to bear upon them, the Cherokees were forced, for the preservation of their Country and their existence, to

negotiate a treaty with the Confederate States. . . . No other alternative was left them, surrounded by the power and influences that they [faced]. (Letter to Abraham Lincoln, September 16, 1862; *Papers of Chief John Ross*.)

107. As soon as the [Union Army's] Indian Expedition marched into the Country, the great mass of the Cherokee people rallied spontaneously around the authorities of the United States. (Ibid.)

108. I . . . hastened to our once lovely home and witnessed the ruins and desolation of the premises—the only buildings standing was [sic] Johnny's chicken house, the carriage house, and Peggy's cabin. . . . Riding through the orchard, [I] found a few peaches, other fruits being gone. I cannot express the sadness of my feelings in rambling over the place. (September 18, 1865, returning to his home at war's end; Ibid.)

109. It is not peace, security and fraternity these lately disloyal leaders want, it is political power. (1866, referring to the Cherokee leaders who had allied themselves to the Confederacy during the Civil War; cited in *After the Trail of Tears: The Cherokees' Struggle for Sovereignty, 1839–1880*, by William G. McLoughlin, University of North Carolina Press, 1993.)

CHIKSIKA

(Late eighteenth to early nineteenth century)

Shawnee, Ohio?

Chiksika was the older brother of Tecumseh (q.v.).

110. When a white man kills an Indian in a fair fight it is called honorable, but when an Indian kills a white man in a fair fight it is called murder. (*A Sorrow in Our Heart*, by Allan W. Eckert, Bantam, 1992.)

111. When a white army battles Indians and wins it is called a great victory, but if they lose it is called a massacre and bigger armies are raised. (Ibid.)

112. The white man seeks to conquer nature, to bend it to his will and to use it wastefully until it is all gone and then he simply moves on leaving the waste behind him and looking for new places to take. The white man is a monster who is always hungry and what he eats is land. (Ibid.)

TEN BEARS

(1792–1872)

Comanche

Ten Bears, a Comanche chief, took part in peace conferences with white officials.

113. You said that you wanted to put us upon a reservation, to build our houses and make us medicine lodges. I do not want them. I was born upon the prairie where the wind blew free and there was nothing to break the light of the sun. I was born where there were no inclosures and where everything drew a free breath. I want to die there. (Speech at Medicine Lodge Council, 1867; *Proceedings of the Indian Peace Commission*, vol. 1, National Archives, Record Group no. 48.)

114. Do not ask us to give up the buffalo for the sheep. (Ibid.)

115. Great Spirit: I want no blood upon my land to stain the grass. I want it all clear and pure, and I wish it so, that all who go through among my people may find it peaceful when they come, and leave peacefully when they go. (*Native American Wisdom*, edited by Kent Nerburn and Louise Mendleboch, New World Library, 1991.)

KEOKUK

(1793?–1848)

Sac, **Illinois**

Keokuk was a Sac chief who spoke out on behalf of his tribe. He was a key spokesman not only in Washington, but also at local peace conferences called by whites. He was also called upon to mediate intertribal disputes.

116. Since the first time that I have met my white brethren in council,

I have been told that the red skins must shake hands. . . . These people [the Sioux] say we are deaf to your advice, and advise you to bore our ears with sticks. I think their ears are so closed against the hearing of all good, that it will be necessary to bore them with iron. (*Niles [Ill.] Weekly Register*, November 4, 1837.)

117. If, among the whites, a man purchased a piece of land, another came upon it, you would drive him off. Let the Sioux keep from our lands, and there will be peace. (Ibid.)

PETALESHARO

(1797–1874?)

Pawnee Loups

Petalesharo, a Pawnee chief, was best known for ending the practice of human sacrifice in the tribal ritual. At one time he was a guest of President James Monroe at the White House.

118. Great Father [President Monroe]: . . . I have heard your words— they have entered one ear and shall not escape the other. (Statement at an 1822 conference in Washington; *Red Men Calling on the Great White Father*, by Katharine C. Turner, University of Oklahoma Press, 1951.)

119. My Great Father: Some of your good chiefs, as they are called [missionaries], have proposed to send some of their good people among us to change our habits, to make us work and live like the white people. . . . You love the manner in which they live. . . . I love the manner in which [my people] live. (Ibid.)

120. We have plenty of buffalo, beaver, deer and other wild animals. We have also an abundance of horses. We have everything we want. We have plenty of land, if you will keep your people off of it. (Ibid.)

121. It is too soon, my Great Father, to send those good men [missionaries] among us. We are not starving yet. We wish you to permit us to enjoy the chase until the game of our country is exhausted. . . . Let us exhaust our present resources before you make us toil and interrupt our happiness. . . . Let me continue to live as I have done, and after I have passed to the Good or Evil Spirit from off the wilderness of my present life the subsistence of my children may become so precarious as to need and embrace the assistance of those good people. (Ibid.)

OPOTHLEYOHOLO

(1798?–1862)

Creek, Georgia

Opothleyoholo, a Creek chief, first fought the United States rather than give up tribal lands. Bowing to what he felt was the inevitable, he moved with his tribe to Indian Territory. During the Civil War, he supported the Union, and was driven out of his land by the Confederate Army.

122. Our people yet abhor the idea of leaving all that is dear to them ... but circumstances have changed their opinions; they have become convinced of their true situation; that they cannot live in the same field with the white man. (1835; *The Politics of Indian Removal,* by Michael D. Green, University of Nebraska Press, 1982.)

123. We Indians are like an island in the middle of the river. The white man comes upon us as a flood. We crumble and fall. (*Great North American Indians: Profiles in Life and Leadership,* by Frederick J. Dockstader, Van Nostrand Reinhold, 1977.)

124. Let us save our people by educating our boys and girls and young men and young women in the ways of the white man. Then they may be planted and deeply rooted about us and our people may stand unmoved in the flood of the white man. (Ibid.)

THE FOUR BEARS

(1800–1837)

Mandan, North Dakota

The Four Bears was a chief of the Mandan tribe. The Mandans are believed to have been the first inhabitants of what later became North Dakota. In 1837 The Four Bears delivered this bitter attack on the whites. He and his tribe had become infected with smallpox, a disease the white man had brought to America.

125. I have never called a white man a dog, but today I do pronounce them to be a set of black-hearted dogs. . . . I do not fear death, my friends. You know it. But to die with my face rotten [from the smallpox], that even the wolves will shrink with horror at seeing me. (*Red & White: Indian Views of the White Man*, by Annette Rosenstiel, Universe Books, 1983.)

126. Listen well to what I have to say, as it will be the last time you will hear me. Think of your wives, children, brothers, sisters, with their faces all rotten, caused by those dogs the whites. Think of all that my friends, and rise all together and not leave one of them alive. (Ibid.)

SPECKLED SNAKE

(Early to mid-nineteenth century)

Cherokee

127. Brothers! We have heard the talk of our great father [President Andrew Jackson]. . . . He says he loves his red children. Brothers! When the white man first came to these shores, the Muscogees gave him land, and kindled him a fire to make him comfortable; and when the palefaces

"I do not fear death . . . [b]ut to die with my face rotten, that even the wolves will shrink with horror at seeing me."

—THE FOUR BEARS, MANDAN

of the south made war on him, their young men drew the tomahawk, and protected his head from the scalping knife. (1830; *Biography and History of the Indians of North America,* by Samuel G. Drake, 11th ed., Boston, 1841.)

128. But when the white man had warmed himself before the Indian's fire, and filled himself with the Indian's hominy, he became very large; he stopped not for the mountain tops, and his feet covered the plains and the valleys. His hands grasped the eastern and the western sea. Then he became our great father. He loved his red children but said: "You must move a little farther, lest I should, by accident, tread on you." With one foot he pushed the red man over the Oconee, and with the other he trampled down the graves of his fathers. But our great father still loved his red children, and he soon made them another talk. He said much; but it all meant nothing but "move a little farther, you are too near me." (Ibid.)

129. He [President Jackson] said, "Go beyond the Oconee and the Oakmulgee, there is a pleasant country." He also said, "It shall be yours forever." Now he says, "The land you live on is not yours; go beyond the Mississippi; there is game, there you may remain while the grass grows or the water runs." (Ibid.)

130. Brothers! Will not our great father come here also? [And tell us that] He loves his red children and his tongue is not forked. (Ibid.)

ELIAS BOUDINOT

(1803?–1839)

Cherokee, Georgia

Elias Boudinot was the first editor of the *Cherokee Phoenix.* He was a member of a Cherokee delegation which went to Washington, D.C., to speak to President Andrew Jackson about the proposed removal of the Cherokees west of the Mississippi. Boudinot returned believing that the Cherokee cause was hopeless. He was later assassinated on the same day as his uncle, Major Ridge (q.v.), and his cousin, John Ridge (q.v.).

131. I have come to the unpleasant and most disagreeable conclusion . . . that our lands, or a large part of them, are about to be seized and taken from us. (25th Congress, 2d Session, *Senate Document 121*, Serial 315.)

132. Now, as a friend of my people, I cannot say *peace, peace*, when there is no peace. I cannot ease their minds with any expectation of a calm, when the vessel is already tossed to and fro, and threatened to be shattered to pieces by an approaching tempest. (Ibid.)

133. If I really believe there is danger, I must act consistently, and give alarm; tell our countrymen our true, or what I believe to be our true, situation. In the case under consideration, I am induced to believe there is danger, "immediate and appalling," and it becomes the people of this country to weigh the matter rightly, act wisely, not rashly, and choose a course that will come nearest befitting the nation. (Ibid.)

BLACK KETTLE

(1803?–1868)

Cheyenne, South Dakota

Black Kettle was a Cheyenne leader who tried to make peace with the white man. He narrowly escaped death at the Sand Creek massacre of 1864, took part in discussions at the Medicine Lodge Council of 1867, and died in battle a year later.

134. I want you to give all the chiefs of the soldiers here to understand that we are for peace, and that we have made peace, that we may not be mistaken by them for enemies. (Address to Colonel John Chivington at Camp Weld, Colorado, September 28, 1864; two months later, Chivington would wipe out nearly half of Black Kettle's band at Sand Creek. *The Sand Creek Massacre*, by Stan Hoig, University of Oklahoma Press, 1961.)

135. I have not come with a little wolf's bark, but have come to talk plain with you. (Ibid.)

136. We must live near the buffalo or starve. (Ibid.)

137. When we came here we came free, without any apprehension, to see you, and when I go home and tell my people that I have taken your hand and the hands of all the chiefs here in Denver, they will feel well, and so will all the different tribes of Indians on the plains, after we have eaten and drunk with them. (Ibid.)

138. Major [Thomas] Fitzpatrick, when he was our agent and brought us presents he did not take them into forts and houses, but would drive his wagons into our villages and empty them there. Every one would help themselves and feel glad. . . . Since the death of Major Fitzpatrick we have had many agents. I don't know as we have been wronged, but it looks so. The amount of goods has diminished; it don't [sic] look right. (Council meeting between Indian leaders and U.S. government representatives, negotiating a new treaty, 1865; *Report of Commissioner of Indian Affairs*, 1865.)

139. These lands that you propose to give to us I know nothing about. There is but a handful here now of the Cheyenne nation, and I would rather defer making any permanent treaty until the others come. . . . There are so few here it would not look right to make a treaty for the whole nation, and so many absent. (Ibid.)

140. I once thought that I was the only man that persevered to be the friend of the white man, but since they have come and cleaned out our lodges, horses, and everything else, it is hard for me to believe white men any more. (*Bury My Heart at Wounded Knee*, by Dee Brown, Holt, Rinehart & Winston, 1971.)

OSCEOLA

(1803?–1838)

Seminole, Alabama

Osceola fought the removal of the Seminoles to reservations west of the Mississippi River. During the Second Seminole War, which began in 1835, Osceola led a highly successful guerrilla campaign against the U.S. Army. He was arrested under a flag of truce and was imprisoned, and he died in captivity.

141. This is the only treaty I will make! (Said as he struck a dagger

Presented with a treaty to sign, he put a dagger through it, saying, "This is the only treaty I will make!"
—OSCEOLA, SEMINOLE

into a treaty document presented in 1835 by American officials. Attributed.)

LITTLE CROW

(1803?–1863)

Santee Sioux, Minnesota

Little Crow, a Santee chief, backed the signing of the Mendota Treaty of 1851. When he went to Washington, D.C., in 1858 to discuss Indian affairs with the white men, some tribesmen accused him of turning his back on his own people. He did, however, take an active part in the Sioux uprising of 1862.

142. Taoyateduta [Little Crow] is not a coward, and he is not a fool! When did he run away from his enemies? When did he leave his braves behind him on the warpath and turn back to his tepee? When he ran from your enemies, he walked behind on your trail with his face to the Ojibways and he covered your backs as a she-bear covers her cubs. Is Taoyateduta without scalps? . . . Behold the scalp locks of your enemies hanging there on his lodgepoles! (*Minnesota History*, vol. 38, September 1962.)

143. Braves! . . . You are full of the white man's devil water. You are like dogs in the Hot Moon when they snap at their own shadows. . . . See! The white men are like the locusts when they fly so thick that the whole sky is a snowstorm. . . . Kill one, two, ten, and ten times ten will come to kill you. (Ibid.)

144. You cannot see the face of your chief; your eyes are full of smoke; your ears are full of roaring waters. Braves! . . . You will die like the rabbits when the hungry wolves hunt them in the Hard Moon. Taoyateduta [Little Crow] is not a coward: he will die with you. (Ibid.)

JOHN RIDGE

(1803–1839)

Cherokee, Georgia

John Ridge was the son of Major Ridge (q.v.). Both played key roles in negotiating a treaty between the Cherokee Nation and President Andrew Jackson. The treaty provided for Cherokee removal to territory west of the Mississippi. The pro-treaty party was vigorously opposed by a Cherokee group led by John Ross (q.v.). Shortly after removal, John Ridge was assassinated on the same day as his father and his cousin, Elias Boudinot (q.v.). All three were seen as traitors by the anti-treaty forces.

145. I may yet die some day by the hand of some poor, infatuated Indian deluded by the counsels of [John] Ross and his minions. . . . I am resigned to my fate, whatever it may be. (After signing the Treaty of

New Echota in 1835; *A Political History of the Cherokee Nation, 1838–1907*, by Morris Wardell, University of Oklahoma Press, 1938.)

146. Genl. Jackson has demonstrated his ancient friendship & truly paternal benevolence to the Cherokees in concluding a treaty of great liberality for their acceptance. It gives the Indian a home, the right of self Government in it & an equal share of the funds accruing from the arrangement. (Letter to Georgia Governor Wilson Lumpkin, May 18, 1835; Georgia Department of Archives and History.)

147. Hitherto a few leading [Cherokee] men were permitted to get all the money & avails of Indian treaties, but it was reserved to this President to change that most unchristian habit of cupidity! (Ibid.)

148. The treaty which is now published to the world is the result of our most solemn considerations—it dispenses full & equal justice to all parties in the Nation and to every individual. The President has assured me that he will stand by this treaty as the Ultimatum of the Government and no other shall be offered to the Cherokee people. . . . The Ross party disbelieve it, & this party composed as it is of Halfbreed Nullifiers wish to change it and suit themselves—that they might prey upon the last avails of an oppressed race. They are, by means of falsehoods, in the field, valley & mountain opposing the ratification of it. . . . The object is procrastination—to outlive Jackson's administration or to compel it to abandon the rights of the Indians to their own keeping and management. Five millions of dollars, managed and disbursed by a few of the Halfbreed race & Georgia-Lawyers would be a speculation which the Rothschilds of Europe would be glad to obtain. (Ibid.)

149. The last hold . . . of this unholy Indian Aristocracy is the *banded outlaws* who are harbored by the Ross party for the purposes of intimidation or assassination. Richard the Third never had better instruments to promote tyranny. Have you not heard of the armed outlaws harbored by the Ross party. . . . Here is a band, a well organized power against the lives of the friendly Indians, the lives of the whites, & their property which sets at defiance your constables & sheriffs & laughs at your Judges & Jurors. And to cap the climax of this league the ablest lawyers of your own state are retained to defend them if taken. . . . There is a remedy in your [the Governor's] power, and it is to organize a guard of thirty men . . . to scour and range in their fastnesses & to search for them in their caves and to suppress their secret meetings. (Ibid.)

"Before the emigrants passed through my country, buffalo, elk, and antelope could be seen. . . . Now, when I look for game, I see only wagons with white tops and men riding upon their horses."
—WASHAKIE, SHOSHONE

WASHAKIE

(1804–1900)

Shoshone, Montana

Washakie, a Shoshone chief, was friendly with the white man. He led battles against the Blackfeet and Crow tribes, but he never warred against the white man. At one time, he was a scout for the military and helped negotiate treaties for them.

150. It was never the intention of the Shoshone tribe . . . to fight the whites; I have, myself, been fired upon by emigrants, but taught my young men that a war with the Great Father [the President] would be disastrous. (July 1858; quoted in indirect discourse by Captain Frederick Lander, superintendent of a road being built through Shoshone country. Cited in a report to the Commissioner of Indian Affairs, *U.S. House Executive Document 108*, 35th Congress, 2d Session, no. 1008.)

151. Before the emigrants passed through my country, buffalo, elk, and antelope could be seen. . . . Now, when I look for game, I see only wagons with white tops and men riding upon their horses. My people are very poor and have fallen back into the valleys of the mountains to dig roots and get meat for their little ones. (Ibid.)

152. I do not propose to fight, notwithstanding the building of this road which will destroy many of our root grounds and drive off our game. . . . We will be much injured by the passage of the new road by emigrants. (Ibid.)

JESSE CHISHOLM

(1805–1868)

Cherokee, Tennessee

Jesse Chisholm was a guide, interpreter, and trader. In 1865 he laid out the famous 800-mile cattle trail that bears his name. It extended from San Antonio, Texas, to Abilene, Kansas.

153. The Chisholm Trail. (Named for Jesse Chisholm.)

WILLIAM SHOREY COODEY

(1806–1849)

Cherokee?

William Shorey Coodey was the nephew of the Cherokee chief John Ross (q.v.). In October 1838, the tribe was removed from

Georgia to be taken to Indian Territory (Oklahoma). Here Coodey describes the beginning of what became known as the Trail of Tears.

154. At noon all was in readiness of moving, the teams were stretched out in a line along the road through a heavy forest, groups of persons formed about each wagon, others shaking the hand of some sick friend or relative who would be left behind. The temporary camp covered with boards and some of bark that for three summer months had been their only shelter and home, were crackling and falling under a blazing flame; the day was bright and beautiful, but a gloomy thoughtfulness was depicted in the lineaments of every face. In all the bustle of preparation there was a silence and stillness of the voice that betrayed the sadness of the heart. (Letter to John Howard Payne, August 13, 1840.)

WHITE BIRD

(1807?–1882?)

Nez Perce

White Bird was a chief of the Nez Perce. At the end of the Nez Perce War, he was trapped with Chief Joseph (q.v.). He refused to surrender and escaped to Canada with a small group.

155. Fight! Shoot them down! We can shoot as well as any of these soldiers. (At the battle of Big Hole River, 1877; *Battle of the Big Hole,* by G. D. Shields, Chicago, 1889.)

BIG EAGLE

(1807–1906)

Santee Sioux, Minnesota

Big Eagle was one of the Sioux chiefs who took part in the 1862 uprising in Minnesota. Years later, he recalled what happened.

156. The whites were always trying to make the Indians give up their life and live like white men—go to farming, work hard and do as they did—and the Indians did not know how to do that, and did not want to anyway. . . . The Indians wanted to live as they did before the Treaty of Traverse des Sioux—go where they pleased and when they pleased; hunt game wherever they could find it, sell their furs to the traders and live as they could. ("Chief Big Eagle's Story of the Sioux Outbreak of 1862," in Minnesota Historical Society, *Collections*, 6: 384–5, 387, 1894).

157. [T]he Indians did not think the traders had done right. The Indians bought goods of them on credit, and when the government payments came the traders were on hand with their books, which showed that the Indians owed so much and so much, and as the Indians kept no books they could not deny their accounts, but had to pay them, and sometimes the traders got all their money. (Ibid.)

158. Then many of the white men often abused the Indians and treated them unkindly. . . . Many of the whites always seemed to say by their manner when they saw an Indian, "I am much better than you," and the Indians did not like this. (Ibid.)

159. It began to be whispered about that now would be a good time to go to war with the whites and get back the lands. . . . It was also thought that a war with the whites would cause the Sioux to forget the troubles among themselves and enable many of them to pay off some old scores. Though I took part in the war, I was against it. I knew there was no good cause for it, and I had been to Washington and knew the power of the whites and that they would finally conquer us. (Ibid.)

160. When the outbreak came Little Crow [q.v.] told some of my band that if I refused to lead them to shoot me as a traitor who would not stand up for his nation, and then select another leader in my place. (Ibid.)

LION BEAR

(Early to mid-nineteenth century)

Dakota

Lion Bear was a Dakota chieftain.

161. Dakotas, the big men are here; they have got Red Iron [q.v.] in a pen like a wolf. They mean to kill him for saying the big men cheat us out of our lands and the money the great Father has sent us. (Speech before Dakota braves, 1862. Shortly afterward, Red Iron was released, which postponed a confrontation. Cited in *My Life and Experiences among Our Hostile Indians,* by Oliver O. Howard, Worthington & Co., 1907.)

162. Dakotas, must we starve like buffaloes in the snow? Shall we let our blood freeze like the little stream? Or shall we make the snow red with the blood of the white braves? (Ibid.)

163. Dakotas, the blood of your fathers talks to you from the graves where we stand. Their spirits come up into your arms and make them strong. Tonight the blood of the white man shall run like water in the rain, and Red Iron shall be with his people. Dakotas, when the moon goes down behind the hills, be ready, and I will lead you against the long knives and the big men who have come to cheat us and take away our lands and put us in a pen for not helping to rob our women and children. (Ibid.)

WILD CAT

(1810?–1857)

Seminole, Florida

Wild Cat, a Seminole chief, unsuccessfully staved off white forces during the Seminole wars. He finally surrendered and was moved to Indian Territory with his tribe.

164. When I was a boy, I saw the white man afar off, and was told that he was my enemy. I could not shoot him as I would a wolf or a bear, yet he came upon me. My horse in fields he took from me. He said he was my friend. He gave me his hand in friendship; I took it, he had a snake in the other; his tongue was forked; he lied and stung me. (Upon his surrender; *Broken Peace Pipes*, by Irwin M. Peithman, Charles C. Thomas, 1964.)

165. I asked for but a small piece of this land, enough to plant and live on far to the south—a spot where I could place the ashes of my kindred—a place where my wife and child could live. This was not granted me. I am about to leave Florida forever and have done nothing to disgrace it. It was my home; I loved it, and to leave it is like burying my wife and child. I have thrown away my rifle and have taken the hand of the white man, and now I say take care of me! (Ibid.)

166. I was in hopes I should be killed in battle, but a bullet never reached me. (*Great North American Indians: Profiles in Life and Leadership*, by Frederick J. Dockstader, Van Nostrand Reinhold, 1977.)

SATANK

(1810?–1871)

Kiowa, South Dakota

Satank, a Kiowa chief and medicine man, participated in council sessions with white officials to bring about peace. In 1871 he led a raid in Texas, which resulted in the deaths of three men. Convicted and sentenced to prison, he was shot while trying to escape.

167. We do not break treaties. We make but few contracts, and them we remember well. The whites make so many they are liable to forget them. (Speech at a Medicine Lodge Council meeting with white officials, 1867; *New York Daily Tribune*, November 30, 1867.)

168. You no doubt are tired of the much talk of our people. Many of them have put themselves forward and filled you with their sayings. (Ibid.)

"I seek no war with anyone. An old man, my fighting days are done."
—DULL KNIFE, CHEYENNE

DULL KNIFE

(1810?–1883)

Cheyenne, Montana

Dull Knife and his tribe participated in the battle of the Little Big Horn. Several months later, their camp was attacked and destroyed by the U.S. Army. Survivors were sent to an Oklahoma reservation. Dull Knife and other members of his tribe fled the reservation, heading back to their homeland in the north. Dull Knife and a tiny group reached the Red Cloud agency, but they were not allowed to stay there. They were sent to another reservation in the north.

169. We thank you for asking us to share your lands. We hope the Great Father will let us come to you. All we ask is to be allowed to live, and to live in peace. (Statement to Red Cloud [q.v.], explaining why he had been hoping to take his people to Red Cloud's reservation; December 1878. Cited in *Reminiscences of a Ranchman*, by Edgar Bronson, Mc-Clure, 1908.)

170. I seek no war with anyone. An old man, my fighting days are done. (Ibid.)

171. We bowed to the will of the Great Father and went far into the south where he told us to go. There we found a Cheyenne cannot live. Sickness came among us that made mourning in every lodge. Then the treaty promises were broken, and our rations were short. Those not worn by diseases were wasted by hunger. To stay there meant that all of us would die. (Ibid.)

172. Our petitions to the Great Father were unheeded. We thought it better to die fighting to regain our old homes than to perish of sickness. (Ibid.)

173. Tell the Great Father . . . if he lets us stay here, Dull Knife's people will hurt no one. Tell him if he tries to send us back we will butcher each other with our own knives. (Statement to U.S. Army Captain Wessells; Ibid.)

SPOKANE GARRY

(1811–1892)

Spokane, Washington

Spokane Garry was chief of the Lower Spokane tribe.

174. If the Great Father [the President] will not give me land at this place, I will not go to another reservation, but will stay here until the whites push me out, and out, and out, until there is no more out. (Speech at council meeting, 1878; Secretary of War, *Annual Report,* 1879–80, 46th Congress, 2d Session.)

175. If we cut ourselves the blood will be red, and so with the whites it is the same, though their skin is white. (*The Spokane Indians: Children of the Sun,* by Robert H. Ruby and John A. Brown, University of Oklahoma Press, 1970.)

POLATKIN

(Nineteenth century)

Spokane, Washington

Polatkin was one of the chiefs of Spokane Garry (q.v.).

176. I love everybody now that I have grey hair. (Response to an appeal by another chieftain for an uprising against the whites; 1856. *The Spokane Indians: Children of the Sun,* by Robert H. Ruby and John A. Brown, University of Oklahoma Press, 1970.)

MARIS BRYANT PIERCE

(1811–1874)

Seneca, New York

Maris Bryant Pierce was an activist. In 1838 Pierce attacked the arguments of the land speculators who wanted to grab Indian lands at bargain prices.

177. In the first place the white man wants our land; in the next place it is said that the offer for it is liberal; in the next place that we shall be better off to remove from the vicinity of the whites and settle in the neighborhood of our fellow red man, where the woods flock with game, and the streams abound with fishes. . . . The fact that the whites want our land imposes no obligation on us to sell it, nor does it hold forth an inducement to do so, unless it leads them to offer a price equal in value to us. We neither know nor feel any debt of gratitude which we owe to them, in consequence of their "loving kindness or tender mercies" toward us, that should cause us to make a sacrifice of our property or our interest, to their wonted avarice . . . which . . . is never sated. (*Red & White: Indian Views of the White Man*, by Annette Rosenstiel, Universe Books, 1983.)

COCHISE

(1812–1874)

Chiricahua Apache

Cochise was an Apache chief. In 1861 he was taken by the U.S. Army under a flag of truce and was mistreated by the soldiers. Afterward, Cochise led a guerrilla campaign against the whites in Arizona for more than ten years. Cochise surrendered in 1871 and lived on a reservation until his death three years later.

178. God made us not as you; we were born like the animals, in the dry grass, not on beds like you. This is why we do as the animals, go about of a night and rob and steal. If I had such things as you have, I would not do as I do, for then I would not need to do so. (Council meeting with General Gordon Granger, 1866; *Kansas State Historical Collections*, 1913–1914.)

179. When I was young I walked all over this country east and west, and saw no other people than the Apaches. After many summers I walked again and found another race of people had come to take it. (Ibid.)

180. Why is it that the Apaches want to die—that they carry their lives on their fingernails? They roam over the hills and plains and want the heavens to fall on them. The Apaches were once a great nation; they are now but few, and because of this they want to die and so carry their lives on their fingernails. (Ibid.)

181. You must speak straight so that your words may go as sunlight to our hearts. (Ibid.)

182. Tell me, if the Virgin Mary has walked throughout all the land, why has she never entered the wigwam of the Apache? Why have we never seen or heard her? (Ibid.)

SMOHALLA

(1815–1907)

Wanapum, Washington

Smohalla was a holy man who preached for a return of the Indian religion. Smohalla tried to explain to the white men why the work they suggested for Indians was contrary to Indian values.

183. My young men shall never work. Men who work cannot dream, and wisdom comes in dreams. (From a late nineteenth-century speech; *The American Indian: The First Victim*, edited by Jay David, Morrow, 1972.)

184. You ask me to plow the ground. Shall I take a knife and tear my mother's breast? Then when I die she will not take me to her bosom to rest. (Ibid.)

185. You ask me to dig for stone! Shall I dig under her skin for her bones? Then when I die I cannot enter her body to be born again. (*Now That the Buffalo's Gone: A Study of Today's American Indians*, by Alvin M. Josephy, Knopf, 1982.)

186. You ask me to cut grass and make hay and sell it, and be rich like white men! But how dare I cut off my mother's hair? (Ibid.)

BLACKFOOT

(?–1877)

Crow

Blackfoot, a Crow chief, took part in treaty discussions and council meetings with white officials.

187. You call the Great Spirit Jesus in your language; we call him in the Crow language E-so-we-wat-se. (Council meeting with white officials, 1873; *Report of Commissioner of Indian Affairs*, 1873.)

188. Those mountains are full of mines. The whites think we don't know about the mines, but we do. We will sell you a big country, all the mountains. Now tell us what you are going to give for our mountains. We want plenty for them. (Ibid.)

OURAY THE ARROW

(1820?–1881)

Ute/Apache, **New Mexico**

Ouray the Arrow was a Ute chief. He walked a fine line between cooperating with the whites and defending Indian interests.

189. The agreement an Indian makes to a United States treaty is like the agreement the buffalo makes with his hunters when pierced with arrows. All he can do is lie down and give in. (*Massacre: The Tragedy of White River*, by Marshall Sprague, Little, Brown, 1957.)

190. I do not like the interest part of the agreement. I would rather have the money in the bank. (Reply to a proposal for the cession of Ute land, in which the Utes would receive interest on the purchase price, September 1873; *Report*, U.S. Secretary of the Interior, 1873.)

"The agreement an Indian makes to a United States treaty is like the agreement the buffalo makes with his hunters when pierced with arrows."
—OURAY THE ARROW,
UTE/APACHE

191. We work as hard as you do. Did you ever try skinning a buffalo? (Reply to a white dignitary who had called Indians lazy; cited in *Great North American Indians: Profiles in Life and Leadership,* by Frederick J. Dockstader, Van Nostrand Reinhold, 1977.)

LITTLE RAVEN

(1820?–1889)

Arapaho, Nebraska

Little Raven was an Arapaho chief. Despite many unfulfilled promises made by the white men, he led his tribe to a peaceful resolution.

192. My young people . . . think I will look like a white man when I come back, because I have been to see the white man in the big house [the President]. (Speech at Cooper Union, New York City, 1871; *Report of Commissioner of Indian Affairs*, 1871.)

193. Long ago the Arapahoes had a fine country of their own. The white man came to see them, and the Indians gave him buffalo meat and a horse to ride on, and they told him the country was big enough for the white man and the Arapahoes, too. (Ibid.)

194. After a while the white men found gold in our country. They took the gold and pushed the Indian from his home. (Ibid.)

195. We want to travel the same road as the white man. We want to have his rifle, his powder, and his ball to hunt with. (Ibid.)

196. I have been wanting many years for Washington to give us our rights. The government sent agents and soldiers out there to us, and both have driven us from our lands. We do not want to fight [but] the white man has taken away everything. (Ibid.)

CROWFOOT

(1821–1890)

Blackfeet

Crowfoot was a chief of the Blackfeet Confederacy.

197. What is life? It is the flashes of a firefly in the night. It is the breath of a buffalo in the winter time. It is the little shadow which runs across the grass and loses itself in the sunset. (*As Long as the Rivers Shall Flow*, War Resisters League, 1974.)

RED CLOUD

(1822–1909)

Oglala Sioux, Nebraska

Red Cloud was a medicine man who became an important warrior chief. He went on the warpath after the whites violated solemn treaty obligations. He led many battles against the whites, the most well known of which were the Fetterman Massacre of 1866 and the Wagon Box Fight of 1867. He won a favorable peace treaty in 1868, but this was later violated by the United States.

198. Hear ye, Dakotas! When the Great Father at Washington [the President] sent us his chief soldier to ask for a path through our hunting grounds, a way for his iron road to the mountains and the western sea, we were told that they wished merely to pass through our country, not to tarry among us, but to seek for gold in the far west. Our old chiefs thought to show their friendship and good will, when they allowed this dangerous snake in our midst. (Council meeting, Fort Laramie, Wyoming, 1866; *Indian Heroes and Great Chieftains*, by Charles A. Eastman, Little, Brown, 1918.)

199. Yet before the ashes of the council fire are cold, the Great Father is building his forts among us. You have heard the sound of the white soldier's axe upon the Little Piney. His presence here is an insult and a threat. It is an insult to the spirits of our ancestors. Are we then to give up their sacred graves to be plowed for corn? Dakotas, I am for war! (Ibid.)

200. When we see the soldiers moving away and the forts abandoned, then I will come down and talk. (*Omaha Weekly World*, June 10, 1868.)

201. Our nation is melting away like the snow on the sides of the hills where the sun is warm, while your people [whites] are like blades of grass in the spring when summer is coming. (*Indian Chiefs*, by Russell Freedman, Holiday House, 1987.)

202. The Great Spirit made us poor and ignorant. He made you [whites] rich and wise and skillful in things which we know nothing about. (*New York Times*, June 17, 1870.)

*"When the white man
comes to my country he
leaves a trail of blood
behind him."*
—RED CLOUD,
OGLALA SIOUX

203. We do not want riches, we want peace and love. (Ibid.)

204. We see a great many soldiers here in our country. We know that the duty of these soldiers is to follow people that are bad throughout the western country. We do not like to see them here. I want you to have pity on us, and have them all taken away, and leave us alone here with the agent of the interior department. (Statement to protest the presence of large numbers of cavalry and infantry troops near the site where peace talks were being held, 1876; *Our Indian Wards*, by George W. Manypenny, Clarke, 1880.)

205. When the white man comes to my country he leaves a trail of blood behind him. (*Bury My Heart at Wounded Knee,* by Dee Brown, Holt, Rinehart & Winston, 1971.)

206. My sun is set. My day is done. Darkness is stealing over me. (Statement to his people, 1903, in which he stepped aside as chief in favor of his son; cited in *Black Hills White Justice: The Sioux Nation Versus the United States, 1775 to the Present,* by Edward Lazarus, HarperCollins, 1991.)

207. The Great Spirit made us, the Indians, and gave us this land we live in. He gave us the buffalo, the antelope, and the deer for food and clothing. We moved on our hunting grounds from the Minnesota to the Platte and from the Mississippi to the great mountains. No one put bounds on us. We were free as the winds and eagle. (Ibid.)

208. I was born Lakota and I have lived as a Lakota and I shall die a Lakota. (Ibid.)

209. Shadows are long and dark before me. I shall soon lie down to rise no more. While my spirit is with my body the smoke of my breath shall be towards the Sun for he knows all things and knows that I am still true to him. (Ibid.)

210. They [the whites] made us many promises, more than I can remember. . . . They never kept but one. They promised to take our land, and they took it! (*American Indians: Answers to Today's Questions,* by Jack Utter, National Woodlands, 1993.)

SPOTTED TAIL

(1823–1881)

Brule Sioux, South Dakota

Spotted Tail, a Sioux chief, took part in many negotiating sessions with the white man. Opponents accused him of selling out his tribe for personal gain, and he was assassinated.

211. We object to the Powder River road. The country which we live in is cut up by the white men, who drive away all the game. That is the

"My father is with me, and there is no Great Father between me and the Great Spirit."
—SPOTTED TAIL,
BRULE SIOUX

cause of our troubles. (Statement to Peace Commission, 1867; *Black Hills White Justice: The Sioux Nation Versus the United States, 1775 to the Present,* by Edward Lazarus, HarperCollins, 1991.)

212. My father is with me, and there is no Great Father between me and the Great Spirit. (Response to a request by other chiefs to accompany them to Washington to see the Great Father, the President. Spotted Tail later did visit Washington. *Black Elk Speaks: Being the Life Story of a Holy Man of the Oglala Sioux,* as told to John G. Neihardt, Morrow, 1932.)

213. This [Black Hills] war did not spring up here in our land; this war was brought upon us by the children of the Great Father who came to take our land from us without price, and who, in our land, do a great many evil things. . . . This has come from robbery—from the stealing of our land. (1876; *Bury My Heart at Wounded Knee,* by Dee Brown, Holt, Rinehart and Winston, 1971.)

214. There is a time appointed to all things. Think for a moment how many multitudes of the animal tribes we ourselves have destroyed, look upon the snow that appears today—tomorrow it is water! Listen to the dirge of the dry leaves, that were green and vigorous but a few moons before! We are a part of that life and it seems that our time has come. (*The Wounded Knee Massacre from the Viewpoint of the Survivors*, edited by James H. McGregor, Wirth Bros., 1940).

215. Some years ago, a good man ... came to us. He talked me out of my old faith; and after a while, thinking that he must know more of these matters than an ignorant Indian, I joined his church and became a Methodist. After a while, he went away, another man came and talked, and I became a Baptist; then another came and talked and I became a Presbyterian. Now another one has come, and wants me to be an Episcopalian. .... All these people tell different stories, and each wants me to believe that his special way is the only way to be good and save my soul. I have about made up my mind that either they all lie, or that they don't know any more about it than I did at the first. I have always believed in the Great Spirit, and worshipped him in my own way. These people don't seem to want to change my belief in the Great Spirit, but to change my way of talking to him. (*Red & White: Indian Views of the White Man*, by Annette Rosenstiel, Universe Books, 1983.)

216. The white people are all thieves and liars. We do not want our children to learn such things. (Commenting on educating Indians at the Carlisle Indian School; *Battlefield and Classroom*, by Richard Henry Pratt, Yale University Press, 1964.)

217. The white man is very smart. He knew there was gold in the Black Hills and he made us agree to give up all that country and now a great many white people are there getting out the gold.... We are not going to give any children to learn such ways. (Ibid.)

LEWIS DOWNING

(1823–1872)

Cherokee

Lewis Downing was elected Cherokee chief after the Civil War.

218. Amid the decay of Indian Nations . . . the five nations [Cherokee, Creek, Chickasaw, Choctaw, and Seminole] . . . have not only survived but increased in numbers, accumulated property, [and] advanced in civilization. . . . All this prosperity under God and His gospel, we owe to our separate national existence and the protection and security afforded by our treaties. (1870; *After the Trail of Tears: The Cherokee Struggle for Sovereignty, 1839–1880,* by William G. McLoughlin, (University of North Carolina Press, 1993.)

219. Dependence does not destroy sovereignty. (The Supreme Court, years before, had declared the Cherokees a "domestic, dependent nation." *Cherokee Advocate,* January 30, 1871.)

WILLIAM WARREN

(1825–1853)

Ojibway, Wisconsin

William Warren wrote about Ojibway legends and traditions. His father, a white man, was descended from a Mayflower pilgrim. During his brief lifetime, Warren was an interpreter, a Minnesota state representative, a newspaper writer, and an author.

220. When an Ojibway dies, his body is placed in a grave, generally in a sitting posture, facing the west. With the articles needed in life for a journey. If a man, his gun, blanket, kettle, fire steel, flint and moccasins, if a woman, her moccasins, axe, portage collar, blanket and kettle. . . . After camping out four nights, and traveling each day through a prairie country, the soul arrives in the land of spirits, where he finds his relatives accumulated since mankind was first created, all is rejoicing, singing and dancing, they live in a beautiful country interspersed with clear lakes and streams, forests and abounding in fruit and game . . . all that the red man most covets in this life. (*History of the Ojibways, Based upon Traditions and Oral Statements,* 1885.)

JOHN ROLLIN RIDGE

(1827–1867)

Cherokee, Georgia

John Rollin Ridge was the grandson of Major Ridge (q.v.). He wrote articles to defend those accused of treachery for supporting the Cherokee removal treaty.

221. His [Major Ridge's] son, John Ridge [q.v.], and his nephew, Elias Boudinot [q.v.], followed the path of this aged pioneer [Major Ridge] of Cherokee civilization, and their names are upon record as the foremost among those who labored to redeem their people from the savage state. They organized the party of civilization. (*New York Tribune*, May 28, 1866.)

ELY PARKER

(1828–1895)

Seneca, New York

Ely Parker studied to be a lawyer but was denied certification because, as an Indian, he was not a citizen. He became a civil engineer. During the Civil War, he joined the staff of General Ulysses Grant, and he drafted the surrender document signed by Robert E. Lee. In 1864 General Grant asked Parker for a memorandum on how the Indian problem might be handled. Nine years later, as president, Grant appointed Parker the first Indian to become commissioner of Indian affairs. Although he was accused of corruption by Grant's political enemies, Parker was cleared of any wrongdoing.

222. In compliance with your request, I have the honor to submit the following proposed plan for the establishment of a permanent and perpetual peace . . . between the United States and various Indian tribes. . . .

"It has of late years become somewhat common, not only for the press, but in the speeches of men of intelligence, and some occupying high and responsible positions, to advocate the policy of their [Indians'] immediate and absolute extermination."
—ELY PARKER, SENECA

First, the transfer of the Indian bureau from the Interior Department back to the War Department. (Memorandum to General U.S. Grant, January 24, 1864; *Senate Executive Document No. 13*, 40th Congress, 1st Session.)

223. Agents appointed from civil life have generally been provided to protect their [Indian] rights, lives and property, and to attend to the prompt and faithful observance of treaty stipulations. But as the hardy pioneer and adventurous miner advanced into the inhospitable regions occupied by the Indians in search of the precious metals, they found no rights possessed by the Indians that they were bound to respect. The faith of treaties solemnly entered into were totally disregarded, and Indian territory wantonly violated. If any tribe remonstrated against the violation of their natural and treaty rights, members of the tribe were inhumanly shot down and the whole treated as mere dogs. Retaliation generally followed, and bloody Indian wars have been the consequence, costing lives and much treasure. (Ibid.)

224. In all troubles arising in this manner the civil agents have been totally powerless to avert the consequences, and when too late the military have been called in to protect the whites and punish the Indians;

when if, in the beginning, the military had had the supervision of the Indians, their rights would not have been improperly molested, or if disturbed in their quietude by any lawless whites, a prompt and summary check to any further aggressions could have been given. (Ibid.)

225. In cases where the government promises the Indians the quiet and peaceable possession of a reservation, and precious metals are discovered or found to exist upon it, the military alone can give the Indians the needed protection and keep the adventurous miner from encroaching upon the Indians until the government has come to some understanding with them. (Ibid.)

226. Most of Indian treaties contain stipulations for the payment annually to Indians of annuities, either in money or goods, or both, and agents are appointed to make these payments whenever government furnishes them the means. I know of no reason why officers of the army could not make all these payments as well as civilians. The expense of agencies would be saved, and, I think, the Indians would be more honestly dealt by. An officer's honor and interest is at stake, which impels him to discharge his duty honestly and faithfully, while civil agents have none of those incentives, the ruling passion with them being generally to avoid all trouble and responsibility, and to make as much money as possible out of their offices. (Ibid.)

227. I would provide for the complete abolishment of the system of Indian traders, which, in my opinion, is a great evil to Indian communities. . . . Indian trading licenses are very much sought after, and when obtained, although it may be for a limited period, the lucky possessor is considered as having already made his fortune. (Ibid.)

228. It has of late years become somewhat common, not only for the press, but in the speeches of men of intelligence, and some occupying high and responsible positions, to advocate the policy of their [Indians'] immediate and absolute extermination. Such a proposition, so revolting to every sense of humanity and Christianity, it seems to me could not for one moment be entertained by any enlightened nation. On the contrary, the honor of the national character and the dictates of a sound policy guided by the principles of religion and philanthropy, would urge the adoption of a system to avert the extinction of a people, however unenlightened they may be. The American government can never adopt the policy of a total extermination of the Indian race within her limits, numbering, perhaps, less than 400,000, without a cost of untold treasure and lives of her people, besides exposing herself to the abhorrence and censure of the entire civilized world. (Ibid.)

229. Then was the cry raised by all those who believed themselves injured or unprovided for, "Nay, this Parker is an Indian genius, he is grown so great and powerful, he doth injure our business and take the bread from the mouths of our families and the money from our pockets; therefore, let us write and put him out of power, so that we may feast as heretofore." (From a letter describing the political attacks on him as commissioner of Indian affairs; *The Life of General Ely S. Parker, Last Grand Sachem of the Iroquois and General Grant's Military Secretary*, vol. 23, Buffalo Historical Society, 1919.)

230. They made their onslaught on my poor innocent head and made the air foul with their malicious accusations. They were defeated, but it was no longer a pleasure to discharge patriotic duties in the face of foul slander and abuse. I gave up a thankless position to enjoy my declining days in peace and quiet. (Ibid.)

STANDING BEAR

(1829?–1908)

Ponca, Nebraska

Standing Bear, a Ponca chief, refused to move his people to an Oklahoma reservation. In 1879 he was taken into custody. The U.S. Army was ordered to take him and his people, by force if necessary, to the new reservation. Through the press and sympathetic attorneys who took his case without fee, Standing Bear won a decision declaring that he was a person and could not be taken and transported without his consent. Government officials, however, interpreted the ruling as applying to Standing Bear and his small group only, and not to other Indians.

231. If you took me away from this land it would be very hard for me. I wish to die in this land. I wish to be an old man here. (*Bury My Heart at Wounded Knee*, by Dee Brown, Holt, Rinehart & Winston, 1971.)

232. I have not wished to give even a part of it [the land] to the Great Father. Though he were to give me a million dollars I would not give him this land. (Ibid.)

233. When people want to slaughter cattle they drive them along until

Ponca Indians skinning a buffalo. The animal was regarded by many tribes as sacred, providing virtually all the necessities of life.

they get them to a corral, and then they slaughter them. So it was with us. (Ibid.)

234. My children have been exterminated. (Ibid.)

235. I am now with the soldiers and officers. I want to go back to my old place north.... I want to save myself and my tribe.... My brothers, it seems to me as if I stood in front of a great prairie fire. I would take up my children and run to save their lives; or if I stood on the bank of an overflowing river, I would take my people and fly to higher ground. (Statement made to Federal District Court Judge Elmer Dundy, 1879; *Nebraska, the Land and the People*, Vol. 1, by Addison E. Sheldon, Lewis, 1931.)

236. Oh, my brothers, the Almighty looks down on me, and knows what I am, and hears my words. May the Almighty send a good spirit to brood over you, my brothers, to move you to help me. (Ibid.)

237. If a white man had land, and someone should swindle him, that man would try to get it back, and you would not blame him. (Ibid.)

238. Look on me, take pity on me, and help me to save the lives of the women and children. My brothers, a power, which I cannot resist, crowds me down to the ground. (Ibid.)

NATIONAL COUNCIL

(1829)

Cherokee

For many years, the unwritten law among the Cherokees forbade the sale of Cherokee land without permission. As pressure was put on the Cherokees to sell their lands and relocate west of the Mississippi, the National Council of the Cherokee Nation decided to put that law into writing.

239. If any citizen or citizens of this [Cherokee] nation should treat and dispose of any lands belonging to this nation without special permission from the national authorities, he or they shall suffer death. (*Cherokee Phoenix*, October 29, 1829.)

240. Any person or persons who shall violate the provisions of this act, and shall refuse, by resistance, to appear at the place designated for trial, or abscond, are hereby declared to be outlaws; and any person or persons of this nation, may kill him or them so offending, in any manner most convenient, within the limits of this nation, and shall not be accountable for the same. (Ibid.)

GERONIMO

(1829–1909)

Chiricahua Apache, Arizona

Geronimo was a medicine man, prophet, and warrior chief of the Chiricahua Apache. He led raids against white settlers in Arizona and New Mexico from 1871 to 1886. Geronimo was in custody several times and escaped; he finally surrendered for the last time in 1887. He finished his life as a farmer on an Oklahoma reservation. He made personal appearances at expositions. President Theodore Roosevelt invited him to ride in his inaugural parade.

241. It [Arizona] is my land, my home, my father's land to which I now ask to be allowed to return. I want to spend my last days there, and be buried among those mountains. If this could be I might die in peace, feeling that my people, placed in their native homes, would increase in numbers, rather than diminish as at present, and that our name would not become extinct. (Letter to President Grant, 1877, following an early capture.)

242. I have several times asked for peace, but trouble has come from the agents and interpreters. (Conference with General George Crook, 1886; *The Truth about Geronimo*, by Britton Davis, Yale University Press, 1929.)

243. Very often there are stories put in the newspapers that I am to be hanged. I don't want that any more. When a man tries to do right, such stories ought not to be put in the newspapers. (Ibid.)

244. I and these others are too old now to follow your Jesus road. But our children are young. They should know about the white man's God.

(*Apache Mothers and Daughters: Four Generations of a Family*, by Ruth McDonald Boyer and Narcissus Duffy Gayton, University of Oklahoma Press, 1992.)

TUSKENEAH

(Early to mid-nineteenth century)

Creek

Tuskeneah was a Creek chief.

245. Your white sons and daughters are moving into my country in a band, and are spoiling my lands and taking possession of the Red peoples improvements that they have made with their own labor. Contrary to the consent of the Nation. Your soldiers have refused to prevent it. (Letter to President Andrew Jackson, 1832; *The Politics of Indian Removal*, by Michael D. Green, University of Nebraska Press, 1982.)

246. These are the kind of [white] characters that settle among us. They steal our property, they swear to lies, they make false accounts against us, they sue us in your State courts for what we know nothing of the Laws that.... are in words that we have no possible means to understanding. (Ibid.)

SATANTA

(1830–1878)

Kiowa

Satanta, chief of the Kiowas, was known as the orator of the plains. A fighter as well as a talker, he led forays against settlers. He was captured and sent to prison, where he committed suicide.

247. The good Indian, he that listens to the white man, gets nothing. The independent Indian is the only one rewarded. (*Bury My Heart at Wounded Knee*, by Dee Brown, Holt, Rinehart & Winston, 1971.)

248. I love the land and the buffalo and will not part with it. . . . I have heard that you intend to settle us on a reservation near the mountains. I don't want to settle. I love to roam over the prairies. There I feel free and happy, but when we settle down, we grow pale and die. (Speech at the Medicine Lodge Council before white officials, 1867; U.S. Bureau of American Ethnology, 17th *Annual Report*, 1895–1896.)

249. I have laid aside my lance, bow, and shield, and yet I feel safe in your presence. (Ibid.)

250. I have told you the truth. I have no little lies hid about me, but I don't know how it is with the commissioners. (Ibid.)

251. A long time ago this land belonged to our fathers, but when I go up to the river I see camps of soldiers on its banks. These soldiers cut down my timber, they kill my buffalo, and when I see that, my heart feels like bursting. (Ibid.)

252. Has the white man become a child that he should recklessly kill and not eat? When the red men slay game, they do so that they may live and not starve. (*New York Times*, October 26, 1867.)

ROMAN NOSE

(1830–1868)

Southern Cheyenne

Roman Nose, a war leader of the Cheyenne, fought attempts by the Union Pacific railroad to go through Indian hunting grounds. He died in battle.

253. Cheyenne warriors are not afraid, but have you never heard of Sand Creek? Your soldiers look just like those who butchered the women and children there. (Addressed to General Winfield Scott Hancock; cited in *Bury My Heart at Wounded Knee*, by Dee Brown, Holt, Rinehart & Winston, 1971.)

254. If the palefaces come farther into our land, there will be scalps of your brethren in the wigwams of the Cheyenne. (Statement to General Innis N. Palmer regarding the Union Pacific railroad; cited in *Great North American Indians: Profiles in Life and Leadership,* by Frederick J. Dockstader, Van Nostrand Reinhold, 1977.)

SIMON POKAGON

(1830–1899)

Pottawattami, Michigan

Simon Pokagon, chief of the Pottawattamis, was a well-known writer on Indian life and culture. When he wrote his autobiography, he wrote it first in his native Indian language and then translated it himself into English. According to one account, Pokagon's father sold the site of what was to become Chicago to the whites.

255. Ash-taw was . . . renowned as a temperance worker. She traveled from place to place, and wherever she found a few families . . . she called the children together to hold a little "pow-wow." . . . She always managed to keep on hand a stock of snakes' eggs . . . about to hatch. She stained them a beautiful red color, placing them on green moss in "wig-was-si ma-kak-ogons" (small, white birch-bark boxes) so as to have them appear to the children as charming as possible. After the children were assembled, she . . . opened the boxes one by one. . . . They all began to inquire what kind of eggs they were, (and) she would make reply, "These are ish-kot-e-waw-bo wan-an-og" (whisky eggs). (*Queen of the Woods,* by Simon Pokagon, 1899.)

256. Then she would add, "Would you like to take some of them?" She would then carefully put into each extended hand some of the charming colored little eggs. On receiving them, childlike they would feel of the little beauties with the tips of their fingers, when to their great surprise, the frail egg shells would crumble away, and from each come forth a little snake squirming and wiggling in their hands. Then with a shriek of horror they would let the young reptiles drop, and scatter like leaves in a whirlwind. (Ibid.)

257. The cruel joke impressed their youthful minds with such a loathsome hate against ish-kot-e-waw-bo (whisky) that their very souls ever after would revolt at the sight, smell, or even thought of the deceptive curse. (Ibid.)

258. This shrewd woman would then make an application of the strong object-lesson, convincing the children that what they had witnessed was but a slight foretaste of the awful reality, and that they who drank, after a while would be tormented with "mi-chi-gin-e-big" (great big snakes), which they could not escape, or even let go of. (Ibid.)

SITTING BULL

(1834–1890)

Hunkpapa Lakota, South Dakota

Sitting Bull never signed a peace treaty with the white man. It was his forces, under Crazy Horse (q.v.), who defeated Custer at the Little Big Horn. Sitting Bull was against the idea of Indians living on reservations, and he fled with his people to Canada. Later, he returned to the United States and was put on a reservation. For a brief time, he made appearances in Buffalo Bill's Wild West Show. There are conflicting accounts of his death. During the time of the Ghost Dance, either U.S. Army soldiers or Indian police tried to arrest him. Some of his supporters came to protect him, and Sitting Bull either was deliberately murdered or died in the shootout that followed.

259. All my warriors were brave and knew no fear. The soldiers who were killed were brave men, too, but they had no chance to fight or run away.... We did not go out of our own country to kill them. They came to kill us and got killed themselves. (Statement after the battle of the Little Big Horn, 1876; *Indian Chiefs,* by Russell Freedman, Holiday House, 1987.)

260. Our land is more valuable than your money. It will last forever. It will not even perish by flames or fire. As long as the sun shines and the waters flow, this land will be here to give life to men and animals. We cannot sell the lives of men and animals; therefore, we cannot sell

"I hate all the white people. You are thieves and liars. You have taken away our land and made us outcasts."
—SITTING BULL,
HUNKPAPA LAKOTA

this land. It was put here for us by the Great Spirit and we cannot sell it because it does not belong to us. (*The Great American Indian Bible,* edited by Louis Hooban, Indian Heritage Council, 1991.)

260a. You can count your money and burn it within the nod of a buffalo's head, but only the Great Spirit can count the grains of sand and the blades of grass of these plains. (Ibid.)

261. What treaty that the white man ever made with us have they kept? Not one. When I was a boy the Sioux owned the world; the sun rose and set on their land; they sent 10,000 men to battle. Where are the warriors today? Who slew them? Where are our lands? Who owns them? . . . What law have I broken? Is it wrong for me to love my own? Is it wicked for me because my skin is red? Because I am Lakota, because I was born where my father died, because I would die for my people and my country? (*Life of Sitting Bull and History of the Indian War of 1890–91,* by W. F. Johnson, Edgewood Publishing, 1891.)

262. I hate all the white people. You are thieves and liars. You have taken away our land and made us outcasts. (Statement to a white audience, 1883; *Bury My Heart at Wounded Knee*, by Dee Brown, Holt, Rinehart & Winston, 1971.)

263. The commissioners bring a paper [the treaty] containing what they wish already written out. It is not what the Indians want, but what the commissioners want. All they have to do is to get the signatures of the Indians. Sometimes the commissioners *say* they compromise, but they never change the document. (*New Sources of Indian History 1850–91*, by Stanley Vestal, University of Oklahoma Press, 1934.)

264. Let us [Indians] put our minds together and see what life we can make for our children. (*Indian Affairs*, Association on Indian Affairs, Fall 1994.)

265. Take the best of the white man's road, pick it up and take it with you. That which is bad leave it alone, cast it away. ("Spiritual Roots of Indian Success," by Henrietta V. Whitemen, in *Contemporary Native American Address*, edited by John R. Maestas, Brigham Young University Press, 1976.)

266. Take the best of the old Indian ways—always keep them. They have been proven for thousands of years. Do not let them die. (Ibid.)

267. Why should the Indian police come against me? We are of the same blood. We are all Sioux. . . . If the white men want me to die, they ought not to put up the Indians to kill me. . . . Let the soldiers come and take me away and kill me, wherever they like. I am not afraid to die. (After receiving word that he was about to be arrested, December 1890; cited by Grasping Eagle in *New Sources*, by Vestal.

268. White Hair [Major James McLaughlin, in charge of Sitting Bull's confinement] wanted me to travel all around [with Buffalo Bill] . . . so he could make a lot of money. Once was enough, I would not go. Then I would not join his church, and ever since he has had it in for me. . . . Why does he keep trying to humble me? Can I be any lower than I am? (Ibid.)

"I am a chief no more, but that is not what grieves me—I am grieved at the ruin of my people."

—KICKING BIRD,
KIOWA

KICKING BIRD

(1835–1875)

Kiowa

Kicking Bird, a Kiowa warrior, first fought the white man and later made peace with him.

269. I am as a stone, broken and thrown away—one part thrown this way, and one part thrown that way. I am a chief no more, but that is not what grieves me—I am grieved at the ruin of my people. (Statement at Medicine Lodge Creek meeting, 1867; *Chronology of Native North American History,* by Duane Champagne, Gale, 1994.)

DELSHAY

(1835–1874)

Tonto Apache

Delshay was a chief during the early years of the Apache wars.

270. I don't want to run over the mountains anymore; I want to make a big treaty. . . . I will keep my word until the stones melt. (*Bury My Heart at Wounded Knee*, by Dee Brown, Holt, Rinehart & Winston, 1971.)

271. God made the white man and God made the Apache, and the Apache has just as much right to the country as the white man. I want to make a treaty that will last, so that both can travel over the country and have no trouble. (Ibid.)

CHIEF JOSEPH

(1840–1904)

Nez Perce, Oregon

Chief Joseph was the leader of the Nez Perce tribe. In 1877, to avoid being forced onto a reservation, he decided to lead his people to freedom in Canada. There were about 500 people in the party, only a third of whom were warriors. The flight of more than a thousand miles through Idaho, Wyoming, and Montana ended at the Bear Paw Mountains of Montana—only thirty miles from the Canadian border. Trapped, starving, and heavily outnumbered, Chief Joseph surrendered. He died on a reservation in the state of Washington.

272. Suppose a white man should come to me and say, "Joseph, I like your horses, and I want to buy them." I say to him, "No, my horses suit me, I will not sell them." Then he goes to my neighbor, and says to him:

"Joseph has some good horses. I want to buy them, but he refuses to sell." My neighbor answers, "Pay me the money and I will sell you Joseph's horses." The white man returns to me, and says, "Joseph, I have bought your horses and you must let me have them." If we sold our lands to the government, this is the way they were bought. (*Our Indian Heritage: Profiles of 12 Great Leaders,* by C. Fayne Porter, Chilton, 1964.)

273. I am tired of fighting. Our chiefs are killed. . . . The old men are all dead. It is the young men who say yes or no. He who led on the young men is dead. It is cold and we have no blankets. The little children are freezing to death. My people, some of them, have run away to the hills, and have no blankets, no food, no one knows where they are— perhaps freezing to death. I want to have time to look for my children and see how many of them I can find. Maybe I shall find them among the dead. Hear me, my chiefs! I am tired, my heart is sick and sad. From where the sun now stands I will fight no more forever. (Statement of surrender to General Nelson Miles, October, 1877; U.S. Secretary of War Report 1877, p. 630.)

274. They [government officials] all say they are my friends and that I shall have justice, but while their mouths all talk right I do not understand why nothing is done for my people. (*North American Review,* vol. 128, 1879.)

275. General Miles promised that we might return to our own country. I believed General Miles or I never would have surrendered. (Ibid.)

276. I have heard talk and talk but nothing is done. Good words do not last long unless they amount to something. Words do not pay for my dead people. They do not pay for my country, now overrun by white men. . . . Good words will not give my people good health and stop them from dying. Good words will not get my people a home where they can live in peace and take care of themselves. I am tired of talk that comes to nothing. It makes my heart sick. (Ibid.)

277. You might as well expect the rivers to run backward as that any man who was born a free man should be contented when penned up and denied liberty to go where he pleases. . . . I have asked some of the great white chiefs where they get their authority to say to the Indian that he shall stay in one place while he sees white men going where they please. They cannot tell me. Let me be a free man—free to stop, free to work, free to trade where I choose, free to choose my own teachers, free to follow the religion of my fathers, free to think and talk and act for myself—and I will obey every law, or submit to the penalty. (Ibid.)

RED IRON

(Mid to late nineteenth century)

Dakota

Red Iron was a tribal chief of the Dakota.

278. The snow is on the ground, and we have been waiting a long time to get our money. We are poor; white Father has plenty. His fires are warm, his tepees keep out the cold. We have nothing to eat. . . . Our hunting season is past. A great many of our people are sick for being hungry. (After making this speech at an 1862 council meeting, Red Iron was briefly imprisoned by the army. *My Life and Experiences among Our Hostile Indians,* by Oliver O. Howard, Worthington & Co., 1907.)

279. We may die because you will not pay us; we may die, but if we do we will leave our bones on the ground where our great Father may see where his Dakota children died. (Ibid.)

280. We have sold our hunting grounds and the graves of our fathers. We have sold our own graves. We have no place to bury our dead, and you will not pay us the money for our lands. (Ibid.)

PALANEAPOPE

(Mid to late nineteenth century)

Yankton Sioux

Palaneapope was a Yankton Sioux chieftain.

281. I think the way the white men treated us is worse than the wolves. We have a way in the winter of putting our dead up on scaffolds up from the ground, but the soldiers cut down the scaffolds and cut off the hair of the head, and if they had good teeth they pulled, and some of them cut off the heads of the dead and carried them away. (Statement to a commissioner of Indian affairs in South Dakota, August, 1865; *Senate Report no. 156*, 39th Congress, 2d Session.)

282. Before the soldiers came along we had good health, but once the soldiers come along they go to my squaws and want to sleep with them, and the squaws being hungry will sleep with them in order to get something to eat, and will get a bad disease, and then turn to their husbands and give them the bad disease. (Ibid.)

283. I think if you will come up to our agency you will laugh in the first place, and then be mad to see our storehouse in the same building with the trader's store. I want the store moved away a mile, so that it won't be so handy to our goods . . . because the trader's store is under the floor where my goods are stored. (Ibid.)

CAPTAIN JACK

(1840?–1873)

Modoc, California

Captain Jack was chief of the Modoc tribe during the Modoc War. In the midst of peace negotiations, he killed U.S. Army General E.R.S. Canby. Shortly after their capture, Captain Jack and his warrior chiefs were put on trial and hanged.

284. If I give up my men that killed the settlers, to let them be tried by your law, will you give up your men that killed our women to let them be tried by our law? (Parley with General E.R.S. Canby, 1873; *Our Indian Heritage: Profiles of 12 Great Leaders*, by C. Fayne Porter, Chilton, 1964.)

285. I have always lived on what I could kill and shoot with my gun and catch in my trap. . . . I . . . have never gone begging. . . . What I have got I have got with my own hands, honestly. . . . [I was told] to live like a white man; and I have always tried to do it, and did do it, until this war started. (Statement at his trial; *Fighting Indians of America*, by David C. Cooke, Dodd, Mead, 1966.)

"If I give up my men that killed the settlers, to let them be tried by your law, will you give up your men that killed our women to let them be tried by our law?"
—CAPTAIN JACK, PONCA

286. I am the voice of my people. Whatever their hearts are, that I talk. (*Bury My Heart at Wounded Knee*, by Dee Brown, Holt, Rinehart & Winston, 1971.)

287. I am not afraid to die. I will not fall on the rocks. When I die, my enemies will be under me. (Ibid.)

GALL

(1840?–1895)

Hunkpapa Lakota, South Dakota

Gall was one of the chiefs at the battle of the Little Big Horn. Later, he became a judge on the Court of Indian Affairs and a representative for tribal interests in Washington.

288. There is one thing I do not like. The whites run our country. If we make peace, the military posts on this Missouri River must be removed and the steamboats stopped from coming up here. (Statement at a conference with white officials, 1868; *New Sources of Indian History 1850–1891*, by Stanley Vestal, University of Oklahoma Press, 1932.)

AMERICAN HORSE

(1840–1908)

Sioux, South Dakota

American Horse tried to keep peace with the white man. Six weeks after the Wounded Knee massacre of 1890, the commissioner of Indian Affairs questioned witnesses in Washington, D.C. One of the witnesses was American Horse.

289. The men were separated, . . . from the women, and they were surrounded by the soldiers. Then came next the village of the Indians that was entirely surrounded by the soldiers also. When the firing began, . . . the people who were standing immediately around the young [Indian] man who fired the first shot were killed right together, and then they [the soldiers] turned their guns, Hotchkiss guns, etc., upon the women who were in the lodge, standing there under a flag of truce, and of course as soon as they were fired upon they fled, the men fleeing in one direction and the women running in two different directions. So that there were three general directions in which they took flight. (Statement of February 11, 1891; *Fourteenth Annual Report of the Bureau of American Ethnology*, part 2, 1896.)

290. There was a woman with an infant in her arms who was killed as she almost touched the flag of truce, and the women and children . . . were strewn all along the circular village until they were dispatched. (Ibid.)

291. Right near the flag of truce a mother was shot down with her infant, the child not knowing that his mother was dead was still nursing, and that especially was a very sad sight. The women as they were fleeing with their babes were killed together, shot right through, and the women who were very heavy with child were also killed. (Ibid.)

292. After most all of them [the Indians] had been killed a cry was made that all those who were not killed or wounded should come forth and they would be safe. Little boys who were not wounded came out of their places of refuge, and as soon as they came in sight a number of soldiers surrounded them and butchered them there. (Ibid.)

CRAZY HORSE

(1842?–1877)

Oglala Sioux, South Dakota

Crazy Horse, a chief of the Oglala Sioux, was part of Sitting Bull's band which attacked and destroyed the forces of General Custer at the battle of the Little Big Horn. Later he surrendered and lived on a reservation. When soldiers came to arrest him, he fled and was mortally wounded.

293. You [white men] say, "Why do you not become civilized?" We do not want your civilization. We would live as our fathers did, and their fathers before them. (*In the Spirit of Crazy Horse*, by Peter Matthiessen, Viking, 1983.)

294. One does not sell the earth upon which the people walk. (*Voices from Wounded Knee 1973*, Akwesasne Notes, 1974.)

294a. We preferred hunting to a life of idleness on the reservations, where we were driven against our will. At times, we did not get enough to eat, and we were not allowed to leave the reservation to hunt. (Deathbed statement at Fort Robinson, Nebraska, 1877; *Twenty Years among Our Savage Indians*, by J. Leo Humfreville, Hartford Publishing, 1897.)

295. We preferred our own way of living. We were no expense to the government. All we wanted was peace and to be left alone. (Ibid.)

296. Soldiers were sent out in the winter, who destroyed our villages. Then "Long Hair" [Custer] came in the same way. They say we massacred him, but he would have done the same to us had we not defended ourselves and fought to the last. Our first impulse was to escape with our squaws and papooses, but we were so hemmed in that we had to fight. (Ibid.)

GEORGE BENT

(1843–1918)

Cheyenne, Missouri?

George Bent was a Cheyenne warrior. On November 29, 1864, hundreds of Cheyenne and Arapaho Indians, led by Black Kettle (q.v.), were massacred at Sand Creek, Colorado. Most of the casualties were women and children. The killings were carried out by militia under the command of Colonel John Chivington. George Bent, wounded in the battle, lay among the dead all day and escaped in the darkness. Half-Cheyenne and half-white, Bent turned his back on the white world after Sand Creek and regarded himself as a Cheyenne for the rest of his life.

297. Black Kettle had a large American flag up on a long lodgepole [at Sand Creek] as a signal to the troop that the camp was friendly. Part of the people were rushing about the camp in great fear. All the time Black Kettle kept calling out not to be frightened, that the camp was under protection and there was no danger. Then suddenly the troops opened fire. (*The Fighting Cheyennes,* by George Grinnell, University of Oklahoma Press, 1956.)

298. Little Bear told me . . . that after the fight he saw soldiers scalping the dead and saw an old woman who had been scalped by the soldiers walk about, but unable to see where to go. Her whole scalp had been taken and the skin of her forehead fell down over her eyes. (Ibid.)

299. Black Kettle, seeing that it was useless to stay longer, started to run, calling out to White Antelope to follow him, but White Antelope refused and stood there ready to die, with arms folded, singing his death song:

Nothing lives long,
Except the earth and the mountains

until he was shot down by the soldiers. (Ibid.)

300. It was a terrible march [to safety after Sand Creek], most of us being on foot, without food, ill-clad and encumbered with the women and children. . . . As we rode into the camp there was a terrible scene. Everyone was crying, even the warriors, and the women and children screaming and wailing. Nearly everyone present had lost some relatives or friends, and many of them in their grief were gashing themselves with their knives until the blood flowed in streams. ("Forty Years with the Cheyennes," by George Bent, *The Frontier*, vol. 4, no. 6, December 1905.)

SARAH WINNEMUCCA

(1844?–1891)

Paiute, Nevada

Sarah Winnemucca was an author, lecturer, and educator. An active lobbyist for Indian rights, she met with the major political figures of her day, including President Rutherford B. Hayes. She was called the "Indian Joan of Arc."

301. After the soldiers had killed all but some little children and babies still tied up in their baskets, the soldiers took them also, and set the camp on fire and threw them into the flames to see them burn alive. (Incident at the Muddy Lake reservation, Nevada, 1865; *Chief Sarah: Sarah Winnemucca's Fight for Indian Rights*, by Dorothy Natus Morrison, Atheneum, 1980.)

302. Many, being on the borders of starvation, have left their houses and wandered we know not where . . . we would all much rather be slain and put out of our misery than to be lingering here—each day bringing new sorrows—and finally to die of hunger and starvation. (Letter to military authorities on the lack of rations for the reservation; Ibid.)

303. I am quite willing to throw off the garments of civilization I now wear and mount my pony. I well remember the time when the hills surrounding this very camp were swarming with hostile Indians, and then the officers talked very sweetly to me. (Statement to officers at Fort McDermitt, Nevada, after requesting food and clothing for her tribe; Ibid.)

304. What I say for my people is so written on my heart that it will never be washed out, never while I live upon this cruel world. (Ibid.)

305. A few years ago you owned this great country. Today the white man owns it all, and you own nothing. Do you know what did it? Education. (Letter to the Indians of Inyo, California, asking for support of her Indian school; Ibid.)

306. You have brains same as the whites, your children have brains. . . . I entreat you to get hold of this [Indian-run] school, and give your support by sending your children, old and young, to it, and when they grow up to manhood and womanhood they will bless you. (Ibid.)

KUSHIWAY

(Mid to late nineteenth century)

Sac/Fox

Kushiway, a visitor to the Carlisle school, addressed the students.

307. Your parents have done something that is wonderful to send you here [Carlisle Indian School] to be educated. Now we look back, our old parents did not know anything; that time is all passed away. (*Battlefield and Classroom*, by Richard Henry Pratt, Yale University Press, 1964.)

308. There is only one tribe that knows much, that are like the white people—that is the Cherokee. They have men today equal to the Great Father: they are educated, they are wise. We other Indians belonging to the different tribes are blind. (Ibid.)

DOUBLEHEAD

(Mid to late nineteenth century)

Creek

Doublehead was a Creek chief.

309. We are afraid if we part with any more of our lands the white people will not let us keep as much as will be sufficient to bury our

dead. (*Native American Wisdom,* edited by Kent Nerburn and Louise Mengleboch, New World Library, 1991.)

EAGLE WING

(Mid to late nineteenth century)

Sioux

Eagle Wing was a Sioux chief.

310. My brothers, the Indians must always be remembered in this land.
Out of our languages we have given names to many beautiful things
which will always speak of us. Minnehaha will laugh of us, Seneca will
shine in our image, Mississippi will murmur our woes. The broad Iowa
and the rolling Dakota and the fertile Michigan will whisper our names
to the sun that kisses them. (*Ploughed Under, the Story of an Indian Chief
Told by Himself,* by William J. Harsha, 1881.)

311. We have been guilty of only one sin—we have had possessions
that the white man coveted. (Ibid.)

QUANAH PARKER

(1845–1911)

Comanche, Texas

Quanah Parker, a Comanche war chief, fought to prevent the
slaughter of the buffalo. Later, he became the chief spokesman
for the Comanches in Washington, D.C.

"This was a pretty country you took away from us, but you see how dry it is now. It is only good for red ants, coyotes, and cattlemen."

—QUANAH PARKER,
COMANCHE

312. We love the white man but we fear your success. This was a pretty country you took away from us, but you see how dry it is now. It is only good for red ants, coyotes, and cattlemen. (*Indian Chiefs*, by Russell Freedman, Holiday House, 1987.)

TWO MOON

(1847–1917)

Cheyenne

Two Moon, a Cheyenne chief, led his forces against General Custer at the battle of the Little Big Horn. More than twenty years later, Two Moon described the battle to Hamlin Garland.

313. While I was sitting on my horse I saw flags come up over the hill to the east like that [he raised his finger-tips]. Then the soldiers rose all at once, all on horses, like this [he put his fingers behind each other to indicate that Custer appeared marching in columns of fours] with a little ways between. Then a bugle sounded, and they all got off horses, and some soldiers led the horses back over the hill. (*McClure's Magazine*, September 1898.)

314. Then the Sioux rode up the ridge on all sides, riding very fast. The Cheyennes went up the left way. Then the shooting was quick, quick. Pop—pop—pop very fast. Some of the soldiers were down on their knees, some standing. Officers all in front. The smoke was like a great cloud, and everywhere the Sioux went the dust rose like smoke. We circled all round him—swirling like water round a stone. We shoot, we ride fast, we shoot again. Soldiers drop, and horses fall on them. Soldiers in line drop, but one man rides up and down the line—all the time shouting. . . . I don't know who he was. He was a brave man. Indians keep swirling round and round, and the soldiers killed only a few. Many soldiers fell. At last all horses killed but five. Once in a while some man would break out and run toward the river, but he would fall. (Ibid.)

315. At last about a hundred men and five horsemen stood on the hill all bunched together. All along the bugler kept blowing his commands. He was very brave too. Then a chief was killed. I hear it was Long Hair [Custer], I don't know, and then five horsemen and the bunch of men, may be so forty, started toward the river. The man on the sorrel horse led them, shouting all the time. He wore a buckskin shirt, and had long black hair and mustache. He fought hard with a big knife. His men were all covered with white dust. I couldn't tell whether they were officers or not. One man all alone ran far down toward the river, then round up over the hill. I thought he was going to escape, but a Sioux fired and hit him in the head. He was the last man. He wore braid on his arms [sergeant]. (Ibid.)

316. All the soldiers were now killed, and the bodies were stripped. After that no one could tell which were officers. (Ibid.)

317. We had no dance that night. We were sorrowful. (Ibid.)

318. Next day four Sioux chiefs and two Cheyennes and I, Two Moon, went upon the battlefield to count the dead. One man carried a little bundle for sticks. When we came to dead men, we took a little stick and gave it to another man, so we counted the dead. There were 388. There were 39 Sioux and seven Cheyennes killed, and about a hundred wounded. (Ibid.)

319. Some white soldiers were cut with knives, to make sure they were dead; and the war women had mangled some. Most of them were left just where they fell. (Ibid.)

PLENTY-COUPS

(1848–1932)

Crow, **Montana**

Plenty-Coups was a Crow chief. Despite his cynicism about whites and their values, he willed his property to the American people for a public park.

320. They [the whites] spoke very loudly when they said their laws were made for everybody; but we soon learned that although they expected us to keep them, they thought nothing of breaking them themselves. They told us not to drink whisky, yet they made it themselves and traded it to us for furs and robes. (*Plenty-Coups, Chief of the Crows,* by Frank B. Linderman, University of Nebraska Press, 1962.)

321. Their Wise Ones said we might have their religion, but when we tried to understand it we found that there were too many kinds of religion among white men for us to understand, and that scarcely any two white men agreed which was the right one to learn. This bothered us a good deal until we saw that the white man did not take his religion any more seriously than he did his laws, and that he kept both of them just behind him, like Helpers, to use when they might do him good in his dealings with strangers. (Ibid.)

FLYING HAWK

(1852–1931)

Oglala Sioux, South Dakota

Flying Hawk, a Sioux chief, fought in several Indian wars. He also battled General Custer at the battle of the Little Big Horn.

322. The tipi is much better to live in: always clean, warm in winter, cool in summer, easy to move. . . . If the Great Spirit wanted men to stay in one place he would make the world stand still. (*Firewater and Forked Tongues, a Sioux Chief Interprets U.S. History,* by M. I. McCreight, Trail's End Publishing Company, 1947.)

SUSETTE LaFLESCHE

(1854–1903)

Ponca/Omaha, Nebraska

Susette LaFlesche, a writer, editor, and lecturer, spoke out on behalf of the rights of Indians. She was the oldest sister of Susan LaFlesche Picotte (q.v.), the first Indian woman to become a medical doctor.

323. I often wonder if there is anything in your [white] civilization which will make good to us what we have lost. (*Native American Doctor: The Story of Susan LaFlesche Picotte,* by Jeri Ferris, Carolrhoda Books, 1991.)

YELLOW WOLF

(1856–1935)

Nez Perce

Yellow Wolf was one of the warriors of Chief Joseph (q.v.). Yellow Wolf and a small group fled to Canada when Chief Joseph surrendered. Later, they returned to the United States and were sent to a reservation in Indian Territory.

324. The whites told only one side. Told it to please themselves. Told much that is not true. Only his own best deeds, only the worst deeds of the Indians, has the white man told. (*Yellow Wolf: His Own Story*, by Lucullus McWhorter, Caxton, 1940.)

325. The air was heavy with sorrow. Some soldiers acted with crazy minds. (Describing a U.S. Army attack on an Indian encampment at the Big Hole River, 1877; Ibid.)

326. I am telling you true! I will die, you will die! This story will be for the people who come after us. For them to see and know what was done here. (Ibid.)

327. Only when approaching the enemy ready to fight life for life can you hear and learn from fellow warriors. Only then are these things told—what Power has been given the warrior, what Power he must use. It is at such time the guard Spirit enters into the warrior's head. Enters that he may defend himself, escaping bullets, arrows, spears, clubs, or knives. To escape with life through the battle. (Ibid.)

328. The Wolf-Power I was given made me a great hunter, a sure scout. (Ibid.)

329. No mountains, no springs, no clear running rivers. Thoughts come of the Wallowa where I grew up, of my own country when only the Indians were there, of tepees along the bending river, of the blue water lake, wide meadows with horse and cattle herds. From the mountain forests, voices seemed calling. I felt as dreaming. Not my living self. (Contrasting the sparse environment of Indian Territory with his boyhood home; cited in *Great North American Indians: Profiles in Life and Leadership*, by Frederick J. Dockstader, Van Nostrand Reinhold, 1977.)

FRANCIS LaFLESCHE

(1857–1932)

Omaha, Nebraska

Francis LaFlesche, an author and anthropologist, was a staff member of the Smithsonian Bureau of American Ethnology. Son of an Omaha chief, he was a half-brother of Susette LaFlesche (q.v.) and Susan LaFlesche Picotte (q.v.).

330. Among my earliest recollections are the instructions wherein we were taught respect and courtesy toward our elders, to say "thank you" when receiving a gift or returning a borrowed article; to use the proper and conventional term of relationship when speaking to another, and never to address anyone by his personal name. (Describing experiences at a Presbyterian missionary school for Indians; *The Middle Five: Indian Boys at School*, Small, Maynard, 1900.)

331. We were also forbidden to pass in front of persons sitting in the tent without first asking permission, and we were strictly enjoined never to stare at visitors, particularly at strangers. (Ibid.)

332. To us there seemed no end to the things we were obliged to do and to the things we were to refrain from doing. (Ibid.)

333. No native American can cease to regret that the utterances of his fathers have been continually belittled when put into English, that their thoughts have frequently been travestied, and their native dignity obscured. (Ibid.)

STANDING BUFFALO

(Mid to late nineteenth century)

Sisseton

Standing Buffalo was a Sisseton chief.

334. Our country is wherever the buffalo range. (1871; *The Odyssey of Chief Standing Buffalo*, by Mark Diedrich, Coyote Books, 1988.)

335. We are chiefs of the plains, we are not poor, but rich, and have plenty of horses and robes. (Ibid.)

WOVOKA

(1858–1932)

Paiute, Nevada

Wovoka, a medicine man, had a vision in 1888. He said that God had told him that Indian lands would be restored, the buffalo and other game would come back, and that the dead would rise. Wovoka said Indians should prepare for these miracles by performing the Ghost Dance. The dance spread across the plains. Many Indians came to believe that the dance would protect them from the white man's bullets. This may have contributed to major misunderstandings on both sides, leading to the Wounded Knee massacre of 1890.

336. When the sun died [was eclipsed] I went up to Heaven and saw God and all the people who had died a long time ago. God told me to come back and tell my people they must be good and love one another, and not fight or steal, or lie. He gave me this dance to give my people. (*Famous Indians, a Collection of Short Biographies*, Bureau of Indian Affairs, 1975.)

CHARLES A. EASTMAN

(1858–1939)

Santee Sioux, Minnesota

Charles Eastman was one of the first Indians to graduate as a medical doctor. Just a month after he received his M.D. from Boston University, he found himself treating the survivors of Wounded Knee. He became a popular writer and advocate for Indian causes. Eastman helped set up dozens of YMCA units for Indians throughout the country. His books on Sioux life were extremely popular.

337. [The Indian] sees no need for setting apart one day in seven as a holy day, since to him all days are God's. (*The Soul of an Indian*, Houghton Mifflin, 1911.)

338. As a child I understood how to give; I have forgotten this grace since I became civilized. I lived the natural life, whereas I now live the artificial. Any pretty pebble was valuable to me then; every growing tree an object of reverence. Now I worship with the white man before a painted landscape whose value is estimated in dollars! Thus the Indian is reconstructed as the natural rocks are ground to powder and made into artificial blocks which may be built into the walls of modern society. (Ibid.)

339. What boy would not be an Indian for a while when he thinks of the freest life in the world? We were close students of nature. We studied the habits of animals just as you study your books. (*Native American Wisdom*, edited by Kent Nerburn and Louise Mendleboch, New World Library, 1991.)

340. Fully three miles from the scene of the [Wounded Knee] massacre we found the body of a woman completely covered with a blanket of snow, and from this point on we found them scattered along as they had been relentlessly hunted down and slaughtered while fleeing for their lives. (*From the Deep Woods to Civilization*, Little, Brown, 1916.)

341. When we reached the spot where the Indian camp had stood [at Wounded Knee], among the fragments of burned tents and other belongings we saw the frozen bodies lying close together or piled one on another. I counted eighty bodies of men who had been in council and

Medicine man killed at Wounded Knee. "[W]e found the body of a woman completely covered with a blanket of snow, and from this point on we found them scattered along as they had been relentlessly hunted down and slaughtered while fleeing for their lives."

—CHARLES A. EASTMAN, SANTEE SIOUX

who were almost as helpless as the women and babes when the deadly fire began, for nearly all their guns had been taken from them. A reckless and desperate young Indian had fired the first shot when the search for weapons was well under way, and immediately the troops opened fire from all sides, killing not only unarmed men, women, and children, but their own comrades who stood opposite them, for the camp was entirely surrounded. (Ibid.)

THOMAS PEGG

(Mid-nineteenth century)

Cherokee

Thomas Pegg was a Cherokee tribal leader during the Civil War. The Cherokee Nation was pressured by both the Union and the Confederacy to join their respective sides.

342. This war has been disastrous in its effect on the welfare of our people. The operations of our government have been paralyzed by the incursions of an overwhelming force. (Statement, 1863; *After the Trail of Tears: The Cherokees' Struggle for Sovereignty, 1839–1880,* by William G. McLoughlin, University of North Carolina Press, 1993.)

343. Our legitimate protection, the government of the United States, was far away and every channel of communication cut off, every military post in our vicinity abandoned.... Our wisest men knew not what to do. (Ibid.)

OOCHALATA

(Mid-nineteenth century)

Cherokee

Oochalata became chief of the Cherokee Nation in 1875.

344. I have received a communication from the Superintendent of Indian Affairs which staggered my belief. . . . His department . . . suspended the law of the United States and the operation of Treaties in relation to intruders. . . . We are then berated as unfit for self-government . . . and more peremptorily required to abandon our right to self-government guaranteed to us by treaty and ours by nature. (Report to Cherokee council regarding the issue of the right to define Cherokee citizenship; *Cherokee Records,* November 13, 1877, Oklahoma Historical Society, Oklahoma City.)

345. From which we are to infer that the Government of the United States have adopted the rule to not observe any Treaty that clashed with the individual opinion of the Secretary of Interior or his subordinate, the Commissioner [of Indian Affairs]. . . . [This means] a new doctrine construing treaty or contracts in writing, to add to it a new clause, after the expiration of 92 years from date of that contract or treaty and without the consent of [the other] party. . . . It is a dangerous doctrine to which I can never agree. (Ibid.)

LITTLE HILL

(Mid-nineteenth century)

Winnebago, **Minnesota**

Little Hill was one of the Winnebago chiefs when the tribe was removed from Minnesota. This took place following the Sioux uprising of 1862.

346. While we lived in Minnesota we used to live in good houses, and always took our Great Father's [the President's] advice, and did whatever he told us to do. (Statement to a member of Congress at Dakota City, Nebraska, 1865; *Our Indian Wards*, by George W. Manypenny, Clarke, 1880.)

347. We used to farm and raise a crop of all we wanted every year. While we lived in Minnesota another tribe of Indians committed depredations against the whites, and then we were compelled to leave Minnesota. . . . We were compelled to leave so suddenly that we were not prepared, not many could sell their ponies and things they had. . . . We had but four days notice. Some left their houses just as they were, with their stoves and household things in them. (Ibid.)

348. It [the new Winnebago area] was not a good country; it was all dust. Whenever we cooked anything it would be full of dust. We found, after a while, that we could not live there. (Ibid.)

IRON SHELL

(Mid-nineteenth century)

Brule Sioux

Iron Shell was a Sioux chief.

349. I will always sign any treaty you will ask me to do, but you have always made away with them—broken them. (Upon signing the Treaty of 1868; *Black Hills White Justice: The Sioux Nation versus the United States, 1775 to the Present*, by Edward Lazarus, HarperCollins, 1991.)

KICKING BEAR

(1853?–1904)

Sioux

Kicking Bear was a leader in the Ghost Dance movement, which had been started by Wovoka (q.v.). After the movement ended, Kicking Bear toured with Buffalo Bill's Wild West Show.

350. I bring you word from your fathers the ghosts, that they are now marching to join you, led by the Messiah who came once to live on earth with the white men, but was cast out and killed by them. (Speech to an Indian council meeting, 1890; *My Friend the Indian,* by James McLaughlin, Houghton Mifflin, 1910.)

WOODEN LEG

(1858–1940)

Cheyenne, **South Dakota**

Wooden Leg was encamped at the Little Big Horn where General Custer was to make his last stand. Wooden Leg was sent to Oklahoma following the battle, but later he moved to Montana. He was an Indian scout for the U.S. Army and was named to the Indian Court.

351. For a long time we did not do much except to drill and work at getting out logs from the timber. I learned to drink whiskey at Fort Keogh . . . I spent my scout pay for whiskey. (*Wooden Leg, a Warrior Who Fought Custer,* by Thomas B. Marquis, University of Nebraska Press, 1957.)

352. Yes, it is pleasant to be situated [on the reservation] where I can sleep soundly at night without fear . . . I wish I could live again through some of the past days of real freedom. (*Great North American Indians: Profiles in Life and Leadership,* by Frederick J. Dockstader, Van Nostrand and Reinhold, 1977.)

CHARLES CURTIS

(1860–1936)

Kaw, **Kansas**

Charles Curtis, trained as a lawyer, entered politics and served as a member of the House of Representatives, U.S. Senate, and, finally, as vice president under Herbert Hoover.

353. There were no high moral principles involved, but I saw what liquor dealers had done and were doing to all sorts of men, how liquor broke them down physically, took away their pride and made them hang around racing stables, to become loafers and beggars. (Explaining his role as prosecuting attorney in Shawnee County, Kansas, where he closed down the speakeasies under state prohibition laws; *From Kaw Tepee to Capitol: The Story of Charles Curtis,* by Don C. Seitz, Frederick A. Stokes, 1928.)

354. I came to Kansas City hoping to receive the nomination for the Presidency. My friends made a gallant fight for me and remained loyal until the last and I cannot find words sufficient to express my gratitude to them. (Acceptance speech after his nomination as vice president in 1928; Ibid.)

355. When the result was announced I gladly bowed to the will of the majority and was ready to begin work for the success of the nominee, Secretary Hoover. I was not a candidate for Vice President and did not seek the nomination, but it is gratifying indeed to have been nominated by this great convention, and I am thankful to the delegates for their expression of confidence in me. (Ibid.)

ISHI

(1862?–1916)

Yahi, California

Ishi was the last survivor of the Yahi, a California tribe believed to have been extinct at the time of his emergence. He
staggered into the town of Oroville, California, in August
1911. He was called the "Wild Man" and had apparently been
in hiding for years. University of California anthropologists
Thomas Waterman and Alfred Kroeber arranged for him to
stay at the Museum of Anthropology, Berkeley, where he
could be studied. Waterman, theorizing that Ishi might be a
survivor of the Yahi, read a list of Yahi words—and below is
the one to which Ishi first responded. Ishi is the Yahi word
for "man."

356. Siwini! Siwini! [Yellow pine! Yellow pine!] (*Our Indian Heritage:
Profiles of 12 Great Leaders*, by C. Fayne Porter, Chilton, 1964.)

BLACK ELK

(1863–1950)

Oglala Sioux, Wyoming

Black Elk was a medicine man and mystic. After General Custer was defeated at the Little Big Horn, Black Elk fled into
Canada with his people. They were later forced back onto
reservations. Black Elk appeared in Buffalo Bill's Wild West
Show. He was at Wounded Knee shortly after the 1890 massacre. Many years later, he dictated his memoirs.

357. [On the reservation] we made these little gray houses of logs ...
and they are square. It is a bad way to live, for there is no power in a
square.... Everything an Indian does is in a circle and that is because

the Power of the World always works in circles, and everything tries to be round. In the old days when we were a strong and happy people, all our power came to us from the sacred hoop of the nation, and so long as the hoop was unbroken, the people flourished. (*Black Elk Speaks, Being the Life Story of a Holy Man of the Oglala Sioux*, as told to John G. Neihardt, Morrow, 1932.)

358. The flowering tree was the living center of the hoop, and the circle of the four quarters nourished it. The east gave peace and light, the south gave warmth, the west gave rain, and the north with its cold and mighty wind gave strength and endurance. (Ibid.)

359. I did not know then [at the time of Wounded Knee] how much was ended. When I look back now from this high hill of my old age, I can still see the butchered women and children lying heaped and scattered all along the crooked gulch as plain as when I saw them with eyes still young. (Ibid.)

360. I can see that something else died there in the bloody mud [of Wounded Knee], and was buried in the blizzard. A people's dream died there. It was a beautiful dream. . . . The nation's hoop is broken and scattered. There is no center any longer and the sacred tree is dead. (Ibid.)

SUSAN LaFLESCHE PICOTTE

(1865–1915)

Omaha, Nebraska

Susan LaFlesche Picotte was the first Indian woman to become a doctor of medicine. She devoted herself to the welfare of her people.

361. I hope to go into their homes and help the women in their housekeeping, teach them a few practical points about cooking and nursing, and especially about cleanliness. (1886; cited in "Dr. Susan LaFlesche Picotte: The Reformed and the Reformer," by Valerie Sherer Mathes, in *Indian Lives: Essays on 19th and 20th Century Native American Leaders*, edited by L. G. Moses and Raymond Wilson, University of New Mexico Press, 1985.)

362. I feel that as a physician I can do a great deal more than as a mere teacher, for the *home* is the foundation of all things for the Indians, and my work I hope will be chiefly in the homes of my people. (Ibid.)

BULL BEAR

(Mid to late nineteenth century)

Cheyenne

Bull Bear was one of a group of military chiefs known as the Dog Soldiers. He took part in the Red River War of 1874–1875, but eventually he ended his days on a reservation.

363. The buffalo is our money. It is our only resource with which to buy what we need and do not receive from the government. (*The Buffalo War: The History of the Red River Indian Uprising of 1874,* by James L. Haley, Doubleday, 1976.)

364. We love them [the buffalo] just as the white man does his money. Just as it makes a white man feel to have his money carried away, so it makes us feel to see others killing and stealing our buffaloes, which are our cattle given to us by the Great Father above to provide us meat to eat and means to get things to wear. (Ibid.)

RED DOG

(Mid to late nineteenth century)

Oglala Sioux

Red Dog fought, unsuccessfully, to keep whites out of the sacred Black Hills.

365. We are all poor because we are all honest. (*Native American Wis-*

dom, edited by Kent Nerburn and Louise Mendleboch, New World Library, 1991.)

WILLIAM P. ROSS

(Mid to late nineteenth century)

Cherokee

William P. Ross, nephew of John Ross (q.v.), was elected chief of the Cherokee Nation in 1872.

366. There are murders and outrages committed in the Cherokee Nation. Alas, there are. . . . And yet those who most loudly wail over such things in the Indian Country are most familiar with them at home. (Statement to House Committee on Territories, February 8, 1874. This was in response to proposed legislation aimed at the Cherokee Nation by neighboring states complaining about crime. *Litton Transcripts,* Oklahoma Historical Society, Oklahoma City.)

367. Kansas, on our borders, had its Benders [gang], its mob at Lacygne, and its shootings along the line of its railroads and border towns. (Ibid.)

368. Arkansas offers rewards for wanted [criminals], it is stated in the issue of a single paper, for fourteen murders, to say nothing of the proceedings of mobs, white and colored, and individual acts of violence which occur in the swamps and mountains of that state. (Ibid.)

369. In Missouri, the Knights of the Hood, in broad daylight cause the gate keepers in city fairs to stand and deliver; mobs stop railway trains, plunder or murder their passengers, shoot down the officers of the law in order to hang men who have been consigned to imprisonment. (Ibid.)

370. There is no undue proportion of unpunished crime in the Cherokee Nation. . . . Life and property are as secure as anywhere else in the surrounding states. (Ibid.)

STANDING ELK

(Mid to late nineteenth century)

Sioux

Standing Elk was a Sioux chief.

371. Your words are like a man knocking me in the head with a stick. What you have spoken has put great fear upon us. Whatever we do, wherever we go, we are expected to say, "Yes! Yes! Yes!"—and when we don't agree at once to what you ask of us in council you always say, "You won't get anything to eat! You won't get anything to eat!" (1876; spoken to U.S. commissioners who threatened to cut off rations if a proposed Black Hills treaty was not signed. Cited in *Black Hills White Justice: The Sioux Nation versus the United States, 1775 to the Present,* by Edward Lazarus, HarperCollins, 1991.)

DICK WASHAKIE

(Mid to late nineteenth century)

Shoshone

Dick Washakie was the son of Washakie (q.v.), the Shoshone chief.

372. The reason the Indian seems to worship the sun to some people is because the Indian believes the sun is a gift from God, our Father above, to enlighten the world and as the sun appears over the horizon they offer up a prayer in acceptance of our Father's gift. (*Washakie,* by Grace Raymond Hebard, Arthur H. Clark, 1930.)

WETATONMI

(Mid to late nineteenth century)

Nez Perce

Wetatonmi was the widow of Ollokot, brother of Chief Joseph (q.v.). This was her recollection of how she felt in October 1877, after her husband had been killed and Chief Joseph had surrendered.

373. It was lonesome, the leaving. Husband dead, friends buried or held prisoners. I felt that I was leaving all that I had but I did not cry. You know how you feel when you lose kindred and friends through sickness—death. You do not care if you die. With us it was worse. Strong men, well women and little children killed and buried. They had not done wrong to be so killed. We had asked to be left in our own homes, the homes of our ancestors. Our going with heavy hearts, broken spirits. But we would be free. . . . All lost, we walked silently on into the wintry night. (*Hear Me My Chiefs!,* by Lucullus V. McWhorter, Caldwell, Idaho, 1952.)

YOUNG-MAN-AFRAID

(Mid to late nineteenth century)

Sioux

Young-Man-Afraid, a Sioux chief, was a friend of Crazy Horse (q.v.) and was part of a delegation that visited Washington, D.C., in 1891 to present Indian grievances.

374. When the white man speaks, the Government and the army see that we obey. When the red man speaks, it goes in one ear and out the other. (Statement to Secretary of the Interior John Noble; *Black Hills White*

Justice: The Sioux Nation versus the United States, 1775 to the Present, by Edward Lazarus, HarperCollins, 1991.)

375. Why were our rations cut down a million pounds? Why have not our winter annuities come? (Ibid.)

376. Why was the Sioux nation called to account for dancing a religious dance? [The Ghost Dance.] (Ibid.)

BAPTISTE GOOD

(Mid to late nineteenth century)

Sioux

Baptiste Good was a Sioux chief.

377. The white man is in the Black Hills just like maggots, and I want you to get them out just as quick as you can. The chief of all thieves [General Custer] made a road into the Black Hills last summer, and I want the Great Father to pay the damages for what Custer has done. (*Bury My Heart at Wounded Knee*, by Dee Brown, Holt, Rinehart & Winston, 1971.)

LITTLE BIG MAN

(Mid to late nineteenth century)

Sioux

Little Big Man was a Sioux chief.

378. I will kill the first chief who speaks for selling the Black Hills. (*Black Hills White Justice: The Sioux versus the United States, 1775 to the Present*, by Edward Lazarus, HarperCollins, 1991.)

CARLOS MONTEZUMA

(1867?–1923)

Yavapai Apache, Arizona

Carlos Montezuma, despite an orphaned childhood of want and neglect, put himself through college and became a doctor. He turned down an offer made by President Theodore Roosevelt to head the Bureau of Indian Affairs, which he despised.

379. The guiding policy seemed to be that the Indian must be cared for like a little child. The feeling was general that if he were allowed to look out for himself, he would be cheated out of his property and would starve. ("Dr. Montezuma, Apache: Warrior in Two Worlds," by Neil M. Clark, *Montana: The Magazine of Western History*, vol. 23, no. 2, April 1973.)

380. It is the same with Indians as with all other people. There is only one way to achieve: do things for yourself. This rule is not abridged for the Indian because his skin is brown or red. (Ibid.)

381. It is perhaps easy to let someone else take care of you. I could have done it. Thousands of my people have been forced to do it. And what has it done for them? Go to the reservations. You will find them there, gamblers, idlers, vicious, committing crimes worse than I could tell you. Why? Because the Indian is taken care of. He does not have to do things for himself. . . . I defy you to do that for anyone and expect him to achieve things that are worthwhile. (Ibid.)

382. Any man, black, red, yellow, brown—or white—can do it [achieve] against obstacles, if he will. But he must do it himself. It cannot be done for him. (Ibid.)

383. The Indian Bureau [Bureau of Indian Affairs] is the only obstacle that stands in the way, that hinders our people's freedom. . . . The Indian Bureau system is wrong. The only way to adjust wrong is abolish it, and the only reform is to let my people go. . . . By doing away with the Indian Bureau you stop making paupers and useless beings and start the making of producers and workers. (*Congressional Record*, 64th Congress, 1st Session, May 12, 1916.)

LUTHER STANDING BEAR

(1868–1939)

Oglala Sioux, South Dakota

Luther Standing Bear, a chief of his people, wrote several books about Indian life and government policy. He was one of the first to attend the Carlisle Indian School in Pennsylvania. He wrote, lectured, performed in Buffalo Bill's Wild West Show, and acted in motion pictures.

384. Soon after I was born, one of our scouts came into camp one day, and very excitedly stated that a big snake was crawling across the prairie. This caused much excitement. Close observation revealed the fact that a stream of smoke was following the supposed snake. It was the first railroad train of the Union Pacific Railroad. (*My People, the Sioux,* by Chief Standing Bear, Boston, 1928.)

385. Only to the white man was nature a "wilderness" and only to him was the land "infested" with "wild" animals and "savage" people. To us it was tame. Earth was bountiful and we were surrounded with the blessings of the Great Mystery. Not until the hairy man from the east came and with brutal frenzy heaped injustices upon us and the families that we loved was it "wild" for us. When the very animals of the forest began fleeing from his approach, then it was that for us the "Wild West" began. (*Land of the Spotted Eagle,* by Chief Standing Bear, Houghton Mifflin, 1933.)

386. The Lakotas are now a sad, silent, and unprogressive people suffering the fate of all oppressed. Today you see but a shattered specimen, a caricature . . . of the man that once was. Did a kind, wise, helpful and benevolent conqueror bring this situation about? Can a real, true, genuinely superior social order work such havoc? (Ibid.)

387. To become a great brave was . . . the highest aspiration [of a young man]. . . . Not only must he have great physical bravery and fighting prowess, but he must meet the severest tests of character. The great brave was a man of strict honor, undoubted truthfulness, and unbounded generosity. (Ibid.)

388. In the natural course of events, every Lakota boy became a hunter, scout, or warrior. . . . When I reached young manhood, the warpath for the Lakota was a thing of the past. The hunter had disappeared with the buffalo, the war scout had lost his calling, and the warrior had taken his shield to the mountain-top and given it back to the elements. The victory songs were sung only in the memory of the braves and even they soon went unsung under a cruel and senseless ban of our overseers. (Ibid.)

389. The old people came literally to love the soil and they sat or reclined on the ground with a feeling of being close to a mothering power. It was good for the skin to touch the earth and the old people liked to remove their moccasins and walk with bare feet on the sacred earth. (Ibid.)

EDWARD GOODBIRD

(1869–?)

Hidatsa, Wyoming

Edward Goodbird became a successful farmer after game became scarce in his area.

390. We Hidatsas believed that this world and everything in it was alive and had spirits; and our faith in these spirits and our worship of them made our religion. My father explained this to me. "All things in this world," he said, "have souls, or spirits. The sky has a spirit; the clouds have spirits; the sun and moon have spirits; so have animals, trees, grass, water, stones, *everything*. These spirits are our gods; and we pray to them and give them offerings, that they may help us in our need." (*Goodbird the Indian, His Story,* edited by Gilbert L. Wilson, 1914.)

391. We Indians did not believe in one Great Spirit, as white men seem to think all Indians do. We did believe that certain gods were more powerful than others. Of these was . . . our elder creator, the spirit of the prairie wolf; and . . . Old-Woman-Who-Never-Dies, who first taught my people to till their fields. (Ibid.)

392. Anyone could pray to the spirits, receiving answer usually in a dream. Indeed, all dreams were thought to be from the spirits; and for this reason they were always heeded, especially those that came by fast-ing and suffering. Sometimes a man fasted and tortured himself until he fell into a kind of dream while yet awake; we called this a vision. (Ibid.)

393. Believing as he did that the world was full of spirits, every Indian hoped that one of them would come to him and be his protector, especially in war. When a lad became about 17 years of age, his parents would say, "You are now old enough to go to war but you should first go out and find your god!" They meant by this that he should not risk his life in battle until he had a protecting spirit. (Ibid.)

394. Whatever he saw in his vision was his god, come to pledge him protection. Usually this god was a bird or beast or it might be the spirit of someone dead; the bird or beast was not a flesh-and-blood animal, but a spirit. (Ibid.)

395. He set out to kill an animal like that seen in his vision, and its dried skin, or a part of it, he kept as his sacred object, or medicine, for in this sacred object dwelt his god. (Ibid.)

DAN KATCHONGVA

(Mid-nineteenth to mid-twentieth century)

Hopi

Dan Katchongva was in his eighties when he testified before a Congressional committee.

396. In ancient times it was prophesied by our forefathers that this land would be occupied by the Indian people and then from somewhere a White Man would come. He will come either with a strong faith and righteous religion which the Great Spirit has also given to him, or he will come after he has abandoned that great Life Plan and fall into a faith of his own personal ideas which he invented before coming here. (Congressional testimony, 1955; *The Great Resistance: A Hopi Anthology,* edited by George Yamada, privately printed, 1957.)

397. It was known that the White Man is an intelligent person, an inventor of many words, a man who knows how to influence people because of his sweet way of talking and that he will use many of these things upon us when he comes. (Ibid.)

398. We knew that this land beneath us was composed of many things that we might want to use later such as mineral resources. We knew that this is the wealthiest part of this continent, because it is here the Great Spirit lives. We knew that the White Man will search for the things that look good to him, that he will use many good ideas in order to obtain his heart's desire, and we knew that if he had strayed from the Great Spirit he would use any means to get what he wants. These things we were warned to watch, and we today know that those prophecies were true because we can see how many new and selfish ideas and plans are being put before us. We know that if we accept these things we will lose our land and give up our very lives. (Ibid.)

TATANGA MANI

(1871–1967)

Stoney

Tatanga Mani was a member of the Stoney Nation.

399. Civilized people depend too much on man-made printed pages. I turn to the Great Spirit's book which is the whole of his creation. You can read a big part of that book if you study nature. You know, if you take all your books, lay them out under the sun, and let the snow and rain and insects work on them for a while, there will be nothing left. But the Great Spirit has provided you and me with an opportunity for study in nature's university, the forests, the rivers, the mountains, and the animals which include us. (*Tatanga Mani, Walking Buffalo of the Stoneys*, by John Walter Grant MacEwan, M. G. Hurtig, 1969).

400. Nobody tries to make coyotes act like beavers or the eagles behave like robins. Christians see themselves as set apart from the rest of the animal and plant world by superiority, even as a special creation. Perhaps the principles of brotherhood which the world needs so urgently come more easily to the Indian. (*Akwesasne Notes*, Mohawk Nation.)

ALEXANDER POSEY

(1873–1908)

Creek, Oklahoma

Alexander Posey, a poet, essayist, and journalist, wrote both humorous and serious pieces about Indian life. In his newspaper column, he wrote satirical articles about serious issues, focusing on the foibles of the white man and his relationship with the Indian. Posey took on the Washington bureaucracy for trying to "Americanize" Indians. These columns were written in the dialect of the time. His serious essays, far more formal in style, were just as effective in their own way.

401. Well, so, Big Man at Washington was made another rule like that one about making the Injun cut his hair off short like a prize fighter or saloon keeper. Big Man he was say this time the Injun was had to change his name just like if the marshal was had a writ for him. So, if the Injun's name is Wolf Warrior, he was had to call himself John Smith, or maybe so Bill Jones, so nobody else could get his mail out of the post office. (*Indian Journal*, April 24, 1903.)

402. Big Man say Injun name like Sitting Bull or Tecumseh was too hard to remember and don't sound civilized like General Cussed Her or old Grand Pa Harry's Son. Hogan he say the Big Man's rule was heap worse than [land] allotment, and Crazy Snake he say he hear white man say all time you could take everything away from a him but you couldn't steal his good name. Guess so thata was alright 'cause they was nothing to a name nohow if you can't borrow some money on it at the bank. (Ibid.)

403. Tookpafka Micco he say he was druther had a deed to his land than a big name in the newspaper. (Ibid.)

404. If [the literary works of Indians] could be translated into English without losing their characteristic flavor and beauty, many of the Indian songs and poems would rank among the greatest poetic productions of all time. Some of them are masterpieces. (*Philadelphia Press*, November 1900.)

405. They [Indian literary works] have splendid dignity, gorgeous word pictures, and reproduce with magic effect every phase of life in the forests—the glint of the fading sunshine falling on the leaves, the faint stirring of the wind, the whirring of the insects. No detail is too small to escape observation and the most fleeting and evanescent of impressions are caught and recorded in the most exquisite language. (Ibid.)

406. The Indian talks in poetry; poetry is his vernacular, not necessarily the stilted poetry of books, but the free and untrammeled poetry of nature, the poetry of the fields, the sky, the river, the sun and the stars. In his own tongue it is not difficult for the Indian to compose, he does it instinctively; but in attempting to write in English he is handicapped. Words seem hard, form mechanical, and it is to these things that I attribute the failure of the civilized Indian to win fame in poetry. (Ibid.)

GERTRUDE SIMMONS BONNIN

(1876–1938)

Yankton Dakota, South Dakota

Gertrude Simmons Bonnin was a writer and Indian activist. After teaching initially, she began writing for major national magazines. She founded the National Council of American Indians, supporting studies of social and economic conditions of American Indians. She pushed for reforms during the Herbert Hoover and Franklin Roosevelt administrations.

407. Trembling with fear and distrust of the palefaces, my teeth chattering from the chilly ride, I crept noiselessly in my soft moccasins along the narrow hall, keeping very close to the bare wall. I was as frightened and bewildered as the captured young of a wild creature. (Arriving, age eight, at a missionary school for Indians; "Impressions of an Indian Childhood," *The Atlantic Monthly*, January 1900.)

408. In the process of my education I had lost all consciousness of the nature world about me. Thus, when a hidden rage took me to the small white-walled prison which I then called my room, I unknowingly turned away from my one salvation. ("An Indian Teacher among Indians," *The Atlantic Monthly*, March 1900.)

409. Alone in my room, I saw like the petrified Indian woman of whom my mother used to tell me. I wished my heart's burdens would turn me to unfeeling stone. But alive, in my tomb, I was destitute! (Ibid.)

410. It is a tragedy to the American Indian and the fair name of America that the good intentions of a benevolent government are turned into channels of inefficiency and criminal neglect. Nevertheless, the American Indian is our fellow man. The time is here when . . . we must acknowledge him. ("Gertrude Simmons Bonnin, 1876–1938: 'Americanize the First American,' " by David L. Johnson and Raymond Wilson, *American Indian Quarterly*, vol. 12, no. 1, Winter 1988.)

411. Revoke the tyrannical powers of Government superintendents over a voiceless people and extend American opportunities to the first American—the Red Man. (Ibid.)

WILL ROGERS

(1879–1935)

Cherokee, Oklahoma

Will Rogers was the foremost humorist of his day. He performed on the stage, in the movies, and over radio. He also wrote a popular newspaper column, in which he commented mostly on politics. His career was cut short by a tragic plane crash.

412. My ancestors did not come over on the Mayflower—they met the boat. (Remark.)

413. My ancestors . . . would have showed better judgment if they had not let yours land. (*Will Rogers, A Biography*, by Donald Day, David McKay, 1962.)

414. Ancestors don't mean a thing in the human tribe. They're as unreliable as a political promise. (Ibid.)

415. I like that picture. It's the only time my people got the best of it. (Ibid; referring to W. J. Wallach's painting of *Custer's Last Stand*.)

416. What's wrong with this world? There ain't but one word will tell you what's wrong, and that's selfishness. (*Teaching the Native American,* by Hap Gilliland, Kendall-Hunt, 1992.)

417. I have regretted all my life that I did not take a chance on the fifth grade. It would certainly come in handy right now, and I never go through a day that I am not sorry for the idea I had of how to go to school and not learn anything. (Ibid.)

418. They sent the Indians to Oklahoma. They had a treaty that said, "You shall have this land as long as grass grows and water flows." It was not only a good rhyme but looked like a good treaty, and it was till they struck oil. Then the government took us again. They said the treaty only refers to "water and grass; it don't say anything about oil." (Syndicated column, February 5, 1928.)

BIG THUNDER

(Late nineteenth century)

Wabanakis

Big Thunder was a Wabanakis chief.

419. The Great Spirit is our father, but the earth is our mother. She nourishes us, that which we put into the ground she returns to us, and healing plants she gives us likewise. If we are wounded, we go to our mother and seek to lay the wounded part against her, to be healed. (*The Indian's Book,* by Natalie Curtis, Harper and Brother, 1907.)

FOUR GUNS

(Late nineteenth century)

Oglala Sioux

Four Guns was an orator.

420. The Indian needs no writing. Words that are true sink deep into his heart where they remain. He never forgets them. On the other hand, if the white man loses his paper, he is helpless. (Speech, 1891; *Native American Reader: Stories, Speeches and Poems*, edited by Jerry D. Blanche, Denali Press, 1990.)

421. I once heard one of their preachers say that no white man was admitted to heaven, unless there were writings about him in a great book. (Ibid.)

JAMES KAYWAYKLA

(?–1963)

Warm Springs Apache, New Mexico

James Kaywaykla was only a child in 1886 when, with the remnants of his tribe, he was forcibly removed from New Mexico and transported to Florida.

422. Until I was about ten years old I did not know that people died except by violence. (*From the Days of Victorio: Recollections of a Warm Springs Apache*, by Eve Ball, University of Arizona Press, 1970.)

423. We had been hunted through the forests and plains of our own land as though we were wild animals. (Ibid.)

424. The White Eyes returned in hordes [following the Civil War] to take our land from us. . . . It was the prospectors and miners whom we considered the most objectionable, for they grovelled in the earth and invoked the wrath of the Mountain Gods by seeking gold, the metal forbidden to man. It is a symbol of the Sun, of Ussen Himself, and sacred to Him. (Ibid.)

425. Most Apaches believe that the body will go through eternity in the condition in which it leaves the earth, and for that reason they abhor mutilation. (Ibid.)

426. Literally the meaning of Ussen is Creator of Life. As nearly as I can judge, our concept of Him is much like the ancient Hebrews' Jehovah. (Ibid.)

427. My people wanted very much to return to the Southwest. The Governor of Arizona said that if a train carrying them reached the border of Arizona Territory it would be dynamited, that Apaches were as dangerous as the rattlesnakes upon which they fed. Of course no Apache ever ate the flesh of any snake. (Ibid.)

JOHN STANDS IN TIMBER

(1884–1967)

Cheyenne

John Stands in Timber was born eight years after his grandfather was killed fighting General Custer at the battle of the Little Big Horn. Early in his youth, he became determined to keep track of the oral literature of his people. The book *Cheyenne Memories*, coauthored with Margot Liberty, was published just after his death.

428. An old storyteller would smooth the ground in front of him with his hand and make two marks in it with his right thumb, two marks with his left, and a double mark with both thumbs together. . . . Then he touched the marks on the ground with both hands and rubbed them together and passed them over his head and all over his body. That meant the Creator had made human beings' bodies and their limbs as he had made the earth, and that the Creator was witness to what was to be told. (*Cheyenne Memories*, by John Stands in Timber and Margot Liberty, Yale University Press, 1967.)

RED FOX

(1870–1976)

Sioux

Red Fox, at the age of six, heard the sounds of gunfire at the battle of the Little Big Horn. His uncle, Crazy Horse (q.v.), was in the process of destroying General Custer's command. During a crowded lifetime, Chief Red Fox met presidents and kings, and he performed at Wild West shows and in the movies.

429. Among the American Indians there was a single concept of religion regardless of tribe or geographic location. They believed that the finite and infinite were expressions of one universal, absolute being that furnished guidelines for their morals and conduct, and motivated every living thing. They called this the Great Spirit. (*The Memoirs of Chief Red Fox*, McGraw-Hill, 1971.)

430. American history, as taught in school textbooks, pictures the development of a nation from the arrival of Columbus to the present in star-spangled language. Censorship has eliminated all malevolent and mischievous behavior from the pages of our past. The Indian is depicted as a savage and the White man as a good Samaritan. (Ibid.)

431. It is true Indians of some tribes painted for war. Many tribes did not. The paint was used for many different things. It was used to show happiness, sorrow, peace, what tribe you belonged to, where you lived, marriage. (Ibid.)

JIM THORPE
(1888–1953)
Sac/Fox, Oklahoma

Jim Thorpe was probably one of the greatest all-around athletes of all time. He was a star athlete while attending Carlisle. During the 1912 Olympics held in Stockholm, Sweden, he won a number of medals in pentathlon and decathlon events. He was stripped of his medals, however, when it was reported that he had been paid for playing professional baseball during the summer, causing him to lose his amateur status. Thorpe went on to play professional baseball and football. In 1982, nearly thirty years after his death, the International Olympic Committee reversed its original ruling, and Jim Thorpe was officially recognized as the winner of the events he had won in 1912.

"[King Gustav] said to me: 'Sir, you are the greatest athlete in the world.' That was the proudest moment of my life."

—JIM THORPE, SAC/FOX

432. Someone started a story that when King Gustav sent for me [during the Olympics], I replied I couldn't be bothered to meet a mere King. . . . The story was not true. I have pictures showing King Gustav crowning me with the laurel wreath and presenting me with the trophies and it is no fabrication that he said to me: "Sir, you are the greatest athlete in the world." That was the proudest moment of my life. (*Pathway to Glory*, by Robert W. Wheeler, Carlton Press, 1975.)

433. Sure! I played baseball in 1909 and 1910 in the Carolina League but I had no idea I was a pro. I got $60 a month for expenses and that's all. I wouldn't even have tried for the Olympic team had I thought I was a pro. (*New York Telegram*, July 21, 1948.)

ELLA DELORIA

(1889–1971)

Sioux, South Dakota

Ella Deloria, an anthropologist, studied under Franz Boas and Ruth Benedict. She wrote about the Dakota language and culture. In her 1944 book *Speaking of Indians*, she dealt with the future of Indians who, during World War II, had gone off to fight or to work in defense plants.

434. Their [American Indian] life has been separated by a wide gulf from that of all other Americans. To quote John Stuart Mill, "a state which dwarfs its men that they may be more docile instruments in its hands *even for beneficial purposes* will find that with small men no great thing can really be accomplished." The italics are mine. (*Speaking of Indians*, by Ella Deloria, Friendship Press, 1994. Reprinted by University of South Dakota Press.)

435. In a way, I believe that this is what has happened to the Indian people. They have always been so supervised and so taken care of that it has been hard to "try their wings" without self-consciousness. And they have been so remote from general American life that they don't always know what to try. (Ibid.)

436. Paternalism and protection and gratuity have left their mark. That is not so strange, nor is such a result peculiar to Indians. Have we not in our own time seen how spoiled and weakened people may become with a little of that sort of thing? (Ibid.)

437. They [Indians] have something to bestir themselves about at last—what a pity it had to be a war! And it has called forth all those dormant qualities that had been thought killed long ago—initiative, industry, alertness. And they had generally retained their innate patience, sympathy, gentleness, religious devotion, tolerance, showing an amazing lack of bitterness—amazing, because they have had plenty to be bitter about. (Ibid.)

MENINOCK

(Late nineteenth to early twentieth century)

Yakima

Chief Meninock was tried in 1915 by the state of Washington for violating the state's code on salmon fishing. He was found guilty. Below are excerpts from his testimony.

438. God created this Indian country and it was like He spread out a big blanket. He put the Indians on it. They were created here in this country, truly and honestly, and that was the time this river started to run. Then God created fish in this river and put deer in these mountains ... and made laws through which has come the increase of fish and game. (*The Washington Historical Quarterly*, July 1928.)

439. Then the Creator gave us Indians life; we awakened and as soon as we saw the game and fish we knew that they were made for us. (Ibid.)

440. For the women God made roots and berries to gather, and the Indians grew and multiplied as a people. (Ibid.)

441. When we were created, we were given our ground to live on, and from that time these were our rights. . . . We had the fish before the missionaries came, before the white man came. (Ibid.)

442. I was not brought from a foreign country and did not come here. I was put here by the Creator. We had no cattle, no hogs, no grain, only berries and roots and game and fish. We never thought we would be troubled about these things, and I tell my people . . . it is not wrong for us to get this food. (Ibid.)

DON C. TALAYESVA
(Late nineteenth to early twentieth century)
Hopi

Don C. Talayesva was a Hopi chief.

443. I grew up believing that Whites are wicked, deceitful people. It seemed that most of them were soldiers, government agents, or missionaries, and that quite a few were Two-Hearts. (ca. 1900; *Sun Chief: The Autobiography of a Hopi Indian*, edited by Leo W. Simmons, New Haven, Conn., 1942.)

NAPOLEON B. JOHNSON
(1891–1974)
Cherokee, Oklahoma

Napoleon B. Johnson was the first president of the National Congress of American Indians, founded in 1944. He served as Vice Chief Justice of the Oklahoma Supreme Court from 1955 until 1965, when he was impeached for bribery.

444. I advocate the assimilation of Indians into the general citizenship wherever and whenever such course is feasible. The time is here for the establishment of a planned program for the progressive liquidation of the U.S. Indian Service. . . . A plan [should be evolved] which leads the American Indians down the road to independence and complete absorption into general citizenship. This is being accomplished through intermarriage; by migration of Indians away from reservations into the non-Indian communities; and by association with non-Indians in the armed forces, war plants, and other industries. (*The Rotarian*, August 1954.)

JACK DEMPSEY

(1895–1983)

Cherokee, Colorado

Jack Dempsey was the world heavyweight boxing champion from 1919 to 1926.

445. Celia [Dempsey's mother] had a strain of Cherokee Indian on her mother's side, which enabled her to see and hear things the rest of us couldn't. At least that's what we thought when we were children. Later we realized she was just smart. (*Dempsey*, by Jack Dempsey with Barbara Piattelli Dempsey, Harper & Row, 1977.)

446. I bathed my face in beef brine to toughen the skin. . . . If I ever got cut, I wouldn't bleed. . . . Eventually, my face got as tough as a saddle. (Ibid.)

SAM AHKCAH

(1896–   )

Navajo

Sam Ahkcah attended a government Indian school. He worked as a mine foreman and rancher before entering Navajo politics. From 1946 to 1954 he was chairman of the Navajo Tribal Council.

447. We must encourage our young people to go on in education. They are our future. We need thousands of young lawyers, doctors, dentists, accountants, nurses and secretaries. We need young men and women who have majored in business administration. ("Sam Ahkcah," by Broderick Johnson and Virginia Hoffman, in *Navajo Biographies*, Rough Rock Demonstration School, 1970.)

448. We don't want them to get an education and take jobs off the reservation. We need them here! (Ibid.)

RUTH MUSKRAT BRONSON

(1897–1982)

Cherokee, Oklahoma

Ruth Muskrat Bronson, an educator, helped Indian youth to appreciate and understand their own culture and heritage.

449. The natives of Alaska are today in much the same predicament the Indians of the United States faced a century and a half ago. They are despised and unwanted by those Alaskans, and there are many of them, who are dominated by the "get rich and get out" psychology that is a relic of the gold-rush days. They are despised and unwanted because they own property which this element in Alaska wants and intends to get at any cost. (Speech to the Indian Rights Association, January 23, 1947; *Indian Truth*, January–April, 1947.)

450. The danger of another Teapot Dome did not pass away with the apprehension of Albert Fall. . . . Alaska is full of possibilities of Federal chicanery yet to be perpetrated on Indians. (Ibid.)

451. One educated Tlingit told me that the "natives of Alaska" occupy a position in many respects no better than that of the Negro in the States. . . . They often have to endure the same kind of exclusions and discriminations. (Ibid.)

ANNA MOORE SHAW

(1898–   )

Pima, Arizona

Anna Moore Shaw has written two books on the Pimas. As a resident of the Salt River Reservation, she taught kindergarten classes on Pima language and culture. She served on the Mutual Self-Help Housing Commission. She was a founder of the reservation's museum.

452. Even as a little child I learned to love Jesus and tried to practice the Golden Rule. But sometimes I envied the old way of life, when Pima children didn't have to go to school and could look forward to colorful tribal dances and festivals. Now, under the influence of the missionaries, the old dances were dying out. I would have no puberty ceremonial, and Circle and Name-Calling dances were almost things of the past. (*A Pima Past*, by Anna Moore Shaw, University of Arizona Press, 1974.)

453. Once father must have sensed my curiosity regarding the ancient traditions. He called my brother and me to him and said, "Willie and Annie, you must always remember that the white *pahl* (preacher) has said that tribal dances and festivals . . . are not for Christians to attend. Those who go to these events are sinners. The devil will get them." (Ibid.)

454. A warrior must be brave and die with a silent throat. (Quoting a relative training a young warrior-to-be; Ibid.)

BEN REIFEL

(1900–1990)

Brule Sioux, South Dakota

Ben Reifel was a Congressman who represented South Dakota from 1961 to 1971. He campaigned for better conditions for

American Indians. Earlier, he had worked in the Bureau of Indian Affairs.

455. We cannot go back to the buffalo economy. We want a modern standard of living the same as whites. (*Extraordinary American Indians,* by Susan Avery and Linda Skinner, Children's Press, 1992.)

HOLLOW HORN

(Early to mid-twentieth century)

Sioux

Hollow Horn was a Sioux medicine man. In 1929 he took part in a sun dance ceremony and made the following prophecy.

456. A day will come in your lifetime when the earth, your mother, will beg you, with tears running, to save her. Ho, if you fail to help her, you [Lakota] and all people will die like dogs. Remember this. (*Black Hills White Justice: The Sioux Nation versus the United States, 1775 to the Present,* by Edward Lazarus, HarperCollins, 1991.)

BEN CALF ROBE

(Twentieth century)

Blackfeet

Ben Calf Robe is an elder of the Blackfeet tribe.

457. People ask me if we will ever get along. When will Indians and whites have respect for each other? I think the time is coming. It will be here when we all have the same color of skin, and we are slowly coming to be that way. (*Shadows of the Buffalo,* by Adolf Hungry Wolf and Beverly Hungry Wolf, Morrow, 1983.)

HARRIETT STARLEAF GUMBS

(Twentieth century)

Shinnecock

Harriett Gumbs is an elder of the Shinnecock tribe.

458. Generations to come will look back and see how 20th-century Americans were the garbage-makers, the poison-producers, the carcinogen-creators. (*Wisdomkeepers: Meetings with Native American Spiritual Elders*, by Steve Wall and Harvey Arden, Beyond Words, 1990.)

459. In exchange for all he's taken from us, all White Man gives us back is "welfare," and even for that little bit he forces our men to leave their homes so their children can get food to eat. (Ibid.)

460. That's rape—raping someone's way of life, raping someone's culture and heritage, raping the land and raping the sea. What kind of legacy is that? We reject it. We want no part of it. (Ibid.)

JOHN ROGERS

(Twentieth century)

Chippewa, Minnesota

John Rogers, now deceased, was a Chippewa chief. He had been taken from the White Earth reservation as a young boy and sent to a boarding school in South Dakota to unlearn Indian ways. He later wrote of his experiences in the book, *Red World and White: Memories of a Chippewa Boyhood*.

461. Her eyes sparkled as the sun on laughing waters. (*The People Named the Chippewa*, by Gerald Vizenor, University of Minnesota Press, 1984.)

462. I had learned to love the primitive life which had for so many, many generations influenced and shaped the existence of my ancestors.

... Nothing the white man could teach me would take the place of what I was learning from the forest, the lakes and the river. (Ibid.)

463. I could read more in the swaying of the trees and the way they spread their branches and leaned to the wind than I could read in any books that they had at school. (Ibid.)

464. I could learn much more from the smiling, rippling waters and from the moss and flowers than from anything the teachers could tell me about such matters. (Ibid.)

465. I could gain knowledge from my daily walks under the trees where the shadows mixed with the shifting sunlight and the wind fanned my cheek with its gentle caress or made me bend, as it did the trees, to its mighty blasts. (Ibid.)

VERNON COOPER

(1905–?)

Lumbee

Vernon Cooper was an elder of the Lumbee tribe, formerly known as the Croatoan.

466. These days people seek knowledge, not wisdom. Knowledge is of the past, wisdom is of the future. (*Wisdomkeepers: Meetings with Native American Spiritual Elders,* by Steve Wall and Harvey Arden, Beyond Words, 1990.)

LOUIS R. BRUCE

(1906–)

Mohawk/Sioux, New York

Louis R. Bruce served as commissioner of Indian affairs. He wanted the Bureau of Indian Affairs to become a service organization to help Indians, rather than a management organization to tell them what to do.

467. I want to see Indians buying cars from Indians on reservations, and buying food in Indian-owned stores, driving on Indian-planned and Indian-built roads, talking on Indian-owned telephone systems, and living in an Indian-managed economy. (*Contemporary American Indian Leaders*, by Marion E. Gridley, Dodd Mead, 1972.)

CARL GORMAN

(1907–)

Navajo, Arizona

Carl Gorman, a Navajo artist, uses tribal motifs in his work.

468. The life of the Navajo is harsh and cruel, a constant battle with nature. Having grown up in the Navajo country, I am keenly aware of this and try to bring out some of this feeling as well as the desire to portray the culture of my people. (*Carl Gorman's World*, by Henry Greenberg and Georgia Greenberg, University of New Mexico Press, 1984.)

469. I have always felt that the traditional [Indian] school of painting is traditional to the Plains Indians, but not to the Navajos, and that I can better express my cultural heritage and myself by using whatever means and technique will best bring out whatever I want to say. (Ibid.)

470. I want to help my Navajo people preserve their beautiful arts and crafts, which are rapidly vanishing. (Interview in the Gallup (N.M.) *Independent*; Ibid.)

471. Indian art is dying out and we Navajo people must do something to prevent this great loss. (Ibid.)

472. Our young Navajo people do not realize the valuable heritage they have. They need training and help. Art offers them an opportunity to do creative work; and at the same time their earnings can be enough to support them if they have the initiative and the industry. (Ibid.)

WILLIAM W. KEELER

(1908–1987)

Cherokee, Texas

William W. Keeler was president of the Phillips Petroleum Company. At one time, he headed the National Association of Manufacturers. He was elected to the Oklahoma Hall of Fame. President Harry Truman appointed him principal chief of the Cherokee Nation. He was later elected to the post by the tribe.

473. Forgive the past and remove resentment from your hearts. Even the strongest person cannot carry such a burden for long. (*Contemporary American Indian Leaders*, by Marion E. Gridley, Dodd Mead, 1972.)

HARRIETT PIERCE

(1910–   )

Seneca, Pennsylvania

Harriet Pierce, a member of the Seneca Bear Clan, is a descendant of Cornplanter (q.v.). In the mid-1960s, she was a leader in the unsuccessful fight to prevent the Army Corps of Engineers from moving an Indian cemetery in Pennsylvania.

474. The white man views land for its money value. We Indians have a spiritual tie with the earth, a reverence for it that whites don't share and can hardly understand. (*Now That the Buffalo's Gone: A Study of Today's American Indians*, by Alvin M. Josephy, Jr., Knopf, 1982.)

ANNIE DODGE WAUNEKA

(1910–   )

Navajo

Dr. Annie Dodge Wauneka, an advocate for political and social causes, was the first Native American to win the Presidential Medal of Freedom. She was the daughter of the last tribal chief and first tribal chairman of the Navajo.

475. Ever since the development of political machinery and bureaucratic organizations among Indians, there has been a sudden perspective of women—and the roles of women—as second-class citizens. The basic reason for discrimination against Indian women stems from the Federal government's intervention in Indian affairs. (Speech at the first Southwest Indian Women's Conference; "Interview with Dr. Annie Dodge Wauneka," by Shirley Hill Witt, in *Frontiers: A Journal of Women Studies,* vol. 6, no. 3, University of Colorado, Fall 1981.)

476. To offset the second-class role, Indian women must become more active in politics and become aware of the educational opportunities open to Native American women. (Ibid.)

EMMA MARKS

(1913–   )

Tlingit, Alaska

Emma Marks, a deeply religious member of the Pentecostal Church, is regarded as one of the finest beadworkers in Alaska. She has been honored for her work by the Alaska State Council on the Arts and the Alaska Governor's Award in the Arts, among others.

477. My grandfather

when I was a child,

still very small . . .

Yes, we smaller children

would sit in a row.

When he was going to tell stories

none of us could get up and run.

But now,

when I try talking with my children

they watch T.V.

(1982; *Haa Tuwunaagu Yis, for Healing Our Spirit: Tlingit Oratory,* edited by Nora Marks Dauenhauer and Richard Dauenhauer, University of Washington Press, 1990.)

ALLAN HOUSER

(1914–1994)

Chiricahua Apache, Oklahoma

Allan Houser was a sculptor, painter, and muralist. His early works appeared at San Francisco's Golden Gate Exposition and the New York World's Fair in 1939. In 1949 he received the first of two Guggenheim Fellowships. By the 1990s, he was being acclaimed as the patriarch of American Indian sculpture.

478. Human dignity is very important to me. I feel that way towards all people, not just Indians. . . . In my work, this is what I strive for— this dignity, this goodness that is in man. I hope I am getting it across. If I am, then I am doing what I have always wanted. (*Houser and Haozous: A Sculptural Retrospective,* The Heard Museum, Phoenix, 1983.)

479. All my life I've worked to emphasize the values that Indians have held for centuries. Especially ideas or concepts of living in harmony with nature. (Ceremony at presentation of a sculpture for the forthcoming National Museum of the American Indian, 1993; cited in "Allan Houser," by Barbara Perlman, in *Native Peoples*, Winter 1995.)

480. This country is recognizing Indians at last, and what we can contribute. (Ibid.)

481. One way of learning art is to choose a master and then try to copy that master; another way is to take off on your own and then try to master whoever you are. (Remark to son, Robert Haozous (q.v.); Ibid.)

LILLIAN VALENZUELA ROBLES

(1916–)

Akagchemem, California

Lillian Valenzuela Robles is an elder activist. She has been a community worker with the Long Beach (California) Unified School District.

482. Each night at 6:30 I walk the perimeter and bless the land with tobacco and sage. I do this to erase the negativity and to let the land know it's not forgotten. Our ancestors must know we haven't forgotten them. (Referring to the sacred Indian site on the California State University campus at Long beach, where faculty housing is planned; quoted in "Voices of My People," by Ken Wibecan, in *Modern Maturity*, December 1993–January 1994.)

483. In order to survive, many of my people had to call themselves Mexicans. In the 1850s, the State of California offered bounties for dead Indians. . . . When whites coming from the East Coast wanted Indian land, they would kill the Indians and take their land. (Ibid.)

JOSEPH C. VASQUEZ

(1917–)

Apache/Sioux, Colorado

Joseph C. Vasquez, a former executive with Hughes Aircraft, has been an advocate on behalf of Native American causes.

484. I do not regret being an Indian, for being one gives me an advantage that others do not have. First, I am an Indian and I am also an American, a good American. I was here yesterday. I am here today. I will be here tomorrow, because I am unique. I belong to a minority with seniority. (*Contemporary American Indian Leaders*, by Marion Gridley, Dodd, Mead, 1972.)

MARY TALLMOUNTAIN

(1918–)

Koyukon Athabascan, Alaska

Mary TallMountain is an author and poet.

485. Alaska is my talisman, my strength, my spirit's home. Despite loss and disillusion, I count myself rich, fertile, and magical. (*I Tell You Now*, edited by Brian Swann and Arnold Krupat, University of Nebraska Press, 1987.)

FREDERICK DOCKSTADER

(1919–   )

Oneida/Navajo, California

Frederick Dockstader is an anthropologist, author, and artist.

486. Only recently has there been any genuine interest in the esthetic product of the Native American. In those instances where it has been expressed, it is largely as souvenir or exotic curiosity products rather than a truly developed appreciation of the esthetic quality. (*Indian Art of the Americas*, Museum of the American Indian, Heye Foundation, 1973.)

487. Even in those specialized institutions devoted to Indian materials or interested in the American West, the treatment is largely sentimental or romantic, frequently reflecting the advance of the frontier in terms of the so-called "conquest" of the Western area. (Ibid.)

488. As long as the Indian is relegated to the production of knick-knacks and tourist souvenirs, his art will never be other than a curiosity occupying a minimum role in the art world. (Ibid.)

489. The greatest problem the younger Indian artist has today is that of being able to select from his Indian background those qualities which are important to him, express them through his art work in a manner which will be acceptable to the Western World, and in so doing, not sacrifice the very quality of Indianness that gives him expression and identity. (Ibid.)

CLYDE WARRIOR

(?–1968)

Ponca

Clyde Warrior was president of the National Indian Youth Council.

490. Our children are learning that their people are not worthy and thus that they individually are not worthy. Even by some stroke of good fortune, prosperity was handed to us "on a platter," that still would not soften the negative judgment our youngsters have of their people and themselves. As you know, people who feel themselves to be unworthy and feel they cannot escape this unworthiness turn to drink and crime and self-destructive acts. (Statement to President Lyndon Johnson's National Advisory Commission on Rural Poverty, February 2, 1967.)

491. Unless there is some way that we as Indian individuals and communities can prove ourselves competent and worthy in the eyes of our youngsters there will be a generation of Indians grow to adulthood whose reaction to their situation will make previous social ills seem like a Sunday School picnic. (Ibid.)

492. For the sake of our psychic stability as well as our physical well-being, we must be free men and exercise free choices. We must make decisions about our own destinies. We must be able to learn and profit by our own mistakes. Only then can we become competent and prosperous communities. (Ibid.)

493. We must be free in the most literal sense of the word—not sold or coerced into accepting programs for our own good, not of our own making or choice. Too much of what passes for grassroots democracy on the American scene is really a slick job of salesmanship. It is not hard for sophisticated administrators to sell tinsel and glitter programs to simple people—programs which are not theirs, which they do not understand and which cannot but ultimately fail and contribute to already strong feelings of inadequacy. Community development must be just what the word implies, Community Development. It cannot be packaged programs wheeled into Indian communities by outsiders which Indians can "buy" or once again brand themselves as unprogressive if they do not "cooperate." (Ibid.)

494. I believe that what is at the heart of this Indian revolution is bureaucracy out of control, over-institutionalization, alienation of individuals, exploitation of people. . . . And American Indians are fed up with this. (1967; *As Long as the Rivers Shall Flow,* War Resisters League, 1974.)

495. If America is so good, if America is so great, if America is so charitable, then why are we forcing people to where the only thing they can do is come out with volcanic eruptions of violence? (Ibid.)

GRACE THORPE

(1921–   )

Sac/Fox, Oklahoma

Grace Thorpe, an Indian activist, was the daughter of Olympic champion Jim Thorpe (q.v.).

496. What has happened to our people all along is that when a change occurs in the Federal Administration, a new commissioner of Indian Affairs and a new director for the Department of Interior are appointed and we have absolutely no continuity. (Personal interview with Robert W. Wheeler; *Pathway to Glory,* by Robert W. Wheeler, Carleton Press, 1975.)

497. Most of our Indian people are torn between the two cultures. In my case, the Indian people look at me as a white, while the white people say I'm an Indian. This leads me to believe that more of our Indian people need to retain their culture, language, and indeed, their Indianness. (Ibid.)

498. I believe a lot of the frustration of our people, the suicide rate and the alcoholism problem, is based on removing them from their Indian world and putting them into the other [white world] without adequate preparation. (Ibid.)

IRA HAYES

(1922–1955)

Pima, Arizona

Ira Hayes was a U.S. Marine who achieved fame during World War II as one of the men photographed by Joe Rosenthal raising the flag over Iwo Jima. Hayes never got used to being a celebrity, which continued in civilian life. After drifting from job to job, he died of alcoholism and exposure.

Ira Hayes, a Pima, pointing to himself taking part in the flag-raising at Iwo Jima.

499. We saw a lot of action, which isn't a very good thing to remember. We lost some of our dear buddies, but they did not die in vain. We accomplished our missions. (Letter to family, February 16, 1944; *The Hero of Iwo Jima and Other Stories*, by William Bradford Huie, New American Library, 1962.)

500. I am back again [overseas with his outfit instead of stateside promoting war bonds] . . . and I like it better this way. I have a reason for coming back. . . . I have not been over here twice for nothing. There were a few guys who went all through the battle of Iwo with me. I've known them for a year, fought together, and were scared most of the time together. And they were back here while I was in the States, just for raising a flag, and getting all the publicity and glory. That I could not see. (Letter to family, June 1945; *The Arizona Republic*, February 22, 1965.)

501. Surprising how much a picture can do. (Ibid.)

502. I wish that guy had never taken that picture. (Attributed.)

JOSEPH NICHOLAS

(1925–   )

Passamaquoddy, Maine

Joseph Nicholas is director of the Waponahki Museum and Resource Center in Pleasant Point, Maine. A World War II veteran, he represents his tribe in the Maine legislature. In 1987 he helped inaugurate the opening of Passamaquoddy Homes Incorporated, a joint venture of the Passamaquoddy tribe of northern Maine and a Finnish company.

503. I'd fought for this country and [after the war] I couldn't even vote. And we didn't receive any G.I. benefits, so we were stuck with our cold homes which were sub-standard. (*Tribal Assets: The Rebirth of Native America*, by Robert H. White, Henry Holt, 1990.)

504. After years of seeing other people's business signs around here saying "Passamaquoddy This" and "Passamaquoddy That," we did have Passamaquoddy Homes Incorporated, and it belongs to us. Non-Indians are beginning to respect Passamaquoddy money. Soon they will respect us as a people. (Ibid.)

ANDY ABIETA

(Twentieth century)

Isleta Pueblo

Andy Abieta was governor of the Isleta Pueblo in New Mexico.

505. When the white man prays, he prays for what *he* wants, for *himself*. When the Indian prays he prays for other people. The last words of the Indian prayer are these: "If there is anything left, let it be for me." You do not hear the Anglos pray that way. It is our way. We shall keep it our way. (*As Long as the Rivers Shall Flow*, War Resisters League, 1974.)

LUTHER CLEARWATER

(Twentieth century)

Sioux

Luther Clearwater is a Rosebud leader.

506. The Indi'n militants keep wantin' to put things way back a hundred years ago. We're gettin' pushed back enough without help! Get ever'body killed or dyin' off, runnin' around crazy and shootin'—that's white man. So many of these nationists get militant and go away and say they talk for their people. They stay out too long, away from home. They don't know how to *be* Indi'n, so busy *actin'* Indi'n. (*Black Hills White Justice: The Sioux Nation versus the United States, 1775 to the Present*, by Edward Lazarus, HarperCollins, 1991.)

LORI CUPP

(Mid to late twentieth century)

Navajo

Lori Cupp is the first Navajo woman to become a surgeon.

507. In the Navajo religion and culture, there is an emphasis on how you relate to everything around you. Everything has to be measured, weighed and harmonious. We call it nizhoni—walking in beauty—and I believe what I do as a surgeon fits into this philosophy. I know my actions directly alter the course of people's lives. (*New York Times*, February 17, 1994.)

508. What an amazing and rare thing it is to actually work inside another human being. At the time, I may be stressed or scared, but I also feel an unbelievable link to something larger—call it God or whatever—a universal spiritual connectedness. (Ibid.)

ROBERT BURNETTE

(1926–)

Standing Rock Sioux, North Dakota

Robert Burnette has long been active in the fight for Indian rights. He served as executive director of the National Congress of American Indians from 1960 to 1963. He was also president of the Rosebud Sioux Tribe and director of the Sioux Tribe's Economic Development Administration. He directed American Indians and Friends, an organization dealing with the civil rights of Native Americans.

509. A warlike struggle, with the Indians as one of the antagonists and the white man as the other, is still being fiercely waged, and, as usual, the Indian is losing. The Indian, though, is at even less of an advantage than he was a century ago. A number of his own, in positions of influence, have gone over to the paleface's side. (*The Tortured Americans*, by Robert Burnette, Prentice-Hall, 1971.)

510. Since he laid down his guns, the Indian has no weapons, literally and figuratively. Thus his struggle to retain his heritage and to survive as an individual may seem foolhardy. Faced with corrupt leadership, an indifferent or malicious Bureau of Indian Affairs, and the absence of any legal remedy for wrongs committed against him, surrounded by greedy real estate, cattle, timber, oil, hunting, fishing, and other interests, his capacity to fight effectively is weak indeed. (Ibid.)

511. General Sherman's definition of a reservation as a place where Indians live, surrounded by thieves, is tragically true. (Ibid.)

512. Considered to be heathens, the Indians were fair game for bloodthirsty missionaries and clergymen, such as Cotton Mather, who extolled the burning alive of a townful of Indian men, women, and children. (Ibid.)

513. As I grew up on the reservation . . . I became aware that not very much had changed for the Indian in several centuries. He no longer had to die on the battlefield . . . ; now he wasted away from tuberculosis, drifted demoralized into alcoholism, and grubbed what . . . mean subsistence he could, lived and died impoverished, powerless, ignored. (Ibid.)

PHILLIP MARTIN

(1926–)

Choctaw, Mississippi

Phillip Martin is chief of the Mississippi band of Choctaws. As a member of the Air Force in postwar Europe, he had been impressed by the will of the Europeans to rebuild. He later drew on that experience to push for Choctaw business enterprises.

514. Schools run by federal bureaucrats produce little bureaucrats. (*Tribal Assets: The Rebirth of Native America,* by Robert H. White, Henry Holt, 1990.)

515. Economic development in Indian Country is more than just capitalization of businesses. Although the American philosophy of separation of business from government is sacred (whether the separation is actual or not), it makes little sense to Indian people. There has never been a private sector on most reservations because they have no precedent for accumulating personal wealth for investment. The tribal government is thus the only source of venture and investment capital. (Ibid.)

516. I can tell you with some certainty that if we had not developed those manufacturing jobs in our tribal enterprise, you would now find the vast majority of those jobs gone to Mexico or Taiwan. (Statement to Congress; Ibid.)

517. To us, the situation with the Bureau [of Indian Affairs] is that "we can't live with it and we can't live without it." (*American Indians: Answers to Today's Questions,* by Jack Utter, National Woodlands, 1993.)

JAKE L. WHITECROW, JR.

(1928–1989)

Quapaw/Seneca, Oklahoma

Jake L. Whitecrow, Jr., was an administrator with the National Indian Health Board. Previously, he had served twenty-seven years in the U.S. Army where he rose to the rank of major.

518. I truly believe that some day, our White brothers, and Black brothers, our Yellow brothers and our Brown brothers will recognize their charge that we must live in harmony within the Universe, one with another and that all rights be recognized and we treat our fellow man the same way we want to be treated. (*NIHB Health Reporter*, National Indian Health Board, December 1993.)

PETER MacDONALD

(1928–   )

Navajo, Arizona

Peter MacDonald was one of the Navajo code talkers who served in the U.S. Marines during World War II. He worked for several years with Hughes Aircraft. He was first elected head of the Navajo Tribal Council in 1970, winning not only reelection, but also an unprecedented third term.

519. Our population has increased from 60,000 to 130,000 in the last 30 years. Most of this population lives in a traditional pastoral economy. We utilize for grazing a land base that was originally too small, and it has not expanded with our population. Thus if we are to retain our culture and remain as a tribal entity on our traditional lands, we must make a rapid transition to a modern agricultural and industrial economy. And to do so, we need our share of the water. (Address to the Colorado

River Water Users Association, December 1972; *The Navajo Nation*, by Peter Iverson, Greenwood Press, 1981.)

520. We must claim what is ours—actively and aggressively. We must assert our rights and continue to press for what is due us. (Third inaugural address, January 1979; Ibid.)

521. We must seek unity within. The time for division and dissension is over. We must reach out to each other, come together and unite. (Ibid.)

522. We must dare to dream great dreams—and then we must dare to put them into action. (Ibid.)

EUGENE R. CRAWFORD

(Mid to late twentieth century)

Navajo, New Mexico

Eugene R. Crawford, now deceased, was one of the Marine code talkers of World War II. By using the Navajo language, they made it impossible for the enemy to break the code. He served in the Solomons, Okinawa, and Iwo Jima.

523. At one point . . . I was captured by U.S. Army soldiers who thought I was Japanese. (*Warriors: Navajo Code Talkers*, by Kenji Kawano, Northland, 1990.)

WILSON KEEDAH, SR.

(Mid to late twentieth century)

Navajo

Wilson Keedah, Sr., was a Marine code talker during World War II. He served on Guadalcanal, Iwo Jima, and Okinawa.

524. I went to war because there were no jobs on the reservation. (*Warriors: Navajo Code Talkers*, by Kenji Kawano, Northland, 1990.)

TEDDY DRAPER, SR.

(Mid to late twentieth century)

Navajo, Arizona

Teddy Draper, Sr., was one of the Marine code talkers of World War II; he served in the Pacific.

525. I participated in the bloody battle of Iwo Jima. . . . They told us to secure communications and telephone wire under combat conditions on the island within three days, but it took about a month. (*Warriors: Navajo Code Talkers*, by Kenji Kawano, Northland, 1990.)

SUN BEAR

(1929–   )

Chippewa, Minnesota

Sun Bear is an author, lecturer, and founder of the Bear Tribe Medicine Society. He has also been a movie actor and a consultant on several television series about the old West.

526. The path of power is different for every individual; it represents the course one should follow through life in order to fulfill his or her purpose on the Earth Mother. It is why you are here. (*The Path of Power*, by Sun Bear, Wabun, and Barry Weinstock, Prentice Hall, 1983.)

527. A lot of folks have the idea that all Indians are noble savages, but that's not true. I think the Great Spirit distributed an equal amount of good people among the races, and an equal amount of ding-a-lings. (Ibid.)

528. Native people have always watched nature; it is their textbook for living. (Ibid.)

JIM EARTHBOY

(?–1988)

Cree/Assiniboine

Jim Earthboy, a veteran of World War II, became interested in the battlefield where Chief Joseph (q.v.) surrendered. It later became a national historical site.

529. Something happened up there at the battlefield. Henry [a friend] and I heard people talking and crying. You know, as long as the battlefield's been there nobody has ever done anything. (Spoken to his wife, 1974; "Annals of the West: Chief Joseph's Revenge," by Mark Stevens, in *The New Yorker*, August 8, 1994.)

JANET McCLOUD

(Mid-twentieth century)

Tulalip

Janet McCloud took part in the fishing rights demonstrations held in Washington State in the mid-1960s. She was one of the early members of the Survival of American Indians Association.

530. The history books are wrong when they talk about "the last Indian wars." They have never stopped! (Statement following the "fish-in" confrontations in Washington State; *Red Power: The American Indians' Fight for Freedom*, by Alvin M. Josephy, Jr., American Heritage, 1971.)

DAISY ALBERT

(Mid-twentieth century)

Hopi

Daisy Albert was an Arizona housewife when she was asked by a national magazine for her thoughts on Indian problems.

531. Some misinformed whites call the real Hopis, those who are sincerely religious and determined to keep the good things given them by the Supreme Being, "hostiles." The real "hostiles" are the whites who are trying to destroy us. (*The Rotarian*, August 1954.)

PETER DILLON

(Mid-twentieth century)

Sioux

Peter Dillon served as chairman of the Black Hills Sioux Nation Council during World War II. The council spoke out on behalf of Sioux claims to the Black Hills.

532. All past history shows that a conquered people has to take what the conqueror gives, just or unjust, but the present will be worse if the boys who are now at the front, who are fighting for what is just and right, not only for our rights, but for the rights of this continent, fail. (Letter, 1944; *Black Hills White Justice: The Sioux Nation versus the United States, 1775 to the Present*, by Edward Lazarus, HarperCollins, 1991.)

WILBUR RIEGERT

(Mid to late twentieth century)

Sioux

Wilbur Riegert was a Sioux leader during the War on Poverty of the late 1960s.

533. Poverty is a noose that strangles humility and breeds disrespect for God and man. (*As Long as the Rivers Shall Flow,* War Resisters League, 1974.)

534. Poverty is a stigma of disgrace, especially in this glorious land of ours. It is inexcusable in a land, and of a people, having more than plenty. (Ibid.)

535. A pointing finger of shame on those who govern and regulate "progress." American Indian family life on reservations is an example of "progressive" poverty brought about by the powers of force, which have left generations to brood over their inability to stem the overwhelming tide of greedy fortune hunters, to have and to hold all they could possess. They have it now, America the beautiful and the bountiful. (Ibid.)

HERBERT BLATCHFORD

(Mid to late twentieth century)

Navajo

Herbert Blatchford, founder of the National Indian Youth Council, became its executive director. He headed the group during the fish-ins held in the state of Washington. Indians fished in those areas from which they had been barred by state law. At one point, representatives of some fifty-six different tribes from all over the United States came to the state to demonstrate their support for those fighting for Indian fishing rights.

536. It was the first full-scale intertribal *action* since the Indians defeated General Custer on the Little Big Horn. (*The New Indians*, by Stan Steiner, Harper & Row, 1968.)

OREN R. LYONS

(1930–)

Onondaga, New York

Oren R. Lyons is an associate professor of American studies at the State University of New York, Buffalo. A distinguished artist, he is a chief of the Turtle Clan of the Onondaga Nation. Lyons is publisher of *Daybreak*, the national Indian news magazine. He has also represented Indian interests at the United Nations.

537. We come here . . . speaking the truth on behalf of people, of the world, of the four-footed, of the winged, of the fish that swim. Someone must speak for them. I do not see a delegation for the four-footed. I see no seat for the eagles. (Speech at United Nations conference in Geneva, Switzerland, 1977; *Native American Reader: Stories, Speeches and Poems*, edited by Jerry D. Blanche, Denali Press, 1990.)

538. We forget and we consider ourselves superior, but we are after all a mere part of the Creation. And we must continue to understand where we are. And we stand between the mountain and the ant, somewhere and only there, as part and parcel of the Creation. (Ibid.)

539. It is our responsibility, since we have been given the minds to take care of these things. The elements and the animals, and the birds, they live in a state of grace. They are absolute, they can do no wrong. It is only we, the two-leggeds, that can do this. (Ibid.)

540. So what is it you guys want from the Elders? Secrets? Mystery? . . . I can tell you right now there are no secrets. There's no mystery. There's only common sense. (Remarks to two non-Indian journalists who were interviewing Native American elders; *Wisdomkeepers: Meetings with Native American Spiritual Elders*, by Steve Wall and Harvey Arden, Beyond Words Pub., 1990.)

541. You break Man's law and you pay a fine or go to jail—maybe. . . . There's another law, the Creator's law. We call it Natural law. . . . If you violate it, you get hit. There's no judge and jury, there's no lawyers or courts, you can't buy a judge or beg your way out of it. (Ibid.)

542. If you kill the water, you kill the life that depends on it, your own included. That's Natural law. It's also common sense. (Ibid.)

543. The history of humankind in North and South America can be divided into two parts: the history of the aboriginal peoples of the Western Hemisphere prior to the landfall of Western man, and the history of North and South America after the voyages of Columbus. These histories can be likened to an iceberg. . . . [S]even-eighths lie beneath the surface of the water. We can see Western occupation above the surface and visible. The aboriginal peoples' time is below the surface and invisible. This 500-year occupation by Western man contrasts with the conservative estimate of 12,000 years of aboriginal occupation. ("The American Indian in the Past," in *Exiled in the Land of the Free*, edited by Oren R. Lyons and John C. Mohawk, Clear Light Publishers, 1992.)

544. It is my observation that we are suffering from the attitudes that come from the Christian doctrine of manifest destiny—that one people will rule the world. Inherent in this is the idea that a chosen people have a divine right—nay mission—to dominate the world. (Commencement address at Syracuse University, New York, 1993.)

545. We have been seasoned in suffering and no one can refute the history of holocaust visited upon the indigenous peoples of the hemisphere. (Ibid.)

546. [B]y killing the salmon in their spawning grounds, by clear cutting the forests without reseeding, by polluting fresh water that all life needs for survival, you have broken the great cycles of regeneration, the fundamental law of natural life. . . . The law that is absolute and merciless. The law that provides life endlessly if we abide, and the law that destroys in exact ratio to transgressions that challenge it. (Ibid.)

547. The white man's religion talks about mastering the earth, which means putting up your towns by water so you can watch your garbage float away. ("R.I.P. Tonto," by Robert Lipsyte, in *Esquire*, February 1994.)

548. When you've taken something from somebody, and they're still there looking at you, it's got to be hard. We haven't disappeared. The land is here and we're still here. Their feet are always moving, but they're not going anywhere, and they're saying, "We'll do this and that with this program," and we're just saying, "You have our land." (Ibid.)

549. The West didn't get wild until the white people got there. There's no such word as *wild* in the Indian languages. The closest we can get to it is the word *free*. We were free people. (Ibid.)

LEONARD CROW DOG

(Mid to late twentieth century)

Lakota

Leonard Crow Dog was the medicine man for the American Indian Movement during the occupation of Wounded Knee in 1973.

550. A reservation Indian is already well-prepared to go to the penitentiary. Before he gets there he has already practiced being in prison. And even on the reservation, many Indians are still having a barbed-wire attitude—I try to teach my children and my people to get rid of the barbed-wire mind. (*In the Spirit of Crazy Horse,* by Peter Matthiessen, Viking, 1983.)

LaDONNA HARRIS

(1931–   )

Comanche, Oklahoma

LaDonna Harris is the founder of Americans for Indian Opportunity, an organization dedicated to improving Indian education and economic opportunity. She is the wife of former U.S. Senator Fred Harris of Oklahoma.

551. Indians have been the victims of fine rhetoric, followed by inaction or worse, for two centuries. Swift action is what is needed. (*Contemporary American Indian Leaders,* by Marion E. Gridley, Dodd, Mead, 1972.)

552. White ideas about Indians are completely phony and I am seeking ways to correct them. We don't sit around doing beadwork and making baskets all the time. (Ibid.)

553. One cannot be "an Indian." One is a Comanche, an Oneida, a Hopi. One can be self-determining, not as "an Indian," but as a Comanche, an Oneida, etc. We progress as communities, not as individuals. We want to maintain ourselves as communities, according to our group identity, not just as mere individuals or as amorphous "Indians." (Statement, 1988; *Native American Reader: Stories, Speeches and Poems*, edited by Jerry D. Blanche, Denali Press, 1990.)

554. We want to maintain ourselves as we are so we can contribute our differences, our particular understanding, to both the national community and to global society. (Ibid.)

555. We [Indians] are not a homogeneous group, and tribal ideas of progress may be radically different from Euro-American ideas. For example, the Northern Cheyenne count as "progress" their ability to maintain environmental quality, rather than the development of their coal resources. (Ibid.)

556. At the moment there is a veritable renaissance going on in tribal America as we come to terms with who we are as tribal people in contemporary society. We are bringing tradition along with us into the future rather than "going back to tradition" and maintaining ourselves like rigid museum pieces. (Ibid.)

LOUIS W. BALLARD

(1931–)

Quapaw/Cherokee, Oklahoma

Louis W. Ballard is a composer whose works have dealt with many aspects of Indian history, such as Wounded Knee. He has been responsible for music education at all federal Indian schools. His work reflects Indian culture, from lullabies and love songs to tribal ceremonial songs.

557. Because I identify with my Indian background, my creative expression has been enhanced and extended to others. (*Contemporary American Indian Leaders*, by Marion E. Gridley, Dodd, Mead, 1972.)

LORRAINE CANOE

(1932–   )

Mohawk, New York

Lorraine Canoe teaches a course on conquered peoples in America at Hunter College, New York. After living in New York City for thirty-five years, she described to a reporter what life was like for a Mohawk in the city.

558. You can find all kinds of things, but the supermarkets do not stock deer meat or boiled corn bread. In no borough are regular Mohawk ceremonies held for each of the year's 13 moons. And it's not easy trying to find someone I can talk Mohawk with. ("Yearning to Breathe Free," by N. R. Kleinfield, *New York Times*, January 3, 1995.)

559. New York is very exciting, but the reservation is my home. (Ibid.)

560. The church is a crutch. It is a white man's religion. They brought it here to conquer us and civilize us. (Ibid.)

JIM BARNES

(1933–   )

Choctaw, Oklahoma

Jim Barnes, a professor of comparative literature at Northeast Missouri State University, founded the Chariton Review Press.

561. I was five years old the last time I heard the mountain lion scream.

That was in Oklahoma, 1938, when times were hard and life was good—and sacred. But a year later, the WPA had done its work: roads were cut, burial mounds were dug, small concrete dams were blocking nearly every stream. The Government was caring for its people. . . . A man could eat again, while all about him the land suffered. (*I Tell You Now*, edited by Brian Swann and Arnold Krupat, University of Nebraska Press, 1987.)

BEN NIGHTHORSE CAMPBELL

(1933–)

Northern Cheyenne, California

Ben Campbell was elected to the U.S. Senate in 1992, representing the state of Colorado. Previously, he had served in the House of Representatives and the Colorado State Legislature. In 1995 he switched from the Democratic to the Republican party.

562. For many people around the world, [1492] will be a year to celebrate the accomplishments of a man who was a product of an emerging industrial society, and his discovery of what was to him an unknown hemisphere. This land, however, was not only inhabited when Columbus arrived, but also shared and cultivated by ethnically diverse peoples who had prospered in every region of these vast "new" lands for many thousands of years. ("Reflections on the Quincentenary," in *Journal of Legal Commentary*, Spring 1992, vol. 7: 517, 1992.)

563. The great cities of Machu Picchu, Tenoshtitlan, Kahokia, and the village cities of the Anasazi reflect industrious and prosperous societies that lived in harmony with Mother Nature, possessing an understanding that humans exist together with, not separate from, the natural world that ensures survival. (Ibid.)

564. It is estimated that more than ten million people, the ancestors of present-day Indian tribes, inhabited North America when Columbus arrived. It is difficult to comprehend the magnitude of the atrocities—intentional, neglectful, or accidental—perpetrated on Indian people by the conquering culture, and later by the very government that assumed

responsibility for their protection. By 1900, the Indian population had dwindled because of imported disease, slavery, forced relocation, and outright genocide, to an estimated 100,000. Today, about two million people are enrolled members of recognized tribes and another ten million Americans claim some Indian ancestry. (Ibid.)

565. Just like that, money started to pour in. I began feeling better, and my standing in the polls began to climb. (Describing what happened at the end of his 1992 campaign, after members of his Cheyenne tribe persuaded him to carry the tuft of an eagle feather and paint parts of his body; *Newsweek,* September 13, 1993.)

566. I can no longer represent the agenda that is put forth by the [Democratic] party, although I certainly agree with many of the things that Democrats stand for. (News conference, announcing his switch in political parties; "Democrats Lose Senate Seat with Switch by Coloradan," by Katharine Q. Seelye, *New York Times,* March 4, 1995.)

567. I've always been considered a moderate, to the consternation of the left wing of the Democratic Party. I imagine my continued modderacy [*sic*] will be now to the consternation of the right wing of the Republican Party. (Ibid.)

568. It [not having a family] made me very self-reliant and independent. If you have nobody to rely on, then you have got to do it yourself. (Statement to biographer; Ibid.)

VINE DELORIA, JR.

(1933–)

Standing Rock Sioux, South Dakota

Vine Deloria, Jr., is a professor of law, political science, religious studies, and history at the University of Colorado, Boulder. The former executive director of the National Congress of American Indians, he is the author of many books on Indian rights.

569. Red Power means we want power over our own lives. . . . We simply want the power, the political and economic power, to run our own lives in our own way. (*The New Indians*, by Stan Steiner, Harper & Row, 1968.)

570. *Custer Died for Your Sins.* (Book title, 1969.)

571. One of the finest things about being an Indian is that people are always interested in you and your "plight." Other groups have difficulties, predicaments, quandaries, problems, or troubles. Traditionally we Indians have had a "plight." (*Custer Died for Your Sins*, by Vine Deloria, Jr., Macmillan, 1969.)

572. One day at a conference we were singing "My Country 'Tis of Thee" and we came across the part that goes:

Land where our fathers died

Land of the Pilgrims' pride . . .

Some of us broke out laughing when we realized that our fathers undoubtedly died trying to keep those Pilgrims from stealing our land. (Ibid.)

573. It has been said of missionaries that when they arrived they had only the Book and we had the land; now we have the Book and they have the land. (Ibid.)

574. Tonto [the "faithful Indian companion" of the Lone Ranger] was everything that the white man had always wanted the Indian to be. He was a little slower, a little dumber, had much less vocabulary, and rode a darker horse. (Ibid.)

575. Somehow Tonto was always there. Like the Negro butler and the Oriental gardener. Tonto represented a silent, subservient subspecies of Anglo-Saxon whose duty was to do the bidding of the all-wise white hero. (Ibid.)

576. It just seems to a lot of Indians that this continent was a lot better off when we were running it. (*New York Times Magazine*, March 8, 1970.)

577. He [a non-Indian] said that he was really sorry about what had happened to Indians, but that there was good reason for it. The continent had to be developed and he felt that Indians had stood in the way and thus had had to be removed. "After all," he remarked, "what did you do to the land when you had it?" I didn't understand him until later when I discovered that the Cuyahoga River running through Cleveland is inflammable. . . . How many Indians could have thought of creating an inflammable river? (*We Talk, You Listen*, by Vine Deloria, Jr., Macmillan, 1970.)

578. The typical white attitude is that Indians can have land as long as whites have no use for it. (Ibid.)

579. With the distribution of funds [if allocated to individual Indians rather than to the tribe as a whole], will come the drug dealers, bootleggers, used car dealers, and appliance salesmen who would normally cross the street to avoid saying hello to an Indian. One great spasm of spending will occur and then the people, as poor as they ever were, will return to normal lives. (Comment on the possible outcome of a 1980 Supreme Court decision to compensate the Sioux for the Black Hills; *Black Hills White Justice: The Sioux Nation versus the United States, 1775 to the Present*, by Edward Lazarus, HarperCollins, 1991.)

580. American Indians seem an enigma to most other Americans. The images portrayed in the movies, whether of noble red man or bloodthirsty savage, recall the stereotypes of western history. Newspaper stories dealing with oil wells, uranium mines, land claims, and the occupation of public buildings and reservation hamlets almost seem to speak of another group altogether and it is difficult to connect the two perceptions of Indians in any single and comprehensible reality. (*Amer-*

ican Indians, American Justice, by Vine Deloria, Jr., and Clifford M. Lytle, University of Texas Press, Austin, 1983.)

581. Literature on Indians provides no clues to understanding the present or remembering the past. Much contemporary literature is a thinly disguised romanticism that looks at Indians as the last and best spiritual hope for a society disheartened and disorganized. (Ibid.)

582. The protections of the Bill of Rights, available to all other Americans, have not been available for American Indians. Not only have the federal courts studiously avoided considering the application of these protections, but Congress and the executive branch have frequently acted as if there were no limitation whatsoever in their power to deal with Indians, and the courts have deferred to this assertion of naked authority. (*Exiled in the Land of the Free,* edited by Oren R. Lyons and John Mohawk, Clear Light Publishers, 1991.)

583. In 1968, the American Indian Civil Rights Act . . . was passed, but this act only served to extend some Bill of Rights protection to tribal members in their relationship with Indian governments. Nothing was authorized that would protect American Indian nations or individuals against the arbitrary actions of the Federal government, protection that both states and individuals enjoy. (Ibid.)

SEVERT YOUNG BEAR

(Mid to late twentieth century)

Sioux

Severt Young Bear is a Sioux activist. Following the 1980 Supreme Court decision to compensate the Sioux for the Black Hills, he spoke out against the ruling.

584. I cannot accept money for the Black Hills because land is sacred to me. . . . [The whites] are trying to change our value system. To be a traditional person is to believe in our own culture, is to believe in yourself as a Lakota person; then you cannot sell the land. (*Black Hills White Justice: The Sioux Nation versus the United States: 1775 to the Present,* by Edward Lazarus, HarperCollins, 1991.)

MARK MARACLE

(Mid to late twentieth century)

Mohawk

Mark Maracle is a militant who backs sovereignty for the Mohawk Nation.

585. The police don't understand how serious we are about history and our claims to the land. They think we are just a bunch of funny colored men with long hair who talk about weird dances and hunting or fishing when we drink too much. This is our history and we were raised with it as you were raised with the Pilgrims and the *Mayflower*. (*One Nation under the Gun*, by Rick Hornung, Pantheon, 1991.)

586. We look at all of the northeast and see our people. Fishing on the coast of Labrador and Newfoundland or running the rapids of the St. Lawrence, or hunting bear and moose, even buffalo in the woods that stretch across New York and into Canada. The police look at us and see six square miles and a bunch of crazies talking shit. They don't understand that we are a lost nation trying to restore the dignity of our past. (Ibid.)

DARREN BONAPARTE

(Mid to late twentieth century)

Mohawk

Darren Bonaparte, a Mohawk reservation resident, comments on casino gambling.

587. It was like, all of a sudden, Las Vegas in your hometown. (On casino gambling on a Mohawk reservation in upstate New York; "Incident at Akwesasne," by Daniel D'Ambrosio, *Gentlemen's Quarterly*, November 1993.)

588. Outside governments have screwed us left and right every chance they got. Stole our land, whittled it down to nothing. We're living on a pillowcase, basically, and finally, because of the white man's greed for gambling, his addictions, cigarettes, cocaine, drugs, guns, whatever, suddenly, we're able to make a profit on their misery. (Ibid.)

VERNON BELLECOURT

(Mid to late twentieth century)

Chippewa, Minnesota

Vernon Bellecourt, who came from a family of twelve children, lived on the reservation until he was fifteen. He operated some small businesses for a time, including a beauty salon and an import firm. In 1968 he helped form the American Indian Movement (AIM), a militant organization fighting for Indian rights.

589. They were going to call the organization the Concerned Indian Americans, CIA. They couldn't use that! So a couple of older, respected women said, "Well, you keep saying that you *aim* to do this, you *aim* to do that. Why don't you call it AIM, the American Indian Movement?" That's how we got our name. (Interview by Richard Ballad, *Penthouse Magazine*, July 1973).

TIM GIAGO

(1934–   )

Oglala Sioux, South Dakota

Tim Giago, born on the Pine Ridge reservation, is a veteran of the Korean War. He is the editor and publisher of the *Lakota Times*, which he established. Giago writes the weekly column,

"Notes from Indian Country." A number of these columns have been compiled in book form.

590. Reservations have become the Mecca for urban Indians, the land base that bespeaks what lies ahead. Without the reservations, there will be no more Indians. It is something the traditional reservation Indian has always known. Our past, present and future is embedded in the lands of our ancestors. How can a Sacred Land ever be called a concentration camp? (*Notes from Indian Country*, vol. 1, Keith Cochran, 1984.)

591. Is self-determination a prelude to termination? Many Indians look at the very word "self-determination" and they say among themselves, "If you remove 'self' and 'de' from the beginning of the word, you end up with 'termination.' " This is a genuine concern among many reservation Indians. (Ibid.)

592. You can still see the bumper stickers on the highway. They read: "Red Power," "Custer wore Arrow shirts," "Hands off my natural resources," or "Remember Wounded Knee." (Ibid.)

593. The issues and the problems that confront Indian people on a day-to-day basis are extremely complex. It takes a lifetime of education to even begin to understand them. (Ibid.)

N. SCOTT MOMADAY

(1934–   )

Kiowa/Cherokee, Oklahoma

N. Scott Momaday is a novelist, essayist, and poet. He won the Pulitzer Prize in 1969 for his novel *House Made of Dawn*, which told the story of a World War II veteran who tried to recover his spirit in the white world. Other honors include the Academy of American Poets Prize and the Native American Literature Prize.

594. The native vision, the gift of seeing truly, with wonder and delight into the natural world, is informed by a certain attitude of reverence and respect. It is a matter of extrasensory as well as sensory perception. In addition to the eye, it involves the intelligence, the instinct, and the imagination. It is the perception not only of objects and forms but also of essences and ideals. (*Contemporary American Indian Leaders,* by Marion Gridley, Dodd Mead, 1972.)

595. I have done three large paintings . . . of what I call the Columbian triad. Each of these is a portrait of Columbus. One is a skeletal, skull-like portrait with a mermaid above it, titled "Admiral of the Ocean," and then there is one of a dark full-face portrait called "Palos," which is the port from which Columbus set sail. The third one is "San Salvador," a depiction of Columbus in a full figure adjacent to an Indian child. Columbus is an emaciated, death-like figure, and the child is pure, innocent, small and naked. It's a confrontation of the old world and the new world. ("Confronting Columbus Again," from "View from the Shore: American Indian Perspectives on the Quincentenary," *Northeast Indian Quarterly,* edited by Jose Barreiro, vol. 7, no. 3, Fall 1990.)

596. Once in his life a man ought to concentrate his mind upon the remembered earth, I believe. He ought to give himself up to a particular landscape in his experience, to look at it from as many angles as he can, to wonder about it, to dwell upon it. He ought to imagine that he touches it with his hands at every season and listens to the sounds that are made upon it. He ought to imagine the creatures there and all the faintest motions of the wind. He ought to recollect the glare of noon and all the colors of the dawn and dusk. (*The Way to Rainy Mountain,* University of New Mexico Press, 1976).

597. We are what we imagine. Our very existence consists in our imagination of ourselves. . . . The greatest tragedy that can befall us is to go unimagined. (First Convocation of American Indian Scholars; *Indian Voices,* edited by J.H. Casto, Indian Historian Press, 1974.)

GERALD VIZENOR

(1934–   )

Chippewa, Minnesota

Gerald Vizenor is a novelist with a background in journalism. He has taught literature and American studies in Minnesota and California.

598. Anthropologists have invented culture; it doesn't have anything to do with Indians. . . . I think they're interesting in their collection of data and the way they sort it and scramble it and reinvent it, but it doesn't have anything to do with tribal people. It never will. (Interview in *Winged Words: American Indian Writers Speak,* by Laura Coltelli, University of Nebraska Press, 1990.)

599. The methodologies of the social sciences separate people from the human spirit. (Ibid.)

DENNIS BANKS

(1937–)

Chippewa, **Minnesota**

Dennis Banks spent fourteen years attending Indian boarding schools. He served several years in the U.S. Air Force. In 1968 he helped found the American Indian Movement (AIM). One of AIM's militant actions was the occupation of Wounded Knee, the site of the 1890 Indian massacre.

600. We have a completely different value system than that of the larger society. . . . We will introduce evidence of how we've had to go underground in order to maintain our traditional religion, our traditional philosophy. (Testimony relating to charges arising out of the Wounded Knee occupation by AIM, February 12, 1974.)

601. We believe that all living things come from our sacred mother earth, all living things, the green things, the winged things of the air, the four-leggeds, the things that crawl and the two-leggeds. . . . But the important thing in our philosophy is that we believe we're the weakest things on earth, that the two-legged is the weakest thing on earth because we have no direction. . . . Now, because we are the weakest things on earth, we do not have license to exploit or manipulate our brothers and sisters and we also know, because of our role in life, that the buffalo and all other relatives of ours teach us, and so we built our civilization. (Ibid.)

602. There is another way [to express our manhood]. That is to grab the bottle, drink it, go down to the other bar and fight your brothers and sisters just to say, "Look, I'm a man," or take the bottle again and go home and mistreat your wife and tell her, "Look, I'm a man." (Ibid.)

603. And there is another way, the way that we will prove that the United States of America in its genocidal policies against Indian people, forced us to be red-white people. That is the other way. It is to cut our hair, put on the ties and become facsimiles of the white man. (Ibid.)

604. There has been . . . a new way to express our manhood, and that's been the American Indian Movement to express our Indianness. . . . I was an accountant by trade in Cleveland, Ohio, and in the Dakota way, if you cut your hair, that means you're in mourning. And it is our contention that a lot of Dakotas now who are misguided cut their hair because they're mourning, because they lost their Indianness. (Ibid.)

605. When I had my hair cut, I was mistaken for a Chicano, for an Arab, a Hawaiian, a Pakistanian, everything but an American Indian. I'm very proud to be Dakota, and when I walk down the street, I want people to know I'm Indian. (Ibid.)

606. They call us the New Indians. Hell, we are the Old Indians, the landlords of this continent, coming to collect the rent. (*Lakota Woman*, by Mary Crow Dog and Richard Erdoes, Grove Weidenfeld, 1990.)

BILLY MILLS

(1938–   )

Sioux, South Dakota

Billy Mills won the gold medal for the 10,000-meter race at the 1964 Olympics held in Tokyo, Japan. Later, he set other track records. In 1970 he became an information officer for the Bureau of Indian Affairs.

607. My Indianness kept me striving to take first and not settle for less in the last yards of the Olympic race. I thought of how our great chiefs kept on fighting when all of the odds were against them as they were against me. I couldn't let my people down. (*Contemporary American Indian Leaders*, by Marion E. Gridley, Dodd, Mead, 1972.)

ROXANNE DUNBAR ORTIZ

(1938–   )

Cheyenne, Oklahoma

Roxanne Dunbar Ortiz is a professor of Native American studies at California State University, Hayward. Her book, *The Great Sioux Nation: Sitting in Judgment on America*, published in 1977, deals with the case of the Wounded Knee occupation of 1973. The defendants argued before the Federal District Court in Lincoln, Nebraska, that under the terms of the Treaty of 1868, the federal government had no jurisdiction over them. The court ruled against them.

608. The Sioux, like other Indian peoples, are now going beyond bare survival and are asserting sovereignty which is leading to drastic changes in United States–Indian relations. The People see two roads available: Nationhood or genocide. The people are choosing nationhood. (*The Great Sioux Nation: Sitting in Judgment on America*, by Roxanne Dunbar Ortiz, American Indian Treaty Council Information Center/Moon Books, 1977.)

609. In asserting sovereignty, the Sioux join other colonies and former colonies all over the world who have been subjected to European and United States colonialism, in declaring integrity as a separate Nation. (Ibid.)

610. No historian would accept accounts of Nazi officials as to what happened in Nazi Germany because those accounts were written to justify that regime. Yet American historians are still subjective about their own history with a few exceptions. They try to justify and rationalize what happened, give excuses or lay blame on a few exceptionally cruel generals or wild frontiersmen. There were too many massacres for them to be accidental. There were too many buffalo for them to become extinct in a period of five years. Genocide is colonial policy, not accident. (Testimony before U.S. District Court, Lincoln, Nebraska, 1974.)

MELVIN THOM

(1939–)

Paiute, Nevada

Melvin Thom, who founded the National Indian Youth Council, served as its president during the "fish-ins" held in Washington State. In the mid-1960s, Indians demanded their treaty rights to fish in designated areas, and did so despite state laws against it.

611. The Indian never fought back before. He just folded his arms and went away angry. In the past he was defeated before the fight began. That's changed. We changed that. Little tribes you hardly ever heard of are still fighting by themselves. They just stay in there and keep fighting. (*The New Indians,* by Stan Steiner, Harper & Row, 1968.)

PAULA GUNN ALLEN

(1939–)

Laguna/Sioux, New Mexico

Paula Gunn Allen, poet and author, has lectured at universities in California and New Mexico. Since 1990 she has been a professor of literature at the University of California, Los Angeles.

612. There is no America without the death of an Indian. And there can be no America without acknowledgment of one of its major sources. (Interview with Franchot Ballinger and Brian Swann, *MELLUS,* Summer 1983.)

613. Every time you flush the toilet, some Navajo goes without water. You understand that. Staying in this hotel in L.A. means that those folks out on the res[ervation] are in trouble because we have all these goodies. And that's true across the board, for every aspect of American life. (Ibid.)

614. There is no American that is not deeply wedded to the Indian. So, you know, exploitation, what does that mean? We've been exploited right out of house and home. (Ibid.)

JERRY FLUTE

(1939–   )

Sisseton-Wahpeton Dakota, South Dakota

Jerry Flute is the executive director of the Association on American Indian Affairs.

615. During Operation Desert Storm, U.S. troops were ordered not to destroy sacred sites of the Iraqi. Yet the same U.S. government continues to destroy sacred sites of Native Americans. (Testimony before the Senate Select Committee on Indian Affairs, Portland, Oregon, February 1993.)

GAIL SMALL

(Mid to late twentieth century)

Northern Cheyenne

Gail Small is a Native American rights activist.

616. Only a dime of every dollar appropriated by Congress for Indians ever reaches the reservations. Most of the moneys are eaten by the massive bureaucracy of the Bureau of Indian Affairs. ("War Stories: Environmental Justice in Indian Country," *Daybreak*, vol. 4, no. 2, 1994.)

617. Promises of overnight wealth to impoverished tribes serve to divide and conquer the people, as federal agencies, energy corporations, and private speculators seek to dump nuclear waste or get rich off Indian land. By necessity, then, Indian tribes are major players in the environmental justice movement. (Ibid.)

618. There are no coal mines on my reservation yet, and no coal leases have been signed. But every year, the tribe debates again whether we can afford to continue refusing the offers of the coal companies. (Ibid.)

DANIEL PEACHES

(1940–)

Navajo, Arizona

Daniel Peaches, a former Arizona state representative, is a Navajo tribal administrator.

619. The policy of the Interior Department regarding the Indians for the 80's should be one of (1) protecting federal trust responsibilities to the Indian people (federal treaties), (2) protect tribal resources, and (3) promote economic development on Indian reservations. (Letter, February 2, 1982; *The Bureau of Indian Affairs*, by Theodore W. Taylor, Westview, 1984.)

620. All federal agencies should allocate funds directly to the Indian tribes, bypassing state governments. (Ibid.)

621. The President's [Reagan's] policy of returning most of the federal responsibilities back to the states would be a disaster for the Indian people. There is simply no mechanism by which states and Indian tribes can have a mutual relationship. (Ibid.)

RUSSELL MEANS

(1940–)

Oglala Sioux, South Dakota

Russell Means, actor and activist, is chairman of the American Indian Anti-Defamation Council. In 1968 Means joined Dennis

Banks (q.v.) and others in the American Indian Movement (AIM). AIM's purposes are to regain land from the United States and to reestablish an Indian nation. Some of its more radical activities included a sit-in at the Bureau of Indian Affairs and the occupation of Wounded Knee, site of the massacre of Indians in 1890.

622. [Columbus] makes Hitler look like a juvenile delinquent. (*Mankiller: A Chief and Her People*, by Wilma Mankiller and Michael Wallis, St. Martin's Press, 1993.)

623. Right now, today, we who live on the Pine Ridge Reservation are living in what white society has designated a "National Sacrifice Area." What this means is that we have a lot of uranium deposits here, and white culture (not us) needs this uranium as energy production material. (*In the Spirit of Crazy Horse*, by Peter Matthiessen, Viking, 1983.)

624. The cheapest, most efficient way for industry to extract and deal with the processing of this uranium is to dump the waste by-products right here at the digging sites. Right here where we live. (Ibid.)

625. It is genocide to dig uranium here and drain the water—no more, no less. (Ibid.)

626. I understand that every living thing comes from one mother, and that is our Mother Earth. It has been said by the old people that only the white man rapes his mother. (Testimony before U.S. District Court, Lincoln, Nebraska, 1974.)

627. We are all brothers and sisters. That includes every living thing, the green things, the winged of the earth, the four-legged, the things that crawl and swim, the mountains, the streams, the rain, the clouds. (Ibid.)

628. They [the U.S. Government] brought in the law enforcement agencies to protect buildings rather than protect people's rights out here. And the end result—Wounded Knee. (*Voices from Wounded Knee*, Akwesasne Notes, 1974.)

629. The President of the United States [Jimmy Carter], to show you what a racist he is, can talk about human rights when my people are suffering genocide not only in the United States but in the entire [Western] hemisphere. (Speech before a United Nations conference in Geneva, Switzerland, 1977; cited in *Native American Reader: Stories, Speeches and Poems*, edited by Jerry D. Blanche, Denali Press, 1990.)

630. There is only one color of mankind that is not allowed to participate in the international community. And that color is the red. The black, the white, the brown, the yellow all participate in one form or another. (Ibid.)

630a. Racism in America against Indian people is so institutionalized and pervasive as to be almost unrecognizable—especially the vicious kind attached to sports teams with names like Indians, Braves, Warriors. People say, "We're honoring you." Well, okay, thank you. But what if we don't feel honored? They say, "C'mon. What harm is it?" The harm is, we're lumped in by the Eurocentric male mind with animals that he puts in zoos and that he kills and hunts for sport, okay? We're lumped in with the lions and tigers. ("MM Interview: Russell Means," by John Edgar Wideman, in *Modern Maturity*, September-October 1995).

ELIZABETH A. WELLS

(1940–)

Mescalero Apache, New Mexico

Elizabeth A. Wells is the founder and director of the Orre Drumrite Walking Heritage, dedicated to the homeless street Indian. Other programs and ceremonies are held on behalf of young adults and children.

631. Remember, our traditional values are based on *order*, the law of the universe; *decency*, the law of humankind; *wisdom*, the gift of the Great Spirit, and *health*, the gift of healing, endow us with the knowledge that our life is our religion; this land is our church; and the universe is our relative. (*Walk in Peace*, by Elizabeth A. Wells, n.d.)

JAMES WELCH

(1940–)

Blackfeet/Gros Ventre, Montana

James Welch, poet and novelist, published his first collection of poetry in 1971.

632. I have seen poems about Indians written by whites and they are either sentimental or outraged over the condition of the Indian. (*South Dakota Review,* vol. 9, no. 2, Summer 1971.)

633. There are exceptions ... but for the most part only an Indian knows who he is ... and hopefully he will have the toughness and fairness to present his material in a way that is not manufactured by conventional stance. (Ibid.)

634. *Never Give a Bum an Even Break.* (Title of poem.)

635. That's a lot of Indian humor—teasing ... plays on words; Indians are very good at puns. (Interview in *Winged Words: American Indian Writers Speak,* by Laura Coltelli, University of Nebraska Press, 1990.)

SHIRLEY BLACK STONE WESTON

(Mid to late twentieth century)

Oglala Sioux

Shirley Black Stone Weston, an Oglala Sioux, recalls old values systems.

636. Generosity, giving, and sharing, these things the Indians had, these things the Indians practiced. I grew up learning these values, experiencing them, and practicing them. ... When I came to college, ... every person [was] for himself or herself. ("I Remember When We Used to Eat Wild Grapes ... ," *Frontiers: A Journal of Women Studies,* vol. 6, no. 3, University of Colorado, Fall 1981.)

SIMON ORTIZ

(1941–)

Acoma Pueblo, New Mexico

Simon Ortiz is an author and poet whose writings reflect the culture and behavior of Native Americans.

637. Indian oral history has not been acceptable to American society not because it has been unwritten but because the Indian system of moral value has not been accepted. A system which is based upon relationships with all things is not efficient within the workings of the American social system. A value system that is all inclusive—in the Indian sense, speaking of a responsibility for all the universe—is unwieldy according to the precepts of the American system which is conveniently exclusive and finds useful only those parts which gain precedence and dominance over others. (*The Great Sioux Nation: Sitting in Judgment on America*, by Roxanne Dunbar Ortiz, American Indian Treaty Council Information Center/ Moon Books, 1977.)

638. I read [in school] whatever was available as I loved reading which was, after all, an extension of my love of language. (*Always the Stories*, in *Simon Ortiz*, by Andrew Wiget, Boise State University, 1986.)

639. I learned [in school] there were no Indians; they were visages of the historical past who rode painted ponies and attacked wagon trains . . . we were expected to identify with white American images of Dick and Jane and Spot and Puff and homes with white picket fences. (Ibid.)

640. Poetry is a way of engendering life, and that is a political stand when it is against what will take away life. . . . Naturally, this inspiration has been labelled dangerous in many cases—and unliterary and unpoetic as well—because it challenges the established oppressive ruling powers that be. (Cited in *Creative Process*.)

641. Native American poets who speak from a tradition of resistance against oppression are speaking for land and life; their poems, personal and social, are political. (Ibid.)

642. As a writer, I've tried to consider most importantly my life as a Native American who is absolutely related to the land and all that means culturally, politically, personally. Nothing is separate from me in that sense, and I am included with the earth and all its aspects and details. (*Native North American Literature*, by Jane Hoehner, Gale, 1994.)

W. RICHARD WEST, JR.

(1943–)

Cheyenne/Arapaho, Oklahoma

W. Richard West, Jr., is the director of the Smithsonian National Museum of the American Indian. Previously, as an attorney in an Indian-owned law firm in Albuquerque, New Mexico, he represented Indian interests in court cases and before Congress.

643. It's estimated that of the 500 or 600 distinct cultures that dwelled within the borders of what is now the United States before 1492, at least 300 remain. (*New York Times*, September 13, 1992.)

644. It seems to me that the guiding set of esthetics in Indian art is inextricably tied to a shared concept of nature and a belief that life exists in things others might see as inanimate. (Ibid.)

645. We want [museum] visitors to come away with a better appreciation of what they've seen, but also with a more informed and sophisticated sense of Indian cultures in general. To accomplish that, you can't just have the predictable glass case of 500 viewing options. You need direction. (Ibid.)

L. DAVID JACOBS

(1943–)

Mohawk, New York

L. David Jacobs served in the U.S. Navy and then received his formal education at the State University of New York and

"It seems to me that the guiding set of esthetics in Indian art is inextricably tied to a shared concept of nature and a belief that life exists in things others might see as inanimate."

—W. RICHARD WEST, JR., ARAPAHO

the University of Utah. An educator and psychologist, he turned to tribal politics in the late 1980s. A chief of the St. Regis Mohawk Tribe, he favors casino gambling run by the reservation.

646. Poverty is our biggest problem, and we have to figure out a way to enrich ourselves in accordance with the law, with the rights that we have as American citizens. (*One Nation under the Gun*, by Rick Hornug, Pantheon, 1991.)

647. On this [American] side of the border, the law gives us a chance to start our bingo and gambling businesses and we should. The gamblers brought money here. They've brought jobs here. In Canada, the government won't allow gambling. That's their problem. Let Ottawa or Quebec keep dishing out grants and subsidies. Washington and Albany want us to go on our own. And it's hard, but it can work if we do it right. The Americans and the Canadians have two separate approaches to our problems. And I'm choosing to stay with the Americans. (Ibid.)

ROBERT HAOZOUS

(1943–)

Apache/Navajo, California

Robert Haozous, the son of artist Allan Houser (q.v.), took on the original spelling of the family name (Ha-o-zous). A major sculptor in his own right, he has his own studio outside Santa Fe.

648. I try to deal honestly and directly with reality in my art and that reality encompasses both ugliness and beauty. (*Houser and Haozous: A Sculptural Retrospective*, The Heard Museum, Phoenix, 1983.)

649. I love the land and I love people and I hope that my work symbolizes this in my own individual way. (Ibid.)

650. My art is contemporary because I live in the present—but also adhere to the belief that one should be inner-directed and that art should reflect its pure source—the soul of its creator. (Ibid.)

LEONARD PELTIER

(1944–)

Ojibwa/Sioux, North Dakota

Leonard Peltier was a leader in the American Indian Movement. In 1977, following a highly controversial trial, he was found guilty of murdering two FBI agents during a shootout.

651. It is not a new development for white society to steal from non-white peoples. When white society succeeds it's called colonialism. When white society's efforts to colonize people are met with resistance, it's called war. But when the colonized Indians of North America meet to stand and resist we are called criminals. What could be more clear than that to treat us as criminals is a farce? (*In the Spirit of Crazy Horse*, by Peter Matthiessen, Viking, 1983.)

HENRY ADAMS

(1944–)

Assinibonne/Sioux, Montana

Henry Adams, an Indian rights activist, has fought for Indian fishing rights. He was an organizer of Indian participation in the Poor People's March on Washington, D.C., in 1968, and led the Indian delegation to Hanoi during the Vietnam war. Most recently, he has been an executive of the Survival of American Indians Association.

652. The state [of Washington] has only one aim. . . . It intends to destroy our fishing equipment, chase us off the rivers, and save the fish for the white men. (*Contemporary American Indian Leaders*, by Marion E. Gridley, Dodd, Mead, 1972.)

653. Treaties are abstract for the most part, almost meaningless except for a few essential elements. One of these is our sovereignty. The self-government part of treaties is the most basic of all . . . the fishing right gives the Indian people that type of tribal community which is necessary. (Ibid.)

654. I will continue to protest . . . until matters are righted, no matter what the "Uncle Tomahawks" and "red apples" say. (Ibid.)

(Editor's note: These derogatory terms are equivalent to the African-American terms "Uncle Tom" and "Oreo cookie.")

SANDRA J. FOX

(1944–   )

Oglala Sioux, South Dakota

Sandra J. Fox has 25 years of experience in Indian education with the Bureau of Indian Affairs and Indian Education Resource Centers. She has written extensively on this subject.

655. The majority of Indian students are "holistic" learners. They learn more easily if they see the whole picture first, then learn the details as a part of the whole. (*Teaching the Native American*, by Hap Gilliland, Kendall-Hunt, 1992.)

JOHN ECHOHAWK

(1945–   )

Pawnee, New Mexico

John Echohawk is a lawyer who works on behalf of Indian rights. He became executive director of the Native American Rights Fund in 1977.

656. The lack of legal protection for Native American religious practices has plagued Indian tribes since Columbus brought European religious intolerance to the New World. ("Native Americans Then and Now," *Earth Journal*, January/February 1994.)

657. One hundred years ago, it was the policy of the U.S. government to stamp out the ancient Native religious practices of reservation Indians, as part of U.S. government policy to assimilate the tribes into "mainstream" American society. (Ibid.)

658. Recent Supreme Court decisions have denied protection for Native religious practices. . . . U.S. forest service bulldozers [clearing away Native American religious sites] accomplish today what U.S. troops did in the 1890s. (Ibid.)

WILMA MANKILLER

(1945–)

Cherokee, Oklahoma

Wilma Mankiller was the first woman to be elected chief of the Cherokee Nation. She first succeeded to the post when her predecessor resigned. She later won reelection on her own.

659. Native Americans regard their names not as mere labels, but as essential parts of their personalities. A native person's name is as vital to his or her identify as the eyes or teeth. (*Mankiller: A Chief and Her People*, by Wilma Mankiller and Michael Wallis, St. Martin's Press, 1993.)

660. Although it is so crucial for us to focus on the good things— our tenacity, our language and culture, the revitalization of tribal communities—it is also important that we never forget what happened to our people on the Trail of Tears. It was indeed our holocaust. (Ibid.)

661. [Sequoya] was always fascinated with the white people's ability to communicate with one another by making distinctive marks on paper—what some native people referred to as "talking leaves." (Ibid.)

662. The Alcatraz experience [when Indians occupied the island] nur-

*"The Alcatraz exper-
ience [when Indians
occupied the island]
nurtured a sense among
us that anything was
possible—even, perhaps,
justice for native
people."*
—WILMA MANKILLER,
CHEROKEE

tured a sense among us that anything was possible—even, perhaps, justice for native people. (Ibid.)

663. The book which became our Indian manifesto [was] *Custer Died
for Your Sins.* (Ibid.)

JOHN MOHAWK

(1945–   )

Seneca, New York

John Mohawk, Ph.D., is an assistant professor in the American
Studies Department at the State University of New York, Buf-

falo. He is the editor of *Daybreak,* a national American Indian news publication. He is a member of the Seventh Generation Fund and chairperson of the board of the Indian Law Resource Center.

664. The identity offered to the Indian was and remains a Catch-22 because there has never been an offer of unequivocal legitimacy. Legitimate Indian governments could not have been destroyed because legitimate Indian governments never existed. By the same token genocide could not have taken place because the peoples and populations who were killed or allowed to expire under oppression were never legitimate peoples. The very identify of the Indian in European and Euro-American eyes was, and to a considerable degree remains, a formula leading to oblivion. ("Indians and Democracy: No One Ever Told Us," in *Exiled in the Land of the Free,* edited by Oren Lyons and John Mohawk, Clear Light Publishers, 1991.)

DAVID C. WARREN

(1945–   )

Choctaw, Mississippi

David C. Warren, a businessman, sells computer software.

665. I am one-quarter Choctaw. My mother's mother was a full-blooded Choctaw. Her name was Marie Pierce Dallas. Although Granny seldom mentioned her ancestry, I was constantly aware of it—her straight jet-black hair, her dark eyes, and her high cheekbones were a constant reminder. She was a grand, proud woman, who bore nine children. Mother was the seventh. Granny lived to the ripe old age of 90. She was instrumental in not only instilling family values, but in helping us become so proud of our Indian heritage. (Personal letter, March 1995.)

666. I remember visiting the reservation in Philadelphia, Mississippi, as a child. I don't recall much, but I do remember sadness, noticing the poor conditions the proud Choctaws were living in. (Ibid.)

MICHAEL DORRIS

(1945–   )

Modoc, Washington

Michael Dorris writes novels, short stories, poetry, essays, and nonfiction. He became a professor of anthropology and Native American studies at Dartmouth, where he met Louise Erdrich (q.v.). They married and have coauthored many literary works.

667. Native American literature is about as descriptive a term as non-Native American literature. If by definition non-Native American literature is about and by people who are not Native Americans, fine, except that doesn't tell you a great deal. (*North Dakota Quarterly*, Winter 1987.)

668. I think what [Louise Erdrich] and I do is either within the tradition of a particular tribe or reservation or it is within the context of American literature. (Ibid.)

669. I don't think that either of us, by any extension of the imagination, could presume or even dare to speak for or write about themes that were important for Navajos or for Iroquois or for people from other regions or other tribal backgrounds. (Ibid.)

JANET CAMPBELL HALE

(1946–   )

Coeur d'Alene, California

Janet Campbell Hale, an author, was brought up on the Coeur d'Alene and Yakima reservations.

670. The government's intention all along was to get us to assimilate into the mainstream of America and to a large extent we have. We all speak English today and we go to school and we work and pay taxes. (During a talk to pupils at the Coeur d'Alene Tribal School, 1992; *Bloodlines: Odyssey of a Native Daughter*, Random House, 1993.)

671. The government would like nothing better, at this point, than to abolish the reservations and get all our tribes to disband, to get rid of us. Only the reservation is our landbase, our home, and we don't want to let go of it. (Ibid.)

672. If Irish or Italian culture dies in America it really isn't that big a deal. They will still exist in Italy and Ireland. Not so with us. There is no other place. North America *is* our old country. (Ibid.)

673. *What if* does not exist. There is nothing but what was and is and we're all stuck with that and have to struggle to do our best with the hand we've been dealt. (Ibid., from introduction.)

674. Fiction speaks in symbolic language, symbols both personal and universal. Fiction and dreams spring from a common well. Dreams, though, speak to the individual—draw attention to suppressed needs, answer troublesome questions, make clear to the dreamer that which was clouded. In the practice of fiction, artists speak not only to the self but to others as well. (Ibid., from essay "Autobiography in Fiction.")

LINDA HOGAN

(1947–)

Chickasaw, Colorado

Linda Hogan writes novels, short stories, poetry, articles, and reviews. She teaches American Indian studies and creative writing in Colorado.

675. Indian women are aware of the difficult position of being female and minority. Tribal women have the lowest wages in the country, and often because of that poverty, Indian children are removed from homes and communities more often than children of any other background. Approximately one-third . . . are removed from homes and placed in foster care or adoptive placement. ("Native American Women: Our Voice, the Air," *Frontiers: A Journal of Women Studies*, vol. 6, no. 3, University of Colorado, Fall 1981.)

676. I'd say there's more racism toward Indian people than toward blacks. (Interview in *Winged Words: American Indian Writers Speak*, by Laura Coltelli, University of Nebraska Press, 1990.)

677. People who are in poverty, people who are in very difficult situations and in pain, have to develop humor or die of despair. (Ibid.)

RICHARD A. HAYWARD

(1947–)

Mashantucket Pequot, Connecticut

Richard A. Hayward is the chairman of the Mashantucket Pequot Tribal Council. The tribe owns and manages the Foxwoods Casino and Resort in Mashantucket, Connecticut. In 1994 Hayward announced a donation of $10 million to the National Museum of the American Indian, the largest single cash donation made in the history of the Smithsonian.

678. Ours is a small tribe, but we have a keen sense of our own history and that of Native America generally. There have been many historic injustices perpetrated on indigenous people of North America, including the slaughter of the Pequots in 1637. But we have survived, and we now flourish. (Announcing a $10 million donation to the National Museum of the American Indian, October 24, 1994; *Smithsonian Runner*, January–February 1995.)

679. In the great tradition of Native Americans everywhere, we believe that it is critical to make a commitment back to Native Americans through this donation. There is obviously no way to turn back the pages of history, but this museum . . . will stand for future generations of Americans as a symbol of understanding, education and tolerance. (Ibid.)

WENDY ROSE

(1948–)

Hopi/Miwok, California

Wendy Rose, a poet, teaches American Indian studies in California. She was the former editor of the *American Indian Quarterly*.

680. It is my greatest but probably futile hope that some day those of us who are ethnic minorities will not be segregated in the literature of America. (*The Third Woman*, edited by Dexter Fisher, Houghton Mifflin, 1980.)

681. *What Happened When the Hopi Hit New York.* (Book title, 1982.)

682. [The centaur reflects] my hybrid status . . . like the centaur, I have always felt misunderstood and isolated—whether with Indians or with non-Indians. (*Songs from This Earth on Turtle's Back*, edited by Joseph Bruchac, Greenfield Review Press, 1983.)

LESLIE SILKO

(1948–)

Laguna, New Mexico

Leslie Silko is a poet, short story writer, and novelist. She is an English professor at the University of Arizona.

683. I am of mixed-breed ancestry, but what I know is Laguna. (*The Man to Send Rain Clouds*, by Kenneth Rosen, Random House, 1975.)

684. My family are the Marmons at Old Laguna on the Laguna Pueblo reservation where I grew up. We are mixed bloods—Laguna, Mexican, white—but the way we live is like Marmons. . . . All those languages, all those ways of living are combined, and we live somewhere on the fringes of all three. (*Voices of the Rainbow,* by Kenneth Rosen, Viking, 1975.)

685. Our origin is unlike any other. My poetry, my storytelling rise out of this source. (Ibid.)

686. The American public has difficulty believing . . . [that] injustice continues to be inflicted upon Indian people because Americans assume that the sympathy or tolerance they feel toward Indians is somehow "felt" or transferred to the government policy that deals with Indians. This is not the case. (*Now That the Buffalo's Gone: A Study of Today's American Indians,* by Alvin M. Josephy, Jr., Knopf, 1982.)

LARRY ECHOHAWK

(1948–   )

Pawnee, Wyoming

Larry Echohawk is a political figure in Idaho. He was first a member of the state's House of Representatives. In 1990, when he was elected attorney general, he became the first Native American to be elected to a statewide executive office. In 1994, however, he was defeated in his race for governor.

687. Politics can't alter sound biology. (Statement to the National Marine Fisheries Service, August 7, 1991; the bureau was placing the chinook salmon on the endangered species list, but there was disagreement on the major cause of the chinook decline.)

688. If you attempt to depend on Idaho water to increase flows without addressing the real killer—the mainstem dams—you will have done what a false prosecution does: put an innocent man in jail and let the real killer go free. Before long the runs will disappear and you will have accomplished nothing. (Ibid.)

689. The mainstem dams have transformed that mighty [Snake] river into a series of slackwater pools, and have slowed the fish's critical journey by a factor of more than seven. Their biological window cannot afford to travel the lower river, and they die by the millions—victims not of low flow but of poor river *velocity.* (Ibid.)

690. As the former Chief Counsel to the Shoshone-Bannock Tribes, I know how much that ceremonial fishery means to them. Yet . . . I asked the tribes to forego exercise of their treaty fishing rights. They refused, arguing—rightly—that they didn't cause the problem and shouldn't have to suffer while downstream neighbors continued to fish. Without pleasure, but with the sure knowledge that it was right, I urged the state to impose a conservation closure—just as it had earlier closed the sport fishery. (Ibid.)

691. No matter which continent your ancestors came from, if you are an American, you are part Indian in your roots. (Address to the Democratic National Convention, New York City, 1992.)

692. My name "Echo Hawk" is the English translation of the name given my great-grandfather in the mid-1880s. To the Pawnee, the hawk is a symbol of a silent warrior. My great-grandfather was known for his bravery, but he was also known as a modest and quiet man. He did not speak of his own deeds, but word of his courage "echoed" throughout the village. And so he was, "Echo Hawk." (Ibid.)

693. The Iroquois have a saying . . . "In our way of life, in our government, with every decision we make, we always keep in mind the Seventh Generation to come. When we walk upon the earth we always plant our feet carefully, because we know the faces of our further generations are looking up at us from beneath the ground." . . . We are, by the reckoning of the years since our party began, the Seventh Generation of Democrats. We can be proud of those before us and those among us who have made the world better—for people of color, and for all people. (Ibid.)

694. So long as we defile our sacred mother earth, as long as the elderly go without health care, as long as men and women labor for bare subsistence, the pain goes on, and the promise is unfulfilled. (Ibid.)

695. The Pawnee used to have 23 million acres of land, almost all of Nebraska. Then they were marched to a small reservation in Oklahoma. I never knew [my great-grandfather] Echo Hawk, but I can imagine what it must have been like to be removed to Oklahoma. (*The New York Times*, September 5, 1994.)

696. I believe in the promise of America. My political credo is very simple: to return something for what you have received. (Ibid.)

697. I told the tribes when I ran for attorney general that I could not be the tribal attorney in the Statehouse. I care very deeply about their issues. I was raised with Indian values and the strongest of those is family. That's what we have to look at, making the family strong. (Commenting on why he opposed casino gambling in the state, despite the fact that it could result in economic gains among the Indian tribes. Ibid.)

JOY HARJO
(1951–)
Creek, Oklahoma

Joy Harjo is a poet, artist, television scriptwriter, and screenwriter.

698. Screenwriting is definitely related to poetry. You're dealing again with the translation of emotions into images. (*Winged Words: American Indian Writers Speak*, by Laura Coltelli, University of Nebraska Press, 1990.)

699. One goal I have . . . is to create a film with a truly tribal vision, viewpoint, in terms of story, camera viewpoints, angles, everything. It hasn't been done, not on the scale I would like to do it. (Ibid.)

GEORGE BALDWIN
(1952–)
Osage/Kaw, Oklahoma

George Baldwin is on the Plan Faculty of California University at Monterey Bay. He was formerly chairman of the Sociology Department at Henderson State University in Arkansas. In 1992 he helped found American Indian Telecommunications to make available modern communcations technology to Native Americans.

700. A lot of people like to romanticize, hold Indians to that image of weaving blankets for sale by the side of the road, and we're weaving all right, but it's gone beyond blankets to information. ("New Technologies, Ancient Cultures," by A.J.S. Rayl, *Omni*, August 1993.)

701. The Information Age is here, and with these technologies, our languages, traditions, and knowledge live. (Ibid.)

LOUISE ERDRICH
(1954–)
Chippewa, Minnesota

Louise Erdrich is an author, editor, and poet. She has also co-authored many literary works with her husband, Michael Dorris (q.v.).

702. *Love Medicine.* (Title of novel, 1984.)

703. My first audience that I would write for, that [Michael Dorris and I] write for, as a couple, is American Indians, hoping that they will read, laugh, cry, really take in the work. (*Winged Words: American Indian Writers Speak*, by Laura Coltelli, University of Nebraska Press, 1990.)

704. One of the problems is the distribution of literature. For instance, how many Indians can afford to buy *Love Medicine* right now? It's pretty expensive and it's the way publishing unfortunately goes on. One of our hopes was to have it available in a nice, cheap edition everywhere. (Ibid.)

MARY BRAVE BIRD
(1956–)
Sioux, South Dakota

Mary Brave Bird was born on the Rosebud reservation. Her first husband, whom she married in a tribal ceremony, was

Leonard Crow Dog (q.v.). Her first child was born during the
Wounded Knee occupation.

705. If you plan to be born, make sure you are born white and male.
It is not the big, dramatic things so much that get us down, but just
being Indian, trying to hang on to our way of life, language, and values
while being surrounded by an alien, more powerful culture. (After describing a life of violence and abuse upon herself, female friends, and
relatives; *Lakota Woman*, by Mary Crow Dog and Richard Erdoes, Grove
Weidenfeld, 1990.)

706. An old medicine man once told me: "Us Lakotas are not like dogs
who can be trained, who can be beaten and keep on wagging their tails,
licking the hand that whipped them. We are like cats, little cats, big cats,
wildcats, bobcats, mountain lions. It doesn't matter what kind, but cats
who can't be tamed, who scratch if you step on their tails." (Ibid.)

707. Racism breeds racism in reverse. (Ibid.)

708. He [a speaker from the American Indian Movement] had himself
wrapped up in an upside-down American flag, telling us that every star
in this flag represented a state stolen from Indians. (Ibid.)

709. The little settlements we lived in . . . were places without hope
where the bodies and souls were being destroyed bit by bit. (Describing
life on the Rosebud reservation of her childhood, *Black Hills White Justice:
The Sioux Nation versus the United States, 1775 to the Present*, by Edward
Lazarus, HarperCollins, 1991.)

710. Jobs were almost nonexistent on the reservation, and outside the
res whites did not hire Indians if they could help it. (Ibid.)

711. Woman beating is part of everyday life on the reservation. The
white man oppresses the half-blood, the half-blood oppresses the full-
blood, and everybody takes out their anger, despair, and feeling of helplessness on the women. (*Ohitika Woman*, by Mary Brave Bird with
Richard Erdoes, Grove, 1993.)

712. The men [on the reservation] have a good and an evil side. Sober,
they are angels. Drunk, their evil side comes out, and they are drunk a
good part of the time. (Ibid.)

713. There is Indian time and white man's time. Indian time means
never looking at the clock. It means doing what you want when you
want it. (Ibid.)

714. In the old days . . . nature was our clock. . . . The sun, the moon,
and the seasons were our timekeepers and that way of looking at time

is still in our subconscious. . . . There is not even a word for time in our language. (Ibid.)

715. Frequently we traveled south across the Mexican border to gather our sacred medicine, peyote. . . . It is legal for us to get it, provided we have a license and can prove that we are tribally enrolled Indians and members of the Native American Church. (Ibid.)

716. It [the sun dance] is the foremost, the most solemn, the most sacred of all our rituals. It is a celebration of life, of the sun, the buffalo, the eagle. It is a self-sacrifice, a suffering for someone you love, to take his or her pain upon yourself. It is not an initiation rite or a way to prove one's courage as was shown in the movie *A Man Called Horse.* That was a misrepresentation. (Ibid.)

JOHN CASTILLO

(1956–)

Apache, California

John Castillo is the executive director of the Southern California Indian Center.

717. There used to be a saying in the 1800s: "Forget the blanket and learn the white man's ways. Now our elders are saying, "Go and learn in the white man's world, but do not forget your Indian ways." ("New Techniques, Ancient Cultures," by A.J.S. Rayl, *Omni*, August 1993.)

INTER-TRIBAL MEETING

(1961)

Sixty-seven Tribes

In 1961 more than 400 Indians from sixty-seven tribes met at the University of Chicago and issued a Declaration of Indian Purpose.

718. When Indians speak of the continent they yielded, they are not referring only to the loss of some millions of acres in real estate. They have in mind that the land supported a universe of things they valued, and loved. With that continent gone, except for the parcels they still retain, the basis of life is precariously held, but they mean to hold the scraps and parcels as earnestly as any small nation of ethnic groups was ever determined to hold to identity and survival. (*Black Hills White Justice: The Sioux Nation versus the United States, 1775 to the Present*, by Edward Lazarus, HarperCollins, 1991.)

SHERMAN ALEXIE

(1966–)

Spokane/Coeur d'Alene, Washington

Sherman Alexie is a poet and short story writer. Much of his work deals with contemporary problems on the reservation, including alcoholism.

719. [Indians] have a way of surviving. But it's almost like Indians can easily survive the big stuff. Mass murder, loss of language and land rights. It's the small things that hurt the most. The white waitress who wouldn't take an order, Tonto, the Washington Redskins. (*The Lone Ranger and Tonto Fistfight in Heaven*, Atlantic Monthly Press, 1993.)

GAETANA DeGENNARO

(1967–)

Tohono O'odham, Arizona

Gaetana DeGennaro, who obtained a degree in anthropology from Hunter College, works at the National Museum of the American Indian in New York City.

720. This is who we are. (Referring to the George Gustav Heye Center at the National Museum of the American Indian in New York; quoted in "Telling the Truth about Native Americans," by Laura Incalcaterra, *Rockland* [N.Y.] *Journal-News*, October 30, 1994.)

721. The museum will help open up people's minds to the stereotypes of Indian people and get rid of those stereotypes. (Ibid.)

722. It [the museum] will let people know we're still living. We have a living culture. (Ibid.)

"INDIANS OF ALL TRIBES"

(1969–1971)

"All Tribes," Alcatraz

On November 9, 1969, fourteen Indian activists occupied Alcatraz Island in San Francisco Bay and held the abandoned prison for nineteen hours. During that time, they offered to "purchase" the island for $24 worth of trinkets. On November 20, eighty-nine Indians took possession. They held the island for nineteen months before the federal government retook it. At one point, the population approached a thousand. During the two occupation periods, several declarations were made by the occupiers. Excerpts follow.

723. Indians of all tribes greet our brothers and sisters of all races and tongues upon our Earth Mother. We here on Indian land, Alcatraz, represent many tribes of Indians. . . . We are quite serious in our demand to be given ownership of this island. . . . We feel that this request is but little to ask from a government which has systematically stolen our lands, destroyed a once beautiful landscape, killed off the creatures of nature, polluted air and water, ripped open the very bowels of our earth in senseless greed, and instituted a program to annihilate the many Indian tribes of this land by theft, suppression, prejudice, termination, and so-called relocation and assimilation. (February 1970; *Congressional Record*, 97th Congress, 2d Session.)

724. We feel that the island is the only bargaining power that we have with the federal government. It is the only way we have to get them to notice us or even want to deal with us. We are going to maintain our occupation, until the island which is rightfully ours is formally granted to us. Otherwise, they will forget us, the way they always have, but we will not be forgotten. (Ibid.)

725. To the Great White Father and All His People. . . . We, the native Americans, re-claim the land known as Alcatraz Island in the name of all American Indians by right of discovery. (*The American Indian: The First Victim*, by Jay David, William Morrow, 1972.)

726. We wish to be fair and honorable in our dealings with the Caucasian inhabitants of this land, and hereby offer the following treaty: We will purchase said Alcatraz Island for twenty-four dollars ($24) in glass beads and red cloth, a precedent set by the white man's purchase of a similar island about 300 years ago. We know that $24 in trade goods for these 16 acres is more than was paid when Manhattan Island was sold, but we know that land values have risen over the years. (Ibid.)

727. We will give to the inhabitants of this island a portion of that land for their own, to be held in trust by the American Indian Affairs and by the Bureau of Caucasian Affairs to hold in perpetuity—as long as the sun shall rise and the rivers go down to the sea. (November 1969, Ibid.)

728. Proclamation to the Great White Father and all his People: We feel that this so-called Alcatraz Island is more than suitable for an Indian Reservation, as determined by the white man's own standard. By this we mean that this place resembles most Indian reservations in that: It is isolated from modern facilities . . . no fresh running water . . . inadequate sanitation . . . no oil or mineral rights . . . no industry . . . unemployment . . . no health care facilities . . . soil is rocky and unproductive . . . no educational facilities . . . population has always been held as prisoners. (*Black Hills White Justice: The Sioux Nation versus the United States, 1775 to the Present*, by Edward Lazarus, HarperCollins, 1991.)

729. Further, it would be fitting and symbolic that ships from all over the world, entering the Golden Gate, would first see Indian land, and thus be reminded of the true history of this nation. This tiny land would be a symbol of great lands once ruled by free and noble Indians. (Ibid.)

JEANNE BEARCRANE

(Mid to late twentieth century)

Crow

Jeanne Bearcrane is an authority on Indian education.

730. One of the greatest strengths of American Indian cultures is the extended family. It is not uncommon to find grandparents, aunts, uncles, cousins, or even friends of the family rearing the Indian child. (*Teaching the Native American*, by Hap Gilliland, Kendall-Hunt, 1992.)

JANICE LaFOUNTAIN

(Late twentieth century)

Crow

Janice LaFountain specializes in Indian education.

731. We must learn to appreciate diversity, not suppress it. How devastating to think of a world in which everyone is the same. (*Teaching the Native American*, by Hap Gilliland, Kendall-Hunt, 1992.)

JOHN LaVELLE

(1960–)

Santee Sioux, Iowa

John LaVelle directs the Center for Support and Protection of Indian Religions and Indigenous Traditions (Center for the SPIRIT).

732. Spiritual genocide. (Commenting on young whites who attempt to copy Native American rituals; quoted in "Borrowers and Wannabes: Impure Faith," by Martin E. Marty, *Christian Century*, June 1–8, 1994.)

WALLACE WELLS, JR.

(Late twentieth century)

Crow Creek Sioux

Wallace Wells, Jr., is a tribal leader.

733. Our tribe has been in a tumult because of the issue of gambling. It has brought out the worst in people. Such as power-hungry leaders who have sold themselves out to greed.... As a tribal leader, I have never been bothered so much in my life by people who want to invest in our tribe—for gambling. (Letter to the editor, *Lakota Times*, January 21, 1992.)

FRED COYOTE

(Mid to late twentieth century)

Wailaki, California

Fred Coyote is a writer and public speaker.

734. I will die an Indian! (*Now That the Buffalo's Gone: A Study of Today's American Indians*, by Alvin M. Josephy, Jr., Knopf, 1982.)

Anonymous Quotations, Prayers, and Proverbs

ANONYMOUS
Montagnais

735. A moving island. (Describing the first sight of a French ship; *After Columbus: Essays in the Ethnohistory of Colonial North America,* by James Axtell, Oxford University Press, 1988.)

ANONYMOUS
Cherokee

736. Boys and girls, the sermon today is do not call yourselves "tribes" and your land "reservations." Stand on your own two feet and insist that you are a NATION and that your land is your TERRITORY. (*Sovereignty and Symbol,* by Gail H. Landsman, University of New Mexico Press, 1988.)

ANONYMOUS

An anonymous student of Carlisle Indian School.

737. Why cannot my people be more independent? Why can they not take care of themselves? Why is it necessary to throw meat to them as to dogs? Surely the best way is for all the children, somehow to learn and practice self-support. (*My Life and Personal Experiences among Our Hostile Indians,* by Oliver O. Howard, Worthington & Co., 1907.)

ANONYMOUS
Delaware

A Delaware medicine man reported what he had been told at the top of a magic mountain by the Master of Life. The account was used by Pontiac (q.v.) to spur other tribes to join in a war against the whites.

738. I am the Maker of heaven and earth, the trees, lakes, rivers, and all things else. I am the Maker of mankind; and because I love you, you must do my will. (*Great Indian Chiefs,* by Albert Britt, McGraw-Hill, 1938.)

739. The land on which you live I have made for you and not for others. Why do you suffer the white man to dwell among you. (Ibid.)

740. My children, you have forgotten the customs and traditions of your forefathers. Why do you not clothe yourselves in skins, as they did, and use the bows and arrows, and the stone-pointed lances, which they used? You have bought guns, knives, kettles, and blankets from the white men, until you can no longer do without them; and what is worse you have drunk the poison firewater, which turns you into fools. Fling all these things away; live as your wise forefathers lived before you. (Ibid.)

ANONYMOUS
Mohawk

741. We shall resist by every means any suggestion, any violation of the treaties, any disturbance of our people in the free use and enjoyment of our land, any usurpation of our sovereignty, and encroachment and oppression. (*Sovereignty and Symbol*, by Gail H. Landsman, University of New Mexico Press, 1988.)

ANONYMOUS
Ojibway

"The Maiden to the Brave."

742. My love is tall and graceful as the young pine waving on the hill, and swift in his course as the noble, stately deer; his hair is flowing, and dark as the blackbird that floats through the air. (*Information Respecting the History of the Indian Tribes of the United States*, by Henry R. Schoolcraft, vol. 5, 1857.)

743. His eyes, like the eagle's, both piercing and bright; his heart, it is fearless and great, and his arm it is strong in the fight, as this bow made of iron-wood which he easily bends. (Ibid.)

744. His arm is as sure in the fight and chase, as the hawk, which never misses its prey. (Ibid.)

745. Ah, and me, ye spirits! of water, of earth, and of sky, while I sing in his praise . . . my voice shall be heard, it shall ring through the sky; and echo, repeating the same, shall cause it to swell in the breadth of the wind; and his fame shall be spread throughout the land, and his name shall be known beyond the lakes. (Ibid.)

ANONYMOUS
Ojibway

"The Brave to the Maiden."

746. Awake! flower of the forest, sky-treading bird of the prairie. Awake! awake! wonderful fawn-eyed One. When you look upon me I am satisfied; as flowers that drink dew. The breath of your mouth is the fragrance of the flowers in the morning, your breath is their fragrance at evening in the moon-of-falling-leaf. (*Path of the Rainbow*, translated by Charles Fenno Hoffman; cited in *Cry of the Thunderbird*, by Charles Hamilton, University of Oklahoma Press, 1972.)

747. When you are beside me my heart sings; a branch it is, dancing, dancing before the Wind-spirit in the moon of strawberries. When you frown upon me, beloved, my heart grows dark . . . the shadows of clouds darken, then with your smiles comes the sun. (Ibid.)

748. Myself! behold me! blood of my beating heart, Earth smiles—the waters smile—even the sky-of-clouds smiles—but I, I lose the way of smiling when you are not near. Awake! awake! my beloved. (Ibid.)

ANONYMOUS
Creek

749. We believe our right to our soil and our government, which is best suited to our peculiar necessities, would be safer if all our race were united together here. That is my earnest wish. Then I think the rising generation could be educated and civilized, and what is still better, christianized, which I believe would be the greatest benefit of all. This would be to our mutual benefit and good. I know I express the minds of our people when I give you this welcome to our life of a higher civilization, which is better than the old life so long led by our race in the past. (Statement of a U.S. commission investigating the potential removal of

Indian tribes to Indian Territory (Oklahoma), 1876; *Our Indian Wards*, by George W. Manypenny, Clarke, 1880.)

ANONYMOUS
Sioux

Anonymous graduate of Carlisle Indian School.

750. Most girls [who graduated from Carlisle] found their life's work in city kitchens and most boys who [did] not drift back to the reservation lost their identity in a shop. (*Black Hills White Justice: The Sioux Nation versus the United States, 1775 to the Present*, by Edward Lazarus, HarperCollins, 1991.)

ANONYMOUS

A leader in the American Indian Movement.

751. We think that the American Indian Movement is not only an advocate for Indian people. It is the spiritual rebirth of our [Indian] nation. It carries the spirituality of our ancient people and of our elder people. So now the American Indian Movement relies very, very heavily on the traditional leaders and the holy men of the various tribes—to give them the direction they need so they can best help the Indian people. (*Now That the Buffalo's Gone*, by Alvin M. Josephy, Jr., Knopf, 1982.)

ANONYMOUS
Apache

In 1871 hundreds of Indians were massacred at Camp Grant, Arizona. Vigilantes from Tucson carried out the attack. What follows are the feelings of one of the chiefs.

752. I no longer want to live; my women and children have been killed before my face, and I have been unable to defend them. Most Indians in my place would take a knife and cut his throat, but I will live to show these people that all they have done, and all they can do, shall not make me break faith with you, so long as you will stand by us and defend us, in a language we know nothing of, to a great governor we never have, nor never shall see. (Statement to Lieutenant Whitman, an American army officer who had tried to warn the Indians of the impending civilian raid, 1871. The lieutenant was removed from this command and transferred to another post. *Our Indian Wards*, by George W. Manypenny, Clarke, 1880.)

753. Get them [the Indians taken captive] back for us; [otherwise] our little boys will grow up as slaves, and our girls, as soon as they are large enough, will be diseased prostitutes to get money for whoever owns them. (Ibid.)

ANONYMOUS
Assiniboine

754. The buffalo gives food from his flesh and clothing from his hide. The marrow, sinew, bones, and the horns can be used by the people, so that a skilled woman can make many different kinds of food and the family does not eat the same thing each day. It is so also with the man, who can make many things from the buffalo for use in war, hunting, and pleasure. All these things the buffalo offers to the ones who heed the talks of the old men and the old women who know that the lives of the people and the growth of children depend on the buffalo. (*The Assiniboines*, edited by Michael S. Kennedy, Norman, Oklahoma, 1961.)

ANONYMOUS

Psychiatrist Robert Coles reported this view of the moon landing, told to him by a young Indian boy.

755. When the white man landed on the moon, my father cried. . . . I told him there weren't any Indians on the moon, so stop crying. He said nothing for a long time. Then he said our spirits were there, too—and he was sure Indians were crying up there, and trying to hide, and hoping that soon they'd go back to their Earth, the white men, where they make so many people unhappy, and where they don't know what to do next. (*New York Review of Books*, March 20, 1975.)

ANONYMOUS

(Late nineteenth century)

Oklahoma Creek, Oklahoma

The Dawes Commission, established in 1893 by President Grover Cleveland, was also known as the Commission to the Five Civilized Tribes. Its job was to end tribal government among the Cherokees, Creeks, Choctaws, Chickasaws, and Seminoles. Certain lands were allotted to each tribe, while other lands were opened up for white settlement.

756. Egypt had its locusts, Asiatic countries their cholera, France its Jacobins, England its black plague, Memphis had the yellow fever . . . but it was left for unfortunate Indian Territory to be afflicted with the worst scourge of the 19th century, the Dawes Commission. (*Native American Testimony*, by Peter Nabokov, Viking Penguin, 1991.)

ANONYMOUS
Pima

757. The hooting of an owl is a bad omen, it is the voice of the deceased returning to tell of a coming catastrophe. In war, however, you should give the owl hoot as a sign to warn of enemy warriors hiding in the thicket. (*A Pima Past*, by Anna Moore Shaw, University of Arizona Press, 1974.)

ANONYMOUS
(Late 1880s)
Pine Ridge Sioux

Many years after the time of the Ghost Dance, an oral historian told anthropologist Ella Deloria (q.v.) what he remembered about it, including some of the Ghost Dance songs.

758. Mother, hand me my sharp knife,

    Mother, hand me my sharp knife,

    Here come the buffalo returning—

    Mother, hand me my sharp knife!

759. Mother, do come back

    Mother, do come back!

    My little brother is crying for you—

    My father says so!

760. The [Ghost Dance] visions varied at the start, but they ended the same way, like a chorus describing a great encampment of all the Dakotas who had ever lived, where all were related and therefore under-

stood each other, where the buffalo came eagerly to feed them, and there was no sorrow but only joy, where relatives thronged out with happy laughter to greet the newcomer. (*Speaking of Indians*, by Ella Deloria, Friendship Press, 1944. Reprinted by University of South Dakota Press.)

ANONYMOUS
Powhatan

A shaman's prediction.

761. Bearded men should come & take away their Country & that there should none of the original Indians be left, within an hundred & fifty years. (*The Reverend John Clayton: His Scientific Writings and Other Related Papers*, edited by Edmund Berkeley and Dorothy Smith Berkeley, Charlottesville, Va., 1965.) (Editor's note: Historians disagree over similar predictions supposedly made before the Europeans came to the New World. Some scholars point out that such predictions were not recorded until after the Europeans arrived. Other scholars point out that since the Native Americans had no written language, the predictions could not have been recorded any earlier.)

ANONYMOUS
Seneca

762. Our Arlington. (Referring to an Indian cemetery in Pennsylvania. In 1964 the Army Corps of Engineers moved its 300 Indian graves to a new location to make way for the floodwaters of a new dam; cited in *Now That the Buffalo's Gone: A Study of Today's American Indians*, by Alvin M. Josephy, Jr., Knopf, 1982.)

ANONYMOUS
Shoshone

Describing a meeting with members of the Lewis and Clark expedition in the northern Rockies in about 1805, the account was given to a fur trader named Warren Ferris in 1831.

763. This state of tranquil happiness was interrupted by the unexpected arrival of two strangers. They were unlike any people hitherto seen, fairer than ourselves, and clothed with skins unknown to us. (*Life in the Rocky Mountains,* by W. A. Ferris and edited by Paul C. Phillips, The Old West Publishing Company, 1940.)

764. They gave us things like solid water, which were sometimes brilliant as the sun, and which sometimes showed us our own faces. Nothing could equal our wonder and delight. We thought them the children of the Great Spirit. (Ibid.)

765. But we were . . . again overwhelmed with fear, for we soon discovered that they were in possession of the identical thunder and lightning [firearms] that had proved in the hands of our foes so fatal to our happiness. (Ibid.)

766. Many of our people were now exceedingly terrified, making no doubt but that they [the white strangers] were leagued with our enemies the Blackfeet, and coming jointly to destroy us. This opinion was strengthened by a request they made for us to go and meet their friends. . . . Our beloved chief . . . convinced us that it was best to conciliate if possible the favor of a people so terribly armed, and who might protect us. [He] induced most of our warriors to follow him and accompany the strangers to their camp. (Ibid.)

767. Upon arriving at the strangers encampment, they found, instead of an overwhelming force of their enemies, a few strangers like the two already with them, who treated them with great kindness, and gave them many things that had not existed before even in their dreams or imaginations. (Ibid.)

ANONYMOUS
Spokane

In the late 1890s, the Spokanes were asked by the government to move to a new reservation. This was the response of one of the chiefs.

768. When we were on our old reservation there came to us men from the government, who spoke as you have spoken. They told us that we would be treated right. . . . They told us that, if we would move to this place, they would give us each a house, fence, seed, wagon and harness. They talked well and we believed them. We came to this place and gave up our old lands. We have no houses and we have no wagons. We gave up all that we had, and the government has given us nothing. If we do as you say, will we not be treated this way again? (Spokane (Wash.) *Spokesman-Review*, October 31, 1897.)

ANONYMOUS
Teton

769. Of all our domain, we loved, perhaps, the Black Hills the most. (*Black Hills White Justice: The Sioux Nation versus the United States, 1775 to the Present,* by Edward Lazarus, HarperCollins, 1991.)

770. The [Teton] named these hills the Sapa, or Black Hills, on account of their color. The slopes and peaks were so heavily wooded with dark pines that from a distance the mountains actually looked black. In the wooden recesses were numberless springs of pure water and numerous small lakes. There were wood and game in abundance and shelter from the storms of the plains. (Ibid.)

771. According to a tribal legend these hills were a reclining female figure from whose breasts flowed life-giving forces and to them the [Teton] went as a child to its mother's arms. (Ibid.)

ANONYMOUS
Winnebago

"What Every Young Man Should Know."

772. If you ever get married, my son, do not make an idol of your wife. The more you worship her, the more will she want to be worshipped. ("The Winnebago Tribe," a chapter by Paul Radin in the *37th Annual Report* of the Bureau of American Ethnology, 1916.)

773. My son, if you keep on listening to your wife, after a while she will never let you go to any feast at all. All your relatives will scold you and your own sisters will think little of you. (Ibid.)

774. For these reasons, my son, I warn you against the words of women. Steel yourself against them. For if you do not do so you will find yourself different from other men. It is not good to be enslaved by a woman. (Ibid.)

775. My son, this also I will tell you. Women can never be watched. If you try to watch them you will merely show your jealousy and your female relatives will also be jealous. After a while you will become so jealous of your wife that she will leave you and run away. You yourself will be to blame for this. You thought too much of a woman and in worshiping her you humbled yourself, and as a consequence she has been taken away from you. All the other women will know of this, and no one will want to marry you again. Everyone will consider you a very bad man. (Ibid.)

ANONYMOUS
Winnebago

"What Every Young Woman Should Know."

776. If you marry a man and you want to be certain of always retaining him, work for him. With work you will always be able to retain your hold on men. If you do your work to the satisfaction of your husband, he will never leave you. (*The Winnebago Tribe,* a chapter by Paul Radin, 37th Annual Report of the Bureau of American Ethnology, 1916.)

777. Remain faithful to your husband. Do not act as though you are married to a number of men at the same time. Lead a chaste life. If you do not listen to what I am telling you and you are unfaithful to your husband, all the men will jeer at you. They will say whatever they wish to [and no one will interfere]. (Ibid.)

778. Do not act haughty to your husband. Whatever he tells you to do, do it. Kindness will be returned to you if you obey your husband, for he will treat you in the same manner. (Ibid.)

779. If a wife has no real interest in her husband's welfare and possessions she will bestow on him no more than any other woman, and the world will ridicule her. (Ibid.)

780. If, on the other hand, you pay more attention to your husband than to your parents, your parents will leave you. Let your husband likewise take care of your parents, for they depend on him. Your parents were instrumental in getting you your husband, so remember that they expect some recompense for it, as likewise for the fact that they raised you. When you visit your husband's people do not go around with a haughty air or act as if you considered yourself far above them. Try to get them to like you. If you are good-mannered you will be placed in charge of the home at which you happen to be visiting. Then your parents-in-law will tell your husband that their daughter-in-law is acting nicely to them. (Ibid.)

ANONYMOUS
Wintu

781. We don't chop down the trees. We only use dead wood. But the white people plow up the ground, pull down the trees, kill everything. The tree says, "Don't. I am sore. Don't hurt me." But they chop it down and cut it up. (*Freedom and Culture,* by Dorothy Lee, Prentice-Hall, 1959.)

782. The spirit of the land hates them [the white people]. . . . They saw up the trees. That hurts them. The Indians never hurt anything, but the white people destroy all. (Ibid.)

783. How can the spirit of the earth like the white man? . . . Everywhere the white man has touched it, it is sore. (Ibid.)

ANONYMOUS
Wyandot

The impact of missionaries is indicated in this report of a dream by a Wyandot woman shortly after a prayer meeting.

784. One night, after being at meeting . . . I lay down to sleep, and dreamed that I saw . . . a high pole set in the ground, and on the top of that pole there was a white child fastened and it gave light to all around in a circle. At the foot of the pole stood the missionary calling the Indians to come into the light, for they were all in the dark. . . . I went; and from the foot of this pole there were two paths: one was a broad road, and it led down hill; the other was a narrow one, and led up a hill. . . . I heard in that house [at the top of the hill] the most delightful singing I ever heard before, and had a great desire to go in. When I came up to the gate, the man spoke to me and said, "You cannot go in now. You must go back and tell all your nation, that if they want to get to heaven they must take this narrow road, for there is no other that leads here." (*History of the Wyandot Mission*, by Finley; cited in *Salvation and the Savage*, by Robert F. Berkhofer, Jr., University of Kentucky Press, 1965.)

PRAYER
Anonymous

785. I seek strength, not to be greater than my brother, but to fight my greatest enemy—myself. (*As Long as the Rivers Shall Flow*, War Resisters League, 1974.)

PRAYER

Osage

---

786. Wakanda, have pity on me—for I am poor.
   Give me what I need,
   Let me win against my enemies.
   Grant me thy aid,
   That I might steal many horses.

(*The Prayers of Man*, compiled by Alfonso M. diNola, edited by Patrick O'Connor, Ivan Obolensky, 1961.)

PRAYER

Pueblos

---

787. Hasten clouds from the four world quarters; Come snow in plenty, that water may be abundant when summer comes; Come ice, cover the fields, that the planting may yield abundance. (*The Prayers of Man*, compiled by Alfonso M. diNola, edited by Patrick O'Connor, Ivan Obolensky, 1961.)

PRAYER
Sioux

788. I promise thee a calico shirt and a dress, O Wakanda. I will also give you a blanket if you grant that I return whole and well to my fireside after having killed a Pawnee. (*The Prayers of Man*, compiled by Alfonso M. diNola, edited by Patrick O'Connor, Ivan Obolensky, 1961.)

PRAYER
Great Plains Indians

789. Morning Star! when you look down upon us, give us peace and refreshing sleep. Great Spirit! bless our children, friends, and visitors through a happy life. May our trails lie straight and level before us. Let us live to be old. We are all your children and ask these things with good hearts. (*The Prayers of Man*, compiled by Alfonso M. diNola, edited by Patrick O'Connor, Ivan Obolensky, 1961.)

PROVERB
Cheyenne

790. A nation is not conquered until the hearts of its women are on the ground. Then it is done, no matter how brave its warriors nor how strong their weapons. (*Lakota Woman*, by Mary Crow Dog and Richard Erdoes, Grove Weidenfeld, 1990.)

PROVERB

Sioux

---

791. A beautiful tepee is like a good mother. She hugs her children to her and protects them from heat and cold, storm and rain. (*Lakota Woman*, by Mary Crow Dog and Richard Erdoes, Grove Weidenfeld, 1990.)

PROVERB

---

792. You cannot judge another person until you have walked a mile in his moccasins. (Traditional.)

Indexes

Author Index

The author index includes groups (for example, "Indians of All Tribes" and the National Council of the Cherokee Nation) as well as individuals. Biographical or background information about an author can be found in the paragraph immediately preceding that author's first quotation. All numbers refer to quote numbers.

Abieta, Andy, 505
Adams, Henry, 652–654
Ahkcah, Sam, 447–448
Albert, Daisy, 531
Alexie, Sherman, 719
Allen, Paula Gunn, 612–614
American Horse, 289–292
Anonymous, 735–784
As-Go-Ye-Wat-Ha. *See* Red Jacket

Baldwin, George, 700–701
Ballard, Louis W., 557
Banks, Dennis, 600–606
Barnes, Jim, 561
Bearcrane, Jeanne, 730
Bedagi. *See* Big Thunder
Bellecourt, Vernon, 589
Bent, George, 297–300
Big Eagle, 156–160
Big Elk, 76

Big Thunder, 419
Black Elk, 357–360
Blackfoot. 187–188
Black Hawk, 49–58
Black Kettle, 134–140
Blatchford, Herbert, 536
Bonaparte, Darren, 587–588
Bonnin, Gertrude Simmons, 407–411
Boudinot, Elias, 131–133
Brave Bird, Mary, 705–716
Bronson, Ruth Muskrat, 449–451
Bruce, Louis R., 467
Buck Watie. *See* Boudinot, Elias
Bull Bear, 363–364
Burnette, Robert, 509–513

Calf Robe, Ben, 457
Campbell, Ben Nighthorse, 562–568
Canoe, Lorraine, 558–560
Captain Jack, 284–287

Castillo, John, 717
Chief Joseph, 272–277
Chiksika, 110–112
Chisholm, Jesse, 153
Clearwater, Luther, 506
Cochise, 178–182
Conassatego, 11–13
Coodey, William Shorey, 154
Cooper, Vernon, 466
Cooweescoowe. See Ross, John
Cornplanter, 30–31
Corn Tassel. See Old Tassel
Coyote, Fred, 734
Crawford, Eugene R., 523
Crazy Horse, 293–296
Crow Dog, Leonard, 550
Crow Dog, Mary. See Brave Bird,
     Mary
Crowfoot, 197
Cupp, Lori, 507–508
Curtis, Charles, 353–355

DeGennaro, Gaetana, 720–722
Deloria, Ella, 434–437
Deloria, Vine, Jr., 569–583
Delshay, 270–271
Dempsey, Jack, 445–446
Dillion, Peter, 532
Dockstader, Frederick, 486–489
Dorris, Michael, 667–669
Doublehead, 309
Downing, Lewis, 218–219
Dragging-Canoe, 25–29
Draper, Teddy, Sr., 525
Dull Knife, 169–173

Eagle Wing, 310–311
Earthboy, Jim, 529
Eastman, Charles A., 337–341
Echohawk, John, 656–658
Echohawk, Larry, 687–697
Erdrich, Louise, 702–704

Flute, Jerry, 615
Flying Hawk, 322
The Four Bears, 125–126
Four Guns, 420–421
Fox, Sandra J., 655

Gall, 288
Garry. See Spokane, Garry
Geronimo, 241–244
Giago, Tim, 590–593
Gist, George. See Sequoya
Good, Baptiste, 377
Goodbird, Edward, 390–395
Gorman, Carl, 468–472
Gumbs, Harriett Starleaf, 458–460

Hale, Janet Campbell, 670–674
Haozous, Robert, 648–650
Harjo, Joy, 698–699
Harris, LaDonna, 551–556
Hayes, Ira, 499–502
Hayward, Richard A., 678–679
Hogan, Linda, 675–677
Hollow Horn, 456
Houser, Allan, 478–481

"Indians of All Tribes," 723–729
Inter-Tribal Meeting, 718
Iron Shell, 349
Ishi, 356

Jacobs, David L., 646–647
Johnson, Napoleon B., 444
Joseph. See Chief Joseph

Kah-nung-cla-geh. See Major Ridge
Katchongva, Dan, 396–398
Kaywaykla, James, 422–427
Keedah, Wilson, Sr., 524
Keeler, William W., 473
Keokuk, 116–117
Kicking Bear, 350
Kicking Bird, 269
King Philip, 7
Kintpuash. See Captain Jack
Krentpoos. See Captain Jack
Kushiway, 307–308

LaFlesche, Francis, 330–333
LaFlesche, Susette, 323
LaFountain, Janice, 731
LaVelle, John, 732
Lion Bear, 161–163
Little Big Man, 378

Little Crow, 142–144
Little Hill, 346–348
Little Raven, 192–196
Little Turtle, 32–36
Logan, 20–24
Lyons, Oren R., 537–549

MacDonald, Peter, 519–522
Mankiller, Wilma, 659–663
Maracle, Mark, 585–586
Marks, Emma, 477
Martin, Phillip, 514–517
McCloud, Janet, 530
McIntosh, William, 78–81
Means, Russell, 622–630a
Meninock, 438–442
Mills, Billy, 607
Minavavana, 43
Mohawk, John, 664
Momaday, N. Scott, 594–597
Montezuma, Carlos, 379–383

National Council, 239–240
Nawica Kjici. *See* Giago, Tim
Nicholas, Joseph, 503–504
Noah. *See* Seattle

Obeale. *See* Cornplanter
Ohiyesa. *See* Eastman, Charles A.
Old Tassel, 14–17
Oochalata, 344–345
Opothleyoholo, 122–124
Ortiz, Roxanne Dunbar, 608–610
Ortiz, Simon, 637–642
Osceola, 141
Ouray the Arrow, 189–191

Palaneapope, 281–283
Parker, Ely, 222–230
Parker, Quanah, 312
Peaches, Daniel, 619–621
Pegg, Thomas, 342–343
Peltier, Leonard, 651
Petalesharo, 118–121
Picotte, Susan LaFlesche, 361–362
Pierce, Harriett, 474
Pierce, Maris Bryant, 177
Pizi. *See* Gall

Plenty-Coups, 320–321
Pokagon, Simon, 255–258
Polatkin, 176
Pontiac, 18–19
Posey, Alexander, 401–406
Powhatan, 4–6
Prayers, 785–789
Proverbs, 790–792
Pushmataha, 44–48

Red Cloud, 198–210
Red Dog, 365
Red Fox, 429–431
Red Iron, 278–280
Red Jacket, 37–42
Reifel, Ben, 455
Ridge, John, 145–149
Ridge, John Rollin, 221
Ridge, Major, 71–75
Riegert, Wilbur, 533–535
Robles, Lillian Valenzuela, 482–483
Rogers, John, 461–465
Rogers, Will, 412–418
Roman Nose, 253–254
Rose, Wendy, 680–682
Ross, John, 99–109
Ross, William P., 366–370

Satank, 167–168
Satanta, 247–252
Seattle, 87–98
Sequoya, 69–70
Shabbona. *See* Shabonee
Shabonee, 77
Shaw, Anna Moore, 452–454
Silko, Leslie, 683–686
Sitting Bull, 259–268
Small, Gail, 616–618
Smohalla, 183–186
Speckled Snake, 127–130
Spokane, Garry, 174–175
Spotted Tail, 211–217
Standing Bear, 231–238
Standing Bear, Luther, 384–389
Standing Buffalo, 334–335
Standing Elk, 371
Stands in Timber, John, 428

Sun Bear, 526–528
Sweet Medicine, 1–3

Tahajadoris, 8–9
Talayesva, Don C., 443
TallMountain, Mary, 485
Tatanga Mani, 399–400
Taoyateduta. *See* Little Crow
Tashunka Witko. *See* Crazy Horse
Tecumseh, 59–67
Teedyuscung, 10
Ten Bears, 113–115
Thom, Melvin, 611
Thorpe, Grace, 496–498
Thorpe, Jim, 432–433
Tuskeneah, 245–246
Two Moon, 313–319

Vasquez, Joseph C., 484
Vizenor, Gerald, 598–599

Walking Buffalo. *See* Tatanga Mani
Warren, David C., 665–666
Warren, William, 220
Warrior, Clyde, 490–495

Washakie, 150–152
Washakie, Dick, 372
Wauneka, Annie Dodge, 475–476
Wayquahgishig. *See* Rogers, John
Weatherford, William, 82–86
Welch, James, 632–635
Wells, Elizabeth A., 631
Wells, Wallace, Jr., 733
West, W. Richard, Jr., 643–645
Weston, Shirley Black Stone, 636
Wetatonmi, 373
White Bird, 155
Whitecrow, Jake L., Jr., 518
Wild Cat, 164–166
Wilson, Jack. *See* Wovoka
Winnemucca, Sarah, 301–305
Wooden Leg, 351–352
Wovoka, 336

Yellow Bird. *See* Ridge, John Rollin
Yellow Wolf, 324–329
Young Bear, Severt, 584
Young-Man-Afraid, 374–376

Zitkala-Sa. *See* Bonnin, Gertrude Simmons

Subject and Key Word Index

All quotations are listed by subject matter. Many may also be found by a key word in the quotation. For example, Chief Joseph's famous quotation, "From where the sun now stands, I will fight no more forever," can be located under the subject "surrender," as well as under the key words "fight" and "sun." Page numbers are preceded by *p.* or *pp.* All other numbers refer to quote numbers.

Abandonment
  (Thomas Pegg), 343
Abenakis
  (Tahajadoris), p. 6 (bio), 9
Aboriginal history
  (Oren R. Lyons), 543–544
Abundance
  (Black Hawk), 49
Academy of American Poets
  (N. Scott Momaday), p. 162 (bio)
Achieve
  (Carlos Montezuma), only one way to achieve, 380
Advice to Young Men
  (Anonymous Winnebago), 772–775
Advice to Young Women
  (Anonymous Winnebago), 776–780
Afterlife
  (William Warren), 220
Agents

(Ely Parker), 223–224, 226
Aging
  (Polatkin), 176
Agreement
  (Ouray the Arrow), agreement the buffalo makes with his hunters, 189
Air Force
  (Phillip Martin), p. 143 (bio)
Alaska
  (Ruth Muskrat Bronson), 449–451
  (Mary TallMountain), Alaska is my talisman, 485
Albany
  (L. David Jacobs), 647
Alcatraz
  ("Indians of All Tribes"), 723–729; more than suitable for an Indian reservation, 728
  (Wilma Mankiller), 662
Alcohol

(Charles Curtis), 353
Alcoholism
  (Mary Brave Bird), 712
  (Robert Burnette), 513
Allocation
  (Daniel Peaches), 620
  (Vine Deloria, Jr.), 579
Almighty
  (Standing Bear), the Almighty looks
  down on me, 236
Alphabet
  (Sequoya), 69–70
American Indian Anti-Defamation
  Council
  (Russell Means), p. 169 (bio)
American Indian Civil Rights Act
  (Vine Deloria, Jr.), 583
American Indian Movement (AIM)
  (Anonymous AIM Leader), 751
  (Dennis Banks), p. 164 (bio)
  (Vernon Bellecourt), 589
  (Mary Brave Bird), 708
  (Leonard Crow Dog), p. 152 (bio)
  (Russell Means), p. 170 (bio)
American Indian Telecommunications
  (George Baldwin), p. 188 (bio)
American Indians and Friends
  (Robert Burnette), p. 142 (bio)
American Revolution
  (Cornplanter), p. 11 (bio)
  (Dragging-Canoe), p. 10 (bio)
Americans for Indian Opportunity
  (LaDonna Harris), p. 152 (bio)
Anasazi
  (Ben Nighthorse Campbell), 563
Ancestors
  (Will Rogers), 412–414
Ancestry
  (Jack Dempsey), 445
Animal
  (Sequoya), like catching a wild ani-
  mal and taming it, 69
Animals
  (Sweet Medicine), 2
Animate
  (William Weatherford), I cannot an-
  imate the dead, 83
Annuity distribution

(John Ridge), 146–147
Ant
  (Oren R. Lyons), we stand between
  the mountain and the ant, 538
Anthropologists
  (Gerald Vizenor), Anthropologists
  have invented culture, 598
Arizona
  (Anonymous Apache), p. 206 (bio)
  (Geronimo), 241
  (Kaywaykla), 427
Arkansas
  (William P. Ross), 368
Arlington
  (Anonymous Seneca), Our Arling-
  ton, 762
Arm
  (Anonymous Ojibway), his arm is
  strong in the fight, 743
Armies
  (Shabonee), The armies of the
  whites are . . . like the sands of the
  sea, 77
Arms
  (Pontiac), 19
Army Corps of Engineers
  (Anonymous Seneca), p. 210 (bio)
  (Harriett Pierce), p. 131 (bio)
Art
  (Frederick Dockstader), 486–489
  (Carl Gorman), 468–472; Indian art
  is dying out, 471
  (Robert Haozous), reality in my art
  . . . encompasses both ugliness and
  beauty, 648; art should . . . reflect
  the soul of its creator, 650
  (Allan Houser), 481
Ashes
  (Wild Cat), the ashes of my kin-
  dred, 165
Assimilate
  (Janet Campbell Hale), govern-
  ment's intention . . . to get us to as-
  similate, 670
Assimilation
  (Anonymous Carlisle Graduate),
  750
  (Anonymous Creek), 749

(Big Eagle), 156
(John Echohawk), 657
(Napoleon B. Johnson), 444
Assistance
(Pontiac), 19
Association on American Indian Affairs
(Jerry Flute), p. 168 (bio)
Athlete
(Jim Thorpe), greatest athlete in the world, 432
Atrocities
(American Horse), 289–292
(Anonymous Apache), 752
(George Bent), 298
(Logan), 21
(Sarah Winnemucca), 301
Audience
(Louise Erdrich), my first audience . . . is American Indians, 703
Avarice
(Maris Bryant Pierce), wonted avarice . . . is never sated, 177
Awake
(Anonymous Ojibway), Awake! Awake! my beloved, 748
Axe
(Tahajadoris), never to drop the axe, 8

Banks, Dennis
(Russell Means), pp. 169–170 (bio)
Barbed-wire mind
(Leonard Crow Dog), 550
Bargaining power
("Indians of All Tribes") only bargaining power that we have, 724
Battle
(Black Hawk), 56
Battle Tactics
(William Weatherford), 85
(Ira Hayes), 499–500
(Wild Cat), hopes I should be killed in Battle, 166
Beadwork
(LaDonna Harris), We don't sit around doing beadwork, 552
Bear Paw Mountains

(Chief Joseph), p. 76 (bio)
Bear Tribe Medicine Society
(Sun Bear), p. 146 (bio)
Beauty
(Lori Cupp), walking in beauty, 507
Believe
(Black Kettle), hard . . . to believe white men, 140
Benders gang
(William P. Ross), 367
Benedict, Ruth
(Ella Deloria), p. 121 (bio)
Benevolent
(Gertrude Simmons Bonnin), good intentions of a benevolent government, 410
Betrayal
(Robert Burnette), 509
Better Off
(Vine Deloria, Jr.), this continent a lot better off, 576
Big Hole River
(White Bird), 155
(Yellow Wolf), 325
Bill of Rights
(Vine Deloria, Jr.), 582, 583
Black Hawk War
(Black Hawk), p. 17 (bio)
Black Hills
(Anonymous Teton), we loved . . . the Black Hills the most, 769; named . . . on account of their color, 770; these Black Hills were a reclining female figure, 771
(Baptiste Good), 377
(Vine Deloria, Jr.), 579
(Little Big Man), 378
(Red Dog), p. 103 (bio)
(Spotted Tail), 213, 217
(Standing Elk), 371
(Severt Young Bear), I cannot accept money for the Black Hills, 584
Black Hills Sioux Nation Council
(Peter Dillon), p. 148 (bio)
Blackfeet
(Anonymous Shoshone), 766
Blackfeet Confederacy
(Crowfoot), p. 55 (bio)

Blackfoot
    (Washakie), p. 42 (bio)
Black Kettle
    (George Bent), p. 83 (bio), 297, 299
Blind
    (Kushiway), we other Indians . . .
    are blind, 308
Blood
    (Lion Bear), make the snow red
    with the blood of the white man,
    162
    (Logan), there runs not a drop of
    my blood, 22
    (Red Cloud), trail of blood, 205
    (Spokane Garry), if we cut our-
    selves, the blood is red, 175
    (Tecumseh), stain the earth red
    with their blood, 60
    (Ten Bears), I want no blood on my
    land, 115
Boas, Franz
    (Ella Deloria), p. 121 (bio)
Bones
    (Red Iron), we will leave our bones
    on the ground, 279
Book
    (Tatanga Mani), the Great Spirit's
    book which is the whole of his cre-
    ation, 399
Born
    (Mary Brave Bird), make sure you
    are born white and male, 705
    (Cochise), we are born like the ani-
    mals, 178
Boston University
    (Charles A. Eastman), p. 94 (bio)
Boudinot, Elias
    (John Rollin Ridge), 221
Boundaries
    (Little Turtle), 35
Bounties
    (Lillian Valenzuela Robles), Califor-
    nia offered bounties for dead Indi-
    ans, 483
Bow
    (Pushmataha), none . . . ever drew
    bow against the United States, 47
Brains

(Sarah Winnemucca), you have
    brains, same as the whites, 306
Brave
    (Luther Standing Bear), to become a
    great brave, 387
Bravery
    (Anna Moore Shaw), 454
    (Sitting Bull), 259
Breath
    (Ten Bears), where everything drew
    a free breath, 113
Brother
    (Cornplanter), when you were
    young and weak, I used to call you
    brother, 30
Brotherhood
    (Jake L. Whitecrow, Jr.), 518
Brothers
    (Russell Means), we are all broth-
    ers, 627
Buffalo
    (Anonymous Assiniboine), The buf-
    falo gives food . . . and clothing,
    754
    (Anonymous Sioux), here come the
    buffalo returning, 758
    (Black Kettle), we must live near
    the buffalo, 136
    (Bull Bear), the buffalo is our
    money, 363; buffalo . . . are our cat-
    tle, 364
    (William McIntosh), the red men
    became like the buffalo, 80
    (Ouray the Arrow), ever try skin-
    ning a buffalo, 191
    (Standing Buffalo), our country . . .
    wherever the buffalo range, 334
    (Ten Bears), give up the buffalo for
    the sheep, 114
Buffalo Bill's Wild West Show
    (Black Elk), pp. 101 (bio)
    (Kicking Bear), p. 99 (bio)
    (Luther Standing Bear), p. 109 (bio)
    (Sitting Bull), p. 72 (bio), 268
Bulldozers
    (John Echohawk), U.S. forest service
    bulldozers accomplish . . . what
    U.S. troops did, 658

Bum
    (James Welch), never give a bum
    an even break, 634
Bumper Stickers
    (Tim Giago), 592
Bureau of Caucasian Affairs
    ("Indians of All Tribes"), 727
Bureau of Indian Affairs
    (Louis R. Bruce), pp. 129–130 (bio)
    (Robert Burnette), 510
    (Sandra J. Fox), p. 178 (bio)
    (Phillip Martin), 517
    (Russell Means), pp. 169–170 (bio)
    (Billy Mills), p. 165 (bio)
    (Carlos Montezuma), p. 108 (bio);
    by doing away with the [BIA] you
    stop making . . . useless beings, 383
    (Ben Reifel), pp. 126–127 (bio)
    (Gail Small), 616
    (Grace Thorpe), 496
Bureaucracy
    (Clyde Warrior), bureaucracy out of
    control, 494
Burial
    (William Warren), 220
Bury
    (Doublehead), will not let us keep
    oland] . . . sufficient to bury our
    dead, 309
Butcher
    (Dull Knife), we will butcher each
    other, 173
Butchered
    (Roman Nose), soldiers look . . .
    like those who butchered, 253

California State University at Long
    Beach
    (Lillian Valenzuela Robles), 482
California University at Monterey Bay
    (George Baldwin), p. 188 (bio)
Camp Grant Massacre
    (Anonymous Apache), p. 206 (bio),
    752
Canada
    (L. David Jacobs), 647
    (Mark Maracle), 586
Canby, General E.R.S.

    (Captain Jack), p. 79 (bio), 284
Captives
    (Anonymous Apache), 752
Care
    (Wild Cat), take care of me, 165
Carlisle
    (Anonymous Carlisle Graduate),
    750
    (Kushiway), p. 85 (bio), 307
    (Spotted Tail), 216
    (Jim Thorpe), p. 119 (bio)
Carlisle School
    (Luther Standing Bear), p. 109 (bio)
Carter, Jimmy
    (Russell Means), 629
Cass, Lewis
    (John Ross), 99
Catch-22
    (John Mohawk), the identity offered
    to the Indian was and remains a
    Catch-22, 664
Cats
    (Mary Brave Bird), we are like cats,
    706
Cemetery
    (Anonymous Seneca), 762
Centaur
    (Wendy Rose), [the centaur reflects]
    my hybrid status, 682
Center for Support and Protection of
    Indian Religions and Indigenous
    Traditions
    (John LaVelle), p. 196 (bio)
Cession
    (John Ross), cession of our posses-
    sory rights in Georgia, 100
Change
    (Sweet Medicine), 1–3
    (Grace Thorpe), 498
Chariton Review Press
    (Jim Barnes), p. 154 (bio)
Cherokee
    (Kushiway), only one tribe that
    knows much . . . the Cherokee, 308
Cherokee Phoenix
    (Elias Boudinot), p. 36 (bio)
Chicago
    (Simon Pokagon), p. 71 (bio)

Chief Joseph
  (Jim Earthboy), p. 147 (bio)
  (Wetatonmi), p. 106 (bio)
  (White Bird), p. 44 (bio)
  (Yellow Wolf), p. 91 (bio)
Chief
  (Kicking Bird), I am a chief no
  more, 269
Chiefs
  (Standing Buffalo), we are the
  chiefs of the plains, 335
Children
  (Sitting Bull), what life we can
  make for our children, 264
Chinook
  (Larry Echohawk), 687
Chisholm Trail
  (Jesse Chisholm), 153
Chivington, Colonel John
  (George Bent), p. 83 (bio)
  (Black Kettle), 134
Chosen People
  (Oren R. Lyons), 544
Christians
  (Tatanga Mani), Christians see
  themselves as . . . a special crea-
  tion, 400
  (Anna Moore Shaw), tribal dances .
  . . not for Christians, 452
Church
  (Lorraine Canoe), the church is a
  crutch, 560
Circles
  (Black Elk), the power of the world
  always works in circles, 357
Civil War
  (Opothleyoholo), p. 33 (bio)
  (Thomas Pegg), p. 96 (bio), 342–343
  (John Ross), p. 27 (bio), 105–108,
  109
Civilization
  (Old Tassel), 15
  (Susette LaFlesche), 323
  (John Rollin Ridge), party of civili-
  zation, 221
  (Sarah Winnemucca), throw off the
  garments of civilization, 303

(Crazy Horse), we do not want
  your civilization, 293
Civilized
  (Anonymous Creek), rising genera-
  tion could be educated and civi-
  lized, 749
Claim
  (Peter MacDonald), we must claim
  what is ours, 520
Cleaned out
  (Black Kettle), cleaned out our
  lodges, horses, and everything else,
  140
Cleanliness
  (Susan LaFlesche Picotte), 361
Co-existence impossibility
  (Opothleyoholo), 122
Coal mining
  (Gail Small), 618
Code talkers
  (Eugene R. Crawford), p. 145 (bio)
  (Teddy Draper, Sr.) p. 146 (bio)
  (Wilson Keedah, Sr.), p. 145 (bio)
  (Peter MacDonald), p. 144 (bio)
Coles, Robert
  (Anonymous Indian Boy), p. 207
  (bio)
Colonialism
  (Roxanne Dunbar Ortiz), 609
  (Leonard Peltier), 651
Color
  (Ben Calf Rove), when we all have
  the same color of skin, 457
  (Russell Means), 630
Columbus, Christopher
  (John Echohawk), Columbus
  brought European religious intoler-
  ance, 656
  (Oren R. Lyons), 543
  (Russell Means), Columbus makes
  Hitler look like a juvenile delin-
  quent, 622
  (N. Scott Momaday), 595
  (Ben Nighthorse Campbell), 562–
  564
  (Red Fox), 430
Commissioner of Indian Affairs
  (Louis R. Bruce), p. 129–130 (bio)

(Ely Parker), p. 62 (bio), 222

Common Sense
(Oren R. Lyons), 540–542

Compact of 1802
(Major Ridge), 72

Compensation
(Vine Deloria, Jr.), 579

Concentration Camp
(Tim Giago), 590

Confederacy
(John Ross), p. 27 (bio), 103, 105–106, 109
(Thomas Pegg), p. 96 (bio)

Confederate Army
(Opothleyoholo), p. 33 (bio)

Connectedness
(Lori Cupp), a universal spiritual C, 508

Conquered
(Cheyenne Proverb), a nation is not conquered until the hearts of its women are on the ground, 790

Conqueror
(Peter Dillon), a conquered people has to take what the conqueror gives, 532

Conquest
(Frederick Dockstader), so-called "conquest" of the Western area, 487

Contemporary
(Robert Haozous), my art is contemporary because I live in the present, 650

Continuity
(Grace Thorpe), we have absolutely no continuity, 496

Conversion
(Anonymous Creek), 749
(Anonymous Wyandot), 784
(Red Jacket), 40–41
(Sitting Bull), 268
(Spotted Tail), 215

Cooperation
(Satanta), 247

Cooper Union
(Little Raven), 192

Coping

(Sherman Alexie), 719

Cornplanter
(Harriett Pierce), p. 131 (bio)

Corral
tanding Bear), to slaughter cattle . . . they get them to a corral, 233

Cost
(Major Ridge), will cost us our lands, our lives, 73

Count
(Sitting Bull), you can count your money . . . but only the Great Spirit can count . . . the blades of grass, 260a

Country
(Little Raven), the country was big enough for the white man and the Arapahos, too, 193
(Delshay), travel over the country and have no trouble, 271

Court of Indian Affairs
(Gall), p. 80 (bio)

Cowardice
(Little Crow), 142

Coyotes
(Tatanga Mani), nobody makes coyotes behave like beavers, 400

Crazy
(Sweet Medicine), you will become crazy and will forget all that I am teaching, 3

Crazy Horse
(Red Fox), pp. 118–119 (bio)
(Sitting Bull), p. 72 (bio)
(Young-Man-Afraid), p. 106 (bio)

Creation
(Meninock), 438

Creator
(John Stands in Timber), the creator has made human beings' bodies . . . as he had made the earth, 428

Credit
(Big Eagle), 157

Credo
(Larry Echohawk), 696

Cresap, Michael
(Logan), 20–21

Crime

(William P. Ross), 366–370
Criminals
  (Leonard Peltier), to stand and re-
  sist we are called criminals, 651
Crook, General George
  (Geronimo), 242
Crow
  (Washakie), p. 42 (bio)
Crow Dog, Leonard
  (Mary Brave Bird), pp. 189–190
  (bio)
Cruel
  (Carl Gorman), life of the Navajo is
  harsh and cruel, 468
Crying
  (George Bent), everyone was crying
  even the warriors, 300
  (Jim Earthboy), people talking and
  crying, 529
Cultural interaction
  (Anonymous Delaware), 740
  (Anonymous Shoshone), 763–767
Culture
  (Carl Gorman), 468–469
  (Janet Campbell Hale), 672
  (Lorraine Canoe), 558
  (Gaetana DeGennaro), we have a
  living culture, 722
Custer, George
  (Herbert Blatchford), 536
  (Black Elk), p. 100 (bio)
  (Crazy Horse), p. 82 (bio), 296
  (Vine Deloria, Jr.), Custer died for
  your sins, 570
  (Flying Hawk), p. 90 (bio)
  (Baptiste Good), 377
  (Red Fox), pp. 118–119 (bio)
  (Sitting Bull), p. 72 (bio)
  (John Stands in Timber), p. 118
  (bio)
  (Two Moon), p. 88 (bio), 315
  (Will Rogers), 415
  (Wilma Mankiller), 663
  (Wooden Leg), p. 99 (bio)

Dakotas
  (Anonymous Sioux), 760
Dallas, Marie Pierce

(David C. Warren), 665
Dams
  (Larry Echohawk), 688–689
Danger
  (Elias Boudinot), there is danger,
  "immediate and appalling," 133
Dartmouth
  (Michael Dorris), p. 182 (bio)
Dawes Commission
  (Anonymous Creek), 756
Day
  (Seattle), day and night cannot
  dwell together, 95
Days
  (Charles A. Eastman), all days are
  God's, 337
Dead
  (Seattle), the invisible dead of my
  tribe, 97
Dealt
  (Janet Campbell Hale), do our best
  with the hand we've been dealt,
  673
Death
  (Paula Gunn Allen), no America
  without the death of an Indian, 612
  (Big Elk), Death will come, 76
  (Red Cloud), 209
  (Red Iron), 279
  (Seattle), death . . . but a change of
  worlds, 98
  (Tecumseh), fear of death, 66
  (Wetatonmi), 373
  (Yellow Wolf), 326
Death Penalty
  (National Council), 239–240
Death Song
  (George Bent), 299
Death Warrant
  (Major Ridge), I have signed my
  death warrant, 75
Deception
  (Black Hawk), 54
Deer
  (Anonymous Ojibway), swift . . . as
  the noble, stately deer, 742
Defiance
  (Anonymous Mohawk), 741

(Little Big Man), 378
(Osceola), 141
(Tecumseh), 65
Deloria, Ella
(Anonymous Pine Ridge Sioux), p. 208 (bio), 760
Demagogues
(John Ross), 101
Democratic National Convention
(Larry Echohawk), 691
Democratic Party
(Ben Nighthorse Campbell), 566–567
Dependence
(Lewis Downing), Dependence does not destroy sovereignty, 219
Desolation
(John Ross), 108
Destroy
(Pontiac), I mean to destroy the English, 18
(Anonymous Wintu), white people destroy all, 782
Destroyed
(Tecumseh), will we let ourselves be destroyed, 65
Devil Water
(Little Crow), 143
Die
(Captain Jack), not afraid to die, 287
(Dull Knife), better to die fighting, 172
(Fred Coyote), I will die an Indian, 734
(Geronimo), die in peace, 241
(Little Crow), you will die, like the rabbits when the hungry wolves hunt them, 144
(Satanta), when we settle down, we grow pale and die, 248
(Anna Moore Shaw), die with a silent throat, 454
(Standing Bear), I wish to die in this land, 231
Differences
(LaDonna Harris), contribute our differences, 554

Dignity
(Allan Houser), strive for . . . dignity, 478
Dime
(Gail Small), only a dime of every dollar . . . reaches the reservations, 616
Disappear
(Red Jacket), we shall disappear forever, 38
Disarmament
(Powhatan), 5
Discovery
("Indians of All Tribes"), claim . . . Alcatraz . . . by right of discovery, 725
Discrimination
(Sherman Alexie), 719
(Ruth Muskrat Bronson), 451
Disease
(Palaneapope), 282
Diversity
(Janice LaFountain), we must learn to appreciate diversity, 731
Division of Labor
(Little Turtle), 36
(Meninock), 439–440
Dogs
(Little Crow), like dogs in the Hot Moon, 143
Dog Soldiers
(Bull Bear), p. 103 (bio)
Dorris, Michael
(Louise Erdrich), p. 189 (bio), 703
Dream
(Black Elk), a people's dream died, 360
Dreams
(Edward Goodbird), all dreams were thought to be from the spirits, 392
(Janet Campbell Hale), Dreams . . . speak to the individual, 674
(Peter MacDonald), dare to dream great dreams, 522
(Smohalla), wisdom comes in dreams, 183
Dundy, Judge Elmer

(Standing Bear), 235
Dust
    (Little Hill), it was all dust, 348

Eagles
    (Oren R. Lyons), no seat for the ea-
    gles, 537
Ear
    (Petalesharo), entered one ear and
    shall not escape, 118
    (Young-Man-Afraid), in one ear
    and out the other, 374
Ears
    (Keokuk), 116
    (Little Crow), your ears are full of
    roaring water, 144
Earth
    (N. Scott Momaday), a man ought
    to concentrate his mind upon the
    remembered earth, 596
    (Luther Standing Bear), good for
    the skin to touch the earth, 389
    (Anonymous Wintu), how can the
    spirit of the earth like the white
    man, 783
    (Harriett Pierce), Indians have a
    spiritual tie with the earth, 474
    (Crazy Horse), one does not sell the
    earth, 294
    (Hollow Horn), the earth, your
    mother, will beg you . . . to save
    her, 456
Echo Hawk
    (Larry Echohawk), 692, 695
Ecology
    (Anonymous Wintu), 781–782, 783
    (Jim Barnes), 561
    (Larry Echohawk), 687–690
    (Harriett Starleaf Gumbs), 458
    (Hollow Horn), 456
    (Oren R. Lyons), 537–542
Economy
    (Louis R. Bruce), living in an In-
    dian-managed economy, 467
    (Pushmataha), 44
    (Ben Reifel), 455
Education
    (Sam Ahkcah), 447–448

(Anonymous Carlisle Graduate),
750
    (Gertrude Simmons Bonnin), 408
    (John Castillo), 717
    (Conassatego), 11–13
    (Tim Giago), 593
    (Kushiway), 307–308
    (Francis LaFlesche), 330–332
    (Tatanga Mani), 399
    (Phillip Martin), 514
    (Opothleyoholo), 124
    (John Rogers), 462–465
    (Will Rogers), 417
    (Spotted Tail), 216–217
    (Annie Dodge Wauneka), 476
    (Sarah Winnemucca), 305
Emigrants
    (Washakie), 150–152
Empathy
    (Proverb), 792
Emuckfaw
    (William Weatherford), 83
Encampment
    (Anonymous Sioux), a great en-
    campment of all the Dakotas who
    had ever lived, 760
Encroachment
    (Tuskeneah), 245–246
Enemies
    (Anonymous Shoshone), leagued
    with our enemies, 766
    (Captain Jack), my enemies under
    me, 287
Enemy
    (Wild Cat), 164
    (Anonymous Prayer), my greatest
    enemy—myself, 785
Enforcement
    (Young-Man-Afraid), 374
Environment
    (Vine Deloria, Jr.), 577
    (Harriett Starleaf Gumbs), 458
    (Oren R. Lyons), 542–547
    (Quanah Parker), 312
    (Satanta), 251
    (Yellow Wolf), 329
Environmental Justice
    (Gail Small), Indian tribes are major

players in the environmental justice movement, 617
Erdrich, Louise
(Michael Dorris), p. 182 (bio), 668
Ethnically diverse
(Ben Nighthorse Campbell), ethnically diverse peoples who had prospered . . . for many thousands of years, 562
Europe
(Phillip Martin), p. 143 (bio)
Evans, Jeremiah
(Sequoya), 69
Evil spirit
(Petalesharo), 121
Execution
(Big Eagle), 160
Executioners
(National Council), 240
Expansion
(Red Jacket), 37
(Speckled Snake), 128–129
Expense
(Crazy Horse), we were no expense to the government, 295
Exploitation
(Paula Gunn Allen), 612–614
Exploited
(Paula Gunn Allen), We've been exploited right out of house and home, 614
Extended Family
(Jeanne Bearcrane), 730
Exterminated
(Standing Bear), my children have been exterminated, 234
Extermination
(Ely Parker), 228
(Red Jacket), 38
Extinction
(Dragging-Canoe), proclaim the extinction of the whole race, 27
Eyes
(Anonymous Ojibway), eyes like the eagle's, piercing and bright, 743
(Little Crow), your eyes are full of smoke, 144

(John Rogers), her eyes sparkled as the sun's laughing waters, 461

Faithfulness
(Anonymous Winnebago), 777
Fall, Albert
(Ruth Muskrat Bronson), 450
Fallen Timbers
(Little Turtle), 32
Fame
(Anonymous Ojibway), 745
Family
(Linda Hogan), 675
Farewell
(Black Hawk), 58
Fate
(John Ridge), I am resigned to my fate, 145
Father
(Big Thunder), the Great Spirit is our Father, 419
Father of Waters
(Major Ridge), give up these lands and go over the great Father of Waters, 74
Fawn-Eyed One
(Anonymous Ojibway), 746
FBI Agents' Murders
(Leonard Peltier), p. 177 (bio)
Fear
(Logan), never felt fear, 23
(Tecumseh), who are the white people that we should fear them?, 60
Ferris, Warren
(Anonymous Shoshone), p. 210 (bio)
Fetterman Massacre
(Red Cloud), p. 56 (bio)
Fiction
(Janet Campbell Hale), Fiction and dreams spring from a common well, 674
Fight
(Chief Joseph), from where the sun now stands, I will fight no more forever, 273
(Dragging-Canoe), treaties may be

all right for men too old to . . .
Fight, 28
(Tecumseh), we must fight each
other's battles, 61
Fighting
(Dull Knife), my fighting days are
done, 170
Fingernails
(Cochise), carry their lives on their
fingernails, 180
Fire
(Standing Bear), in front of a great
prairie fire, 235
Firearms
(Anonymous Shoshone), 765
Firewater
(Tecumseh), poisonous firewater, 68
(Anonymous Delaware), you have
drunk the poison firewater, 740
First American
(Gertrude Simmons Bonnin), the
first American—the Red Man, 411
Fish
(Meninock), we had the fish . . . be-
fore the white man came, 441
Fish-in demonstrations
(Janet McCloud), 530
Fishing rights
(Henry Adams), 652–653
(Larry Echohawk), 690
(Meninock), 439, 441–442
Fish-ins
(Herbert Blatchford), p. 149 (bio)
(Melvin Thom), p. 167 (bio)
Fitzpatrick, Thomas
(Black Kettle), 138
Five civilized tribes
(Lewis Downing), 218
Flag
(George Bent), 297
(Mary Brave Bird), every star in
this flag represented a state stolen
from Indians, 708
Flag-raising photo
(Ira Hayes), p. 138 (bio), 500–502
Flood
(Opothleyoholo), white man comes
upon us as a flood, 123

Florida
(James Kaywaykla), p. 117 (bio)
(Wild Cat), 165
Flowers
(Anonymous Ojibway), flowers that
drink dew, 746
Flush
(Paula Gunn Allen), every time you
flush the toilet, some Navajo goes
without the water, 613
Food
(Minavana), the Great Spirit . . . has
provided food for us in these . . .
lakes and . . . mountains, 43
Forefathers
(Anonymous Delaware), live as
your wise forefathers lived, 740
Forest
(William McIntosh), we were like
the trees of the forest, 78
Forgiveness
(William W. Keeler), 473
Forked Tongue
(Speckled Snake), 130
Fort Keogh
(Wooden Leg), 351
Fort McDermitt
(Sarah Winnemucca), 303
Foxwoods Casino
(Richard A. Hayward), p. 184 (bio)
Free
(Red Cloud), free as the winds and
eagle, 207
Freedom
(Chief Joseph), 277
(Satanta), 248
(Wooden Leg), the past days of real
freedom, 352
French
(Tahajadoris), p. 6 (bio), 8–9
French and Indian War
(Cornplanter), p. 11 (bio)
(Pontiac), p. 9 (bio)
(Teedyuscung), p. 6 (bio)
Friend
(Logan), the friend of white men,
21
Friendship

(Pushmataha), 44–45
Frightened
(Gertrude Simmons Bonnin), frightened and bewildered as the young of a wild creature, 407
Fringes
(Leslie Silko), we live somewhere on the fringes, 684
Frustration
(Grace Thorpe), 498

Gambling
(Darren Bonaparte), 587–588
(Larry Echohawk), 697
(L. David Jacobs), 647
(Wallace Wells, Jr.), 733
Game
(Washakie), When I look for game, I see only wagons with white tops, 151
Garbage
(Oren R. Lyons), watch your garbage float away, 547
Garland, Hamlin
(Two Moon), p. 88 (bio)
Garry, Spokane
(Polatkin), p. 50 (bio)
Generation Gap
(Emma Marks), 477
Generosity
(Logan), 20
Genocide
(Dennis Banks), 603
(Ben Nighthorse Campbell), imported disease, slavery, forced relocation, and outright genocide, 564
(John LaVelle), spiritual genocide, 732
(Russell Means), 625
(John Mohawk), 664
(Roxanne Dunbar Ortiz), nationhood or genocide, 608; Genocide is colonial policy, not accident, 610
Georgia Legislature
(William McIntosh), 78
Georgia Militia
(William Weatherford), 85
Ghost Dance

(Kicking Bear), p. 99 (bio), 350
(Sitting Bull), p. 72 (bio)
(Wovoka), p. 93 (bio), 336
(Young-Man-Afraid), 376
Ghost Dance Songs
(Anonymous Sioux), 758–759
GI benefits
(Joseph Nicholas), didn't receive any G.I. benefits, 503
Gift
(N. Scott Momaday), the gift of seeing truly, 594
Glory
(Black Hawk), path to glory is rough, 52
(Ira Hayes), publicity and glory, 500
Gold
(James Kaywaykla), gold, the metal forbidden to man, 424
(Little Raven), 194
Golden Gate Exposition
(Allan Houser), p. 133 (bio)
Gold-rush
(Ruth Muskrat Bronson), relic of the gold-rush days, 449
Good Indian
(Satanta), the good Indian . . . gets nothing, 247
Good luck charm
(Ben Nighthorse Campbell), 565
Good Spirit
(Petalesharo), 121
Government
(Thomas Pegg), our government has been paralyzed, 342
Grace
(Oren R. Lyons), a state of grace, 539
Granger, General Gordon
(Cochise), 178
Grant, Ulysses
(Geronimo), 241
(Ely Parker), p. 62 (bio)
Grasping Eagle
(Sitting Bull), 267
Grass

(Red Cloud), your people are like
blades of grass, 201
(Seattle), his people . . . are like the
grass that covers the . . . prairies,
88
(Smohalla), 186
(Speckled Snake), while the grass
grows or the river runs, 129
Gratitude
(Maris Bryant Pierce), we neither
know nor feel any debt of grati-
tude, 177
Graves
(Red Cloud), sacred graves to be
plowed for corn, 199
(Red Iron), we have sold our own
graves, 280
Great Father
(Dull Knife), 169, 171, 173
(Little Hill), took our Great Father's
advice, 346
(Red Cloud), 198–199
(Spotted Tail), there is no Great Fa-
ther between me and the Great
Spirit, 212
Greatness
(Seattle), the greatness of tribes
now almost forgotten, 90
Great Spirit
(Anonymous Shoshone), children of
the Great Spirit, 764
(Big Elk), 76
(Black Hawk), 52
(Edward Goodbird), we Indians did
not believe in one Great Spirit, 391
(William McIntosh), 78
(Red Fox), 429
(Sun Bear), 527
(Tecumseh), 61, 65
Grief
(George Bent), 300
Grievances
(Young-Man-Afraid), 374–376
Grovel
(Tecumseh), grovel to none, 67
Guadalcanal
(Wilson Keedah, Sr.), p. 145 (bio)
Guggenheim Fellowship

(Allan Houser), p. 133 (bio)
Guns
(Powhatan), I insist the guns and
swords . . . be removed, 5

Hair
(Alexander Posey), 401
Hair cutting
(Dennis Banks), 604–605
Halfbreed race
(John Ridge), 148
Hancock, General Winfield Scott
(Roman Nose), 253
Hand
(Black Kettle), taken your hand, 137
(William McIntosh), we took the
white man by the hand, 79
Haozous, Robert
(Allan Houser), 481
Happy Hunting Grounds
(Major Ridge), 72
Harmony
(Lori Cupp), 507
(Jake L. Whitecrow, Jr.), harmony
within the Universe, 518
Harris, Fred
(LaDonna Harris), p. 152 (bio)
Harrison, William Henry
(Tecumseh), p. 19 (bio), 63
Hate
(Sitting Bull), I hate all the white
people, 262
Haughty
(Anonymous Winnebago), do not
act haughty toward your husband,
778
Hawk
(Anonymous Ojibway), the hawk
. . . never misses its prey, 774
Hayes, Rutherford B.
(Sarah Winnemucca), p. 84 (bio)
Healing
(Big Thunder), 419
Heart
(Sarah Winnemucca), written on
my heart, 304
Heathens
(Robert Burnette), 512

Heaven
    (Anonymous Wyandot), 784
    (Anonymous Delaware), I am the
    Maker of heaven and earth, 738
    (Four Guns), no white man . . . ad-
    mitted to heaven . . . unless there
    are writings . . . in a great book,
    421
Helplessness
    (Anonymous Apache), 752
Henderson State University
    (George Baldwin), p. 188 (bio)
Heritage
    (Larry Echohawk), 691
    (Carl Gorman), 472
    (Red Cloud), 208
    (David C. Warren), 665
History
    (Red Fox), 430
    (Roxanne Dunbar Ortiz), 610
    (Janet McCloud), history books are
    wrong, 530
Hitler, Adolph
    (Russell Means), 622
Holistic education
    (Sandra J. Fox), 655
Holocaust
    (Oren R. Lyons), the history of ho-
    locaust visited upon the indigenous
    peoples, 545
    (Wilma Mankiller), Trail of Tears
    was . . . our holocaust, 660
Home
    (Susan LaFlesche Picotte), the home
    is the foundation, 362
Hoop
    (Black Elk), our power came . . .
    from the sacred hoop, 357–358; the
    flowering tree was the living center
    of the hoop, 358; the nation's hoop
    is broken, 360
Hoover, Herbert
    (Gertrude Simmons Bonnin), p. 114
    (bio)
    (Charles Curtis), p. 100 (bio), 355
Hope
    (Mary Brave Bird), places without
    hope, 709

Horseshoe Bend
    (William Weatherford), p. 24 (bio)
Hostiles
    (Daisy Albert), the real hostiles are
    the whites, 531
House Committee on Territories
    (William P. Ross), 366
Houser, Allan
    (Robert Haozous), p. 176 (bio)
Hughes Aircraft
    (Peter MacDonald), p. 144 (bio)
    (Joseph C. Vasquez), p. 135 (bio)
Human Sacrifice
    (Petalesharo), p. 32 (bio)
Humble
    (Sitting Bull), trying to humble me,
    268
Humor
    (Linda Hogan), develop humor or
    die of despair, 677
    (James Welch), 635
Hunted
    (James Kaywaykla), hunted . . . as
    though we were wild animals, 423
    (Powhatan), to be so hunted that I
    cannot rest, 6
Hunter College
    (Lorraine Canoe), p. 154 (bio)
    (Gaetana DeGennaro), p. 192 (bio)
Hunting
    (Pontiac), 19
    (Satanta), 252
Hunting Ground
    (Little Turtle), the greater and best
    part of your brothers' hunting
    ground, 35
Hunting Rights
    (Old Tassel), 16–17
Husband
    (Anonymous Winnebago), 776–780
Hypocrisy
    (Plenty-Coups), 320–321

Iceberg
    (Oren R. Lyons), these histories can
    be likened to an iceberg, 543
Ideas

(Dan Katchongva), new and selfish
ideas, 398
Identity
  (Anonymous Carlisle Graduate),
  750
  (Gaetana DeGennaro), 720
  (LaDonna Harris), 553
  (Inter-Tribal Meeting), determined
  to hold to identity, 718
  (Simon Ortiz), 639
  (Grace Thorpe), 497
  (Joseph C. Vasquez), 484
  (James Welch), 633
Idleness
  (Crazy Horse), we preferred hunt-
  ing to a life of idleness, 294a
Images
  (Simon Ortiz), images of Dick and
  Jane, 639
Imagine
  (N. Scott Momaday), we are what
  we imagine, 597
Imprisonment
  (Lion Bear), 161
Indian
  (Luther Clearwater), don't know
  how to *be* Indi'n, so busy *actin'* In-
  di'n, 506
  (James Welch), only an Indian
  knows who he is, 633
Indian agent
  (Black Kettle), 138
Indian art
  (W. Richard West, Jr.), guiding set
  of esthetics in Indian art, 644
Indian Law Resource Center
  (John Mohawk), p. 181 (bio)
Indian life
  (Ella Deloria), 434
Indianness
  (Frederick Dockstader), the quality
  of Indianness, 489
  (Billy Mills), 607
  (Grace Thorpe), 497
Indian police
  (Sitting Bull), 267
Indian Rights Association
  (Ruth Muskrat Bronson), 449

Information Age
  (George Baldwin), 701
Ingratitude
  (Speckled Snake), 127–128
Injustice
  (Vine Deloria, Jr.), 582–583
  (Leslie Silko), 686
Injustices
  (Richard A. Hayward), historic in-
  justices perpetrated on indigenous
  people, 678
Interaction
  (Pushmataha), 44
Interior Department
  (Grace Thorpe), 496
International Olympic Committee
  (Jim Thorpe), p. 119 (bio)
Interpreter
  (Cornplanter), 31
Inter-tribal disputes
  (Keokuk), 116–117
Intruders
  (Oochalata), 344
Investment
  (Phillip Martin), no precedent for
  . . . investment, 515
Irony
  ("Indians of All Tribes"), 726–728
Iroquois
  (Larry Echohawk), 693
Island
  (Red Jacket), we stand a small is-
  land, 38
Iwo Jima
  (Eugene R. Crawford), p. 145 (bio)
  (Teddy Draper, Sr.), 525
  (Ira Hayes), p. 138 (bio)
  (Wilson Keedah, Sr.), p. 145 (bio)

Jackson, Andrew
  (Elias Boudinot), p. 36 (bio)
  (Pushmataha), p. 16 (bio)
  (John Ridge), p. 40 (bio), 146–148
  (John Ross), p. 27 (bio), 99
  (Speckled Snake), 127–130
  (Tuskeneah), 245
  (William Weatherford), p. 24 (bio),
  82–86

Jamestown
  (Powhatan), p. 4 (bio)
Japanese
  (Eugene R. Crawford), thought I
  was Japanese, 523
Jealousy
  (Anonymous Winnebago), 775
  (Powhatan), 4
Jesus
  (Blackfoot), you call the Great Spirit
  Jesus, 187
  (Geronimo), too old . . . to follow
  your Jesus road, 244
Joan of Arc
  (Sarah Winnemucca), p. 84 (bio)
Jobs
  (Phillip Martin), jobs gone to Mex-
  ico or Taiwan, 516
Johnson, Lyndon
  (Clyde Warrior), 490
Jones, Evan
  (John Ross), 101
Jurisdiction
  (Roxanne Dunbar Ortiz), p. 166
  (bio)
Justice
  (Captain Jack), 284
  (Chiksika), 110
  (Cornplanter), 31
  (Oren R. Lyons), 541

Kahokia
  (Ben Nighthorse Campbell), 563
Kansas
  (William P. Ross), 367
Kill
  (Sitting Bull), let the soldiers . . . Kill
  me, 267
Killer
  (Larry Echohawk), let the real killer
  go free, 688
King Charles
  (King Philip), 7
King Gustav
  (Jim Thorpe), 432
King Philip's War
  (King Philip), p. 5 (bio)
Knick-Knacks

  (Frederick Dockstader), Knick-
  Knacks and tourist souvenirs, 488
Knights of the Hood
  (William P. Ross), 369
Knowledge
  (Vernon Cooper), Knowledge is of
  the past, 466
  (John Rogers), gain knowledge
  from my walks, 465
Kroeber, Alfred
  (Ishi), p. 101 (bio)

Labrador
  (Mark Maracle), 586
Lacygne
  (William P. Ross), 367
LaFlesche, Susette
  (Francis LaFlesche), p. 92 (bio)
Lakotas
  (Luther Standing Bear), the Lakotas
  are now a sad, silent, and unpro-
  gressive people, 386
Lance
  (Satanta), I have laid aside my
  lance, 249
Land
  (Anonymous Cherokee), your land
  is your territory, 736
  (Anonymous Delaware), the land
  . . . I have made for you, 739
  (Cochise), 179
  (Vine Deloria, Jr.), 578
  (Doublehead), 309
  (Inter-Tribal Meeting), the land sup-
  ported a universe of things they
  valued, 718
  (Robert Haozous), I love the land
  and I love people, 649
  (Oren R. Lyons), you have our
  land, 548
  (Major Ridge), we obtained the
  land from the living God, 72
  (William McIntosh), we will give
  you land for yourselves and for
  your children, 78
  (Old Tassel), their cry is more land,
  14
  (Simon Ortiz), related to the land

... culturally, politically, personally, 642
(Petalesharo), we have plenty of land, 120
(Red Cloud), 210
Land claims
(Mark Maracle), 585
Land ownership
(Sitting Bull), 260
Land purchase
(Chief Joseph), 272
Land rights
(Meninock), 441
Land sale
(National Council), 239
Landlords
(Dennis Banks), we are the landlords of this continent, coming to collect the rent, 606
Lands
(Elias Boudinot), our lands ... are about to be seized, 132
Language
(Black Hawk), how smooth ... the language of the whites, 50
(Simon Ortiz), my love of language, 638
Language recognition
(Ishi), 356
Las Vegas
(Darren Bonaparte), Las Vegas in your hometown, 587
Law
(Oren R. Lyons, 541
(Plenty-Coups), 320
Laws
(Tuskeneah), Laws that ... are in words that we have no possible means to understanding, 246
(Major Ridge), laws which ... harass our braves, 72
Laziness
(Black Hawk), 55
Lee, Robert E.
(Ely Parker), p. 62 (bio)
Legitimacy
(John Mohawk), 664
Lewis and Clark expedition

(Anonymous Shoshone), p. 210 (bio)
Liberty, Margot
(John Stands in Timber), p. 118 (bio)
Lies
(Satanta), I have no little ties, 250
Life
(Crowfoot), 197
(Charles A. Eastman), I lived the natural life ... now I live the artificial, 338
Lincoln, Abraham
(John Ross), p. 27 (bio)
Liquor
(Anonymous Delaware), 740
Literature
(Vine Deloria, Jr.), Much contemporary literature is thinly disguised romanticism, 581
(Michael Dorris), Native American literature is about as descriptive a term as non-Native American literature, 667
(Louise Erdrich), one of the problems is the distribution of literature, 704
Little Bear
(George Bent, 298
Little Big Horn
(Crazy Horse), p. 82 (bio), 296
(Dull Knife), p. 48 (bio)
(Flying Hawk), p. 90 (bio)
(Gall), p. 80 (bio)
(Herbert Blatchford), 536
(John Stands in Timber), p. 118 (bio)
(Red Fox), p. 118 (bio)
(Sitting Bull), p. 72 (bio) 259
(Two Moon), 313–314, 316–319, 325
(Wooden Leg), p. 99 (bio)
Little Crow
(Big Eagle), 160
Locusts
(Little Crow), white men are like the locusts, 143
Long Beach (Calif.) School District

(Lillian Valenzuela Robles), p. 134 (bio)
Lord Dunmore
  (Logan), p. 9 (bio), 20
Lose
  (Seattle), everything to lose and nothing to gain, 92
Lost
  (Wetatonmi), all lost, we walked silently on into the wintry night, 373
Love
  (Polatkin), I love everybody now that I have grey hair, 176
Love Medicine
  (Louise Erdrich), 702, 704
Loves
  (Speckled Snake), loves his red children, 127, 130
Love songs
  (Anonymous Ojibway), 742–748
Lumpkin, Wilson
  (John Ridge), 146

Machu Picchu
  (Ben Nighthorse Campbell), 563
Mahicans
  (Tahajadoris), 9
Maine Legislature
  (Joseph Nicholas), p. 140 (bio)
Male-female relationships
  (Anonymous Winnebago), 772–780
A Man Called Horse
  (Mary Brave Bird), 716
Manhattan
  ("Indians of All Tribes"), 726
Manhood
  (Dennis Banks), 602, 604
Manifest Destiny
  (Oren R. Lyons), the Christian doctrine of manifest destiny—that one people will rule the world, 544
Manifesto
  (Wilma Mankiller), our Indian manifesto, 663
Manners
  (Francis LaFlesche), 330–332
Massacre

(Chiksika), when a white army loses . . . it is called a massacre, 111
Massacred
  (Crazy Horse), They say we massacred him [Custer], but he would have done the same, 296
Massasoit
  (King Philip), p. 5 (bio)
Mather, Cotton
  (Robert Burnette), 512
Mayflower
  (Mark Maracle), 585
  (Will Rogers), my ancestors did not come over on the Mayflower, 412
  (William Warren), p. 61 (bio)
McLaughlin, Major James
  (Sitting Bull), 268
Medicine
  (Edward Goodbird), 395
Medicine Lodge
  (Kicking Bird), 269
Medicine Lodge Council
  (Black Kettle), p. 37 (bio)
  (Satank), 167
  (Satanta), 248
Men
  (Conassatego), send us . . . their sons . . . and we will . . . make men of them, 13
Messiah
  (Kicking Bear), 350
Mexicans
  (Lillian Valenzuela Robles), in order to survive . . . had to call themselves Mexicans, 483
Mile
  (Proverb), walk a mile in his moccasins, 792
Miles, General Nelson
  (Chief Joseph), 273, 275
Militants
  (Luther Clearwater), militants keep wantin' to put things way back a hundred years, 506
Military supervision
  (Ely Parker), 222–226
Mill, John Stuart
  (Ella Deloria), 434

Million
    (Standing Bear), were he to give me
    a million dollars, 232
Mineral resources
    (Dan Katchongva), 398
Mines
    (Blackfoot), those mountains are
    full of mines, 188
Mining
    (Smohalla), 185
    (Sweet Medicine), 3
Minnesota
    (Little Hill), 346–347
Minority
    (Joseph C. Vasquez), I belong to a
    minority with seniority, 484
Misery
    (Darren Bonaparte), make a profit
    on their misery, 588
    (Sarah Winnemucca), put out of our
    misery, 302
Misrepresentation
    (Black Hawk), vindicate my charac-
    ter from misrepresentation, 51
Missionaries
    (Vine Deloria, Jr.), 573
    (Petalesharo), 119, 121
Missionary
    (Anonymous Wyandot), 784
Mississippi
    (Speckled Snake), 129
Missouri
    (William P. Ross), 369
Missouri River
    (Gall), 288
Mixed ancestry
    (Leslie Silko), 683–685
Moccasins
    (Proverb), walk a mile in his moc-
    casins, 792
Modoc War
    (Captain Jack), p. 79 (bio)
Mohican
    (Tecumseh), 64
Money
    (Bull Bear), the buffalo is our
    money, 363

    (Ouray the Arrow), money in the
    bank, 190
Monroe, James
    (Petalesharo), p. 32 (bio), 118
Monster
    (Chiksika), the white man is a mon-
    ster who is always hungry, 112
Moon
    (Anonymous Indian Boy), when the
    white man landed on the moon,
    755
Moon landing
    (Anonymous Indian Boy), 755
Morning
    (Seattle), morning must flee the ris-
    ing sun, 95
Mother
    (Big Thunder), the earth is our
    mother, 419
Mother Earth
    (Larry Echohawk), defile our sacred
    Mother Earth, 694
    (Russell Means), 626
Mother Lodge
    (John Ross), 102
Mother Nature
    (Ben Nighthorse Campbell), lived in
    harmony with Mother Nature, 563
Mourn
    (Logan), who is there to mourn, 24
Mourning
    (Dull Knife), mourning in every
    lodge, 171
Muddy Lake Reservation
    (Sarah Winnemucca), 301
Muscogees
    (Speckled Snake), 127
Museum of Anthropology
    (Ishi), p. 101 (bio)
Music
    (Louis W. Ballard), 557
Mutilation
    (James Kaywaykla), 425
    (Palaneapope), 281

Names
    (Eagle Wing), we have given names
    to many beautiful things, 310

(Wilma Mankiller), names [are] essential parts of . . . personalities, 659
(Alexander Posey), 401–403
Narragansett
(Tecumseh), 64
Nation
(Mark Maracle), we are a lost nation, 586
National Association of Manufacturers
(William W. Keeler), p. 131 (bio)
National Congress of American Indians
(Robert Burnette), p. 142 (bio)
(Vine Deloria, Jr.), p. 157 (bio)
(Napoleon B. Johnson), p. 123 (bio)
National Council of American Indians
(Gertrude Simmons Bonnin), p. 114 (bio)
National Indian Health Board
(Jake L. Whitecrow, Jr.), p. 144 (bio)
National Indian Youth Council
(Herbert Blatchford), p. 149 (bio)
(Melvin Thom), p. 167 (bio)
(Clyde Warrior), p. 136 (bio)
National Marine Fisheries Service
(Larry Echohawk), 687
National Museum of the American Indian
(Gaetana DeGennaro), p. 192 (bio), 720–722
(Richard A. Hayward), p. 184 (bio), 678–679
(Allan Houser), 479
(W. Richard West, Jr.), p. 174 (bio), 645
National Sacrifice Area
(Russell Means), 623
Nationhood
(Roxanne Dunbar Ortiz), Nationhood or genocide, 608
Native American Literature Prize
(N. Scott Momaday), p. 162 (bio)
Native American Rights Fund
(John Echohawk), p. 178 (bio)
Native sons

(Major Ridge), I am one of the native sons, 71
Nature
(Chiksika), the white man seeks to conquer nature, 112
(Charles A. Eastman), we were close students of nature, 339
(Allan Houser), living in harmony with nature, 479
(Sun Bear), nature . . . is their textbook for living, 528
(W. Richard West, Jr.), shared concept of nature, 644
Navajo Tribal Council
(Sam Ahkcah), p. 124 (bio)
(Peter MacDonald), p. 144 (bio)
Nazi Germany
(Roxanne Dunbar Ortiz), 610
Nebraska
(Larry Echohawk), the Pawnee used to have . . . almost all of Nebraska, 695
Necessity
(Major Ridge), unbending, iron necessity, 73
Neglect
(Gertrude Simmons Bonnin), inefficiency and criminal neglect, 410
Negotiations
(Red Cloud), 200
Negro
(Ruth Muskrat Bronson), a position . . . no better than that of the Negro, 451
Neutrality
(John Ross), 104–105
Newfoundland
(Mark Maracle), 586
New Mexico
(James Kaywaykla), p. 117 (bio)
Newspaper stories
(Geronimo), 243
New World
(King Philip), p. 5 (bio)
New York
(Mark Maracle), 586
(Wendy Rose), when the Hopi hit New York, 681

New York City
  (Lorraine Canoe), p. 154 (bio)
New York World's Fair
  (Allan Houser), p. 133 (bio)
Nez Perce War
  (White Bird), p. 44 (bio)
Nicholson, Joseph
  (Cornplanter), 31
Night
  (Seattle), The Indian's night prom-
  ises to be dark, 96
Noble, John
  (Young-Man-Afraid), 374
Northeast Missouri State University
  (Jim Barnes), p. 154 (bio)
Northern Cheyenne
  (LaDonna Harris), 555
Nursing
  (American Horse), the child not
  knowing . . . his mother was dead
  was still nursing, 291

Oak
  (Pushmataha), tidings like the
  sound of the fall of a mighty oak,
  48
Oakmulgee
  (Speckled Snake), 129
Oconee
  (Specked Snake, 128–129
Oil
  (Will Rogers), 418
Ojibways
  (Little Crow), 142
Okinawa
  (Eugene R. Crawford), p. 145 (bio)
  (Wilson Keedah, Sr.), p. 145 (bio)
Oklahoma
  (Dull Knife), p. 49 (bio)
  (Will Rogers), 418
Oklahoma Hall of Fame
  (William W. Keeler), p. 131 (bio)
Oklahoma Supreme Court
  (Napoleon B. Johnson), p. 123 (bio)
Old country
  (Janet Campbell Hale), North
  America is our old country, 672
Ollokot

  (Wetatonmi), p. 106 (bio)
Olympics
  (Billy Mills), p. 165 (bio)
  (Jim Thorpe), p. 119 (bio), 432–433
Omen
  (Anonymous Pima), hooting of an
  owl is a bad omen, 757
Operation Desert Storm
  (Jerry Flute), 615
Oral history
  (Simon Ortiz), Indian oral history
  has not been acceptable, 637
Orator
  (Satanta), orator of the plains, p. 69
  (bio)
Origin
  (Leslie Silko), our origin is unlike
  any other, 685
Orre Drumrite Walking Heritage
  (Elizabeth A. Wells), p. 171 (bio)
Ottawa
  (L. David Jacobs), 647
Out
  (Spokane Garry), until there is no
  more out, 174
Outcasts
  (Sitting Bull), you . . . have made
  us outcasts, 262
Outlaws
  (John Ridge), banded outlaws . . .
  for the purposes of intimidation or
  assassination, 149
Owl
  (Anonymous Pima), hooting of an
  owl is a bad omen, 757

Paint
  (Red Fox), 431
  (Seattle), disfigure their faces with
  black paint, 91
Palmer, General Innis N.
  (Roman Nose), 254
Parents
  (Anonymous Winnebago), 780
Passamaquoddy Homes Incorporated
  (Joseph Nicholas), p. 140 (bio), 504
Paternalism
  (Ella Deloria), 435–436

(Carlos Montezuma), 379–381
Pawnee
(Big Elk), p. 22 (bio)
Peace
(Black Kettle), we are for peace, 134
(Elias Boudinot), there is no peace, 132
(Dull Knife), to live in peace, 169
(Gall), 288
(Keokuk), 117
(King Philip), I shall treat of peace only with the King, 7
(Little Turtle), prudent to listen to . . . offers of peace, 34
(Red Cloud), 203
(Tahajadoris), we shall never make peace, 8
(Teedyuscung), 10
Peace plan
(Ely Parker), 222
Peace terms
(William Weatherford), 86
Pebble
(Charles A. Eastman), any pretty pebble was valuable, 338
Pequot
(Tecumseh), 64
Persecution
("Indians of All Tribes"), 723
Peyote
(Mary Brave Bird), 715
Philadelphia
(Little Turtle), 36
Philadelphia, Mississippi
(David C. Warren), 666
Phillips Petroleum
(William W. Keeler), p. 131 (bio)
Physician
(Susan LaFlesche Picotte), as a physician I can do a great deal more, 362
Picotte, Susan LaFlesche
(Francis LaFlesche), p. 92 (bio)
(Susette LaFlesche), p. 90 (bio)
Pilgrims
(Vine Deloria, Jr.), 572
(King Philip), p. 5 (bio)
(Mark Maracle), 585

Pine
(Anonymous Ojibway), graceful as the young pine, 742
Pine Ridge Reservation
(Russell Means), 623
Pipe
(Tecumseh), we must smoke the same pipe, 61
Pity
(Pontiac), take pity on us, your children, 19
Plight
(Vine Deloria, Jr.), Indians have had a "plight," 571
Plow
(Smohalla), plow the ground, 184
Poems
(Simon Ortiz), their poems, personal and social, are political, 641
(James Welch), poems about Indians written by whites, 632
Poetry
(Simon Ortiz), Poetry is a way of engendering life, 640
(Alexander Posey), 404–405; the Indian talks in poetry, 406
Pokanoket
(Tecumseh), 64
Policy
(Leslie Silko), 686
Policy issues
(Daniel Peaches), 619–621
Political attacks
(Ely Parker), 229–230
Politics
(Larry Echohawk), Politics can't alter sound biology, 687
Pontiac
(Anonymous Delaware), p. 202 (bio)
Poor
(Red Cloud), Great Spirit made us poor, 202
(Red Dog), poor because we are all honest, 365
(Standing Buffalo), we are not poor but rich, 335
Poor People's March

(Henry Adams), p. 177 (bio)
Population
  (Ben Nighthorse Campbell), 564
  (Geronimo), 241
Populations
  (Red Cloud), 201
Poverty
  (L. David Jacobs), Poverty is our
  biggest problem, 646
  (Wilbur Riegert), Poetry is a noose
  that strangles, 533; Poetry . . . is a
  stigma of disgrace, 534; "progres-
  sive" poverty brought about by . . .
  force, 535
Powder River Road
  (Spotted Tail), 211
Power
  (Big Eagle), power of the whites,
  159
  (John Ross), 109
  (Standing Bear), a power which I
  cannot resist, 238
  (Sun Bear), the path of power is
  different for every individual, 526
Prayer
  (Andy Abieta), 505
  (Great Plains Indians), 789
  (Osage Prayer), 786
  (Pueblos Prayer), 787
  (Sioux Prayer), 788
Prays
  (Andy Abieta), the white man
  prays . . . for himself . . . the Indian
  prays . . . for other people, 505
Predictions
  (Anonymous Powhatan), 761
Presidential Medal of Freedom
  (Annie Dodge Wauneka), p. 132
  (bio)
Presidential politics
  (Charles Curtis), 354–355
Pride
  (Fred Coyote), 734
Primitive
  (John Rogers), I had learned to love
  the primitive life, 462
Prison
  (Leonard Crow Dog), reservation

Indian . . . has already practiced be-
  ing in prison, 550
Pro
  (Jim Thorpe), no idea I was a pro,
  433
Problems
  (Tim Giago), 593
Progress
  (LaDonna Harris), tribal ideas of
  progress, 555
Promises
  (Anonymous Spokane), 768
  (Chief Joseph), 274–275
  (Red Cloud), 210
Propaganda
  (Yellow Wolf), 324
Prophecy
  (Hollow Horn), 456
  (Dan Katchongva), 396, 398
  (Sweet Medicine), 1–3
Prosperity
  (John Ross), the prosperity of our
  people fixed upon a permanent ba-
  sis, 99
Prostitutes
  (Anonymous Apache), our girls . . .
  will be diseased prostitutes, 753
Protection
  (Edward Goodbird), 393–394
  (Seattle), 94
Pulitzer Prize
  (N. Scott Momaday), p. 162 (bio)
Punishment
  (Black Hawk), 53

Qualities
  (Ella Deloria), dormant qualities
  that had been thought killed long
  ago, 437
Quebec
  (L. David Jacobs), 647

Racism
  (Mary Brave Bird), Racism breeds
  racism in reverse, 707
  (Linda Hogan), more racism toward
  Indian people, 676
  (Russell Means), Racism in America

against Indian people . . . institutionalized and pervasive, 630a

Rapes
(Russell Means), only the white man rapes his mother, 626

Raping
(Harriett Starleaf Gumbs), raping someone's way of life, 460

Rattlesnakes
(Kaywaykla), dangerous as the rattlesnakes upon which they fed, 427

Read
(John Rogers), read more in the swaying of the trees, 463

Reagan, Ronald
(Daniel Peaches), 621

Recognition
(Allan Houser), 480

Red ants
(Quanah Parker), [the land] is only good for red ants, coyotes, and cattlemen, 312

Red Cloud
(Dull Knife), p. 49 (bio), 169

Red Iron
(Lion Bear), 161, 163

Red man
(Seattle), the red man has ever fled the approach of the white man, 95; when the last red man shall have perished, 97

Red Power
(Vine Deloria, Jr.), Red Power . . . means power over our own lives, 569

Red River War
(Bull Bear), p. 103 (bio)

Redundancy
(Luther Standing Bear), 388

Regeneration
(Oren R. Lyons), you have broken the great cycles of regeneration, the fundamental law of natural life, 546

Religion
(Daisy Albert), 531
(Anonymous Delaware), 738
(Anonymous Wyandot), 783
(Lorraine Canoe), 560

(John Echohawk), 656–658
(Geronimo), 244
(Edward Goodbird), 390–395
(Dan Katchongva), 396, 398
(Oren R. Lyons), the white man's religion talks about mastering the earth, 547
(Plenty-Coups), the white man did not take his religion any more seriously than he did his laws, 321
(Red Jacket), 39–41; you want to force your religion upon us, 40
(Anna Moore Shaw), 452–453
(Wovoka), 336

Remembrance
(N. Scott Momaday), 596

Removal
(William Shorey Coodey), 154
(Little Hill), 347
(John Ridge), p. 40 (bio)
(Major Ridge), p. 21 (bio)
(John Ross), p. 27 (bio); such removal will be injurious, 100

Renaissance
(LaDonna Harris), a . . . renaissance going on in tribal America, 556

Republican Party
(Ben Nighthorse Campbell), 567

Resentment
(William W. Keeler), remove resentment from your hearts, 473

Reservation
(Anonymous Spokane), 768
(Robert Burnette), reservation . . . surrounded by thieves, 511
(Janet Campbell Hale), the reservation is our landbase, 671
(Lorraine Canoe), the reservation is my home, 559
(Leonard Crow Dog), 550
("Indians of All Tribes"), 728
(Wilson Keedah, Sr.), no jobs on the reservation, 524
(Carlos Montezuma), 381
(Satanta), 248
(Ten Bears), 113
(David C. Warren), 666
(Wooden Leg), 352

Reservations
    (Crazy Horse), idleness on the res-
    ervations, 294a
    (Tim Giago), without the reserva-
    tions, there will be no more Indi-
    ans, 591
    (Janet Campbell Hale), government
    would like . . . to abolish the reser-
    vations, 670
Resistance
    (Spokane Garry), 174
    (Melvin Thom), 611
Respect
    (Joseph Nicholas), learning to re-
    spect Passamaquoddy money, 504
    (Ben Calf Robe), respect for each
    other, 457
Responsibility
    (Simon Ortiz), responsibility for all
    the universe, 637
Revenge
    (The Four Bears), 126
    (Logan), this called on me for re-
    venge, 22
    (William Weatherford), a mean
    spirit of revenge, 86
Revolution
    (Clyde Warrior), 494
Revolutionary War
    (Red Jacket), p. 14 (bio)
Riches
    (Red Cloud), we do not want
    riches, 203
Ridge, John
    (Elias Boudinot), p. 36 (bio)
    (John Rollin Ridge), 221
Ridge, Major
    (Elias Boudinot), p. 36 (bio)
    (John Ridge), p. 40 (bio)
    (John Rollin Ridge), p. 62 (bio), 221
Rights
    (Ely Parker), no rights possessed by
    the Indians that they were bound
    to respect, 223
    (Seattle), the red man no longer has
    rights, 89
Ritual
    (John Stands in Timber), 428

River
    (Vine Deloria, Jr.), creating an in-
    flammable river, 577
    (Standing Bear), on the bank of an
    overflowing river, 235
Rivers
    (Chief Joseph), you might as well
    expect the rivers to run backwards,
    277
Road
    (Red Cloud), iron road, 198
    (Washakie), building of this road . .
    . will destroy many of our root
    grounds and drive off our game,
    152
Rock River
    (Black Hawk), 49
Roosevelt, Franklin
    (Gertrude Simmons Bonnin), p. 114
    (bio)
Roosevelt, Theodore
    (Geronimo), p. 68 (bio)
    (Carlos Montezuma), p. 108 (bio)
Rosebud Reservation
    (Mary Brave Bird), p. 189 (bio), 709
Rosenthal, Joe
    (Ira Hayes), p. 138 (bio)
Ross, John
    (William Shorey Coodey), p. 44
    (bio)
    (John Ridge), p. 40 (bio), 145, 148–
    149
    (William P. Ross), p. 104 (bio)
Rothschilds
    (John Ridge), 148
Ruin
    (Kicking Bird), grieved at the ruin
    of my people, 269

Sacred
    (Black Elk), the sacred tree is dead,
    360
Sacred object
    (Edward Goodbird), in this sacred
    object dwelt his god, 395
Sacred sites
    (Jerry Flute), 615
Saddle

(Jack Dempsey), my face got as
tough as a saddle, 446
Sadness
(William Shorey Coodey), sadness
of the heart, 154
Salesmanship
(Clyde Warrior), slick job of sales-
manship, 493
Salt River Reservation
(Anna Moore Shaw), p. 126 (bio)
Sand Creek
(Roman Nose), 253
Sand Creek Massacre
(George Bent), p. 83 (bio), 297–300
(Black Kettle), p. 37 (bio)
Satire
(Alexander Posey), 401–403
Savage
(Red Fox), Indian depicted as a sav-
age, 430
(John Rollin Ridge), redeem their
people from their savage state, 221
Savages
(Sun Bear), the idea that all Indians
are noble savages, 527
Sayings
(Satank), filled you with their say-
ings, 168
Scalp
(Black Hawk), white men do not
scalp, they poison, 57
Scalping
(George Bent), 298
Scalps
(Little Crow), 142
(Roman Nose), there will be scalps,
254
Scores
(Big Eagle), settle old scores, 159
Scourge
(Anonymous Creek), worst scourge
of the 19th century, 756
Screenwriting
(Joy Harjo), Screenwriting is . . . re-
lated to poetry, 698
Second Seminole War
(Osceola), p. 38 (bio)
Secret society

(John Ross), 101–102
Segregated
(Wendy Rose), segregated in the lit-
erature of America, 680
Self-determination
(Tim Giago), 591
(Clyde Warrior), 492–493
Self-government
(Oochalata), berated as unfit for
self-government, 344
Self-image
(Clyde Warrior), 490–492
Selfishness
(Will Rogers), What's wrong with
this world? . . . selfishness, 416
Self-reliance
(Ben Nighthorse Campbell), 568
(Carlos Montezuma), 379–382
Self-sufficiency
(Anonymous Carlisle Student), 737
(Louis R. Bruce), 467
(Captain Jack), 285
Sell
(Sitting Bull), we cannot sell this
land, 260
Senate Select Committee on Indian
Affairs
(Jerry Flute), 615
Sequoya
(Wilma Mankiller), 661
Sequoya redwoods
(Sequoya), p. 21 (bio)
Serpents
(Tecumseh), white people are like
poisonous serpents, 59
Settlement
(Dragging Canoe), settlement of
this land dark and bloody, 29
Seventh Generation
(Larry Echohawk), 693
Seventh Generation Fund
(John Mohawk), p. 181 (bio)
Shadows
(Red Cloud), Shadows are long and
dark, 209
Shawnee County, Kansas
(Charles Curtis), 353
She-bear

(Little Crow), as a she-bear covers her cubs, 142
Sherman, William
(Robert Burnette), 511
Ship
(Anonymous Montagnais), 735
Shoot
(White Bird), shoot as well as any . . . soldiers, 155
Sin
(Eagle Wing) we have been guilty of only one sin, 311
Sioux Uprising of 1862
(Big Eagle), p. 45 (bio), 159–160
(Little Crow), p. 39 (bio)
(Little Hill), p. 97 (bio)
Site desecration
(Lillian Valenzuela Robles), 482
Skin
(Sitting Bull), Is it wicked for me because my skin is red?, 261
Sky-treading bird
(Anonymous Ojibway), 746
Slaughter
(Richard A. Hayward), slaughter of the Pequots, 678
Slavery
(John Ross), 102
Slaves
(Anonymous Apache), our little boys will grow up as slaves, 753
(Minavavana), we are not your slaves, 43
(Old Tassel), not created us to be your slaves, 17
Sleeps
(Little Turtle), chief who never sleeps, 33
Smallpox
(The Four Bears), p. 34 (bio), 125–126
Smiles
(Anonymous Ojibway), with your smiles comes the sun, 747
Smith, John
(Powhatan), 4–6
Smithsonian
(Richard A. Hayward), p. 184 (bio)
(Francis LaFlesche), p. 92 (bio)

(W. Richard West, Jr.), p. 174 (bio)
Snake
(Black Hawk), they followed us like the snake, 55
(Luther Standing Bear), a big snake crawling across the prairie, 384
(Red Cloud), dangerous snake in our midst, 198
(Wild Cat), he had a snake in the other , 164
Snake eggs
(Simon Pokagon), 255
Snakes
(Simon Pokagon), 256, 258
Snow
(Dragging-Canoe), whole nations have melted away like snow, 25
(Red Cloud), Our nation is melting away like the snow, 201
(Tecumseh), as snow before a summer sun, 64
Social sciences
(Gerald Vizenor), methodologies of the social sciences, 599
Society
(Charles A. Eastman), artificial blocks which may be built into the walls of modern society, 338
Soldiers
(Red Cloud), duty of these soldiers is to follow people who are bad, 204
Solomons
(Eugene R. Crawford), p. 145 (bio)
Sorrow
(Yellow Wolf), air was heavy with sorrow, 325
Southern California Indian Center
(John Castillo), p. 191 (bio)
Southwest Indian Women's Conference
(Annie Dodge Wauneka), 475
Souvenir
(Frederick Dockstader), souvenir or exotic curiosity products, 486
Sovereignty
(Anonymous Mohawk), 741

(Lewis Downing), 218; Dependence does not destroy sovereignty, 219

Speak
(Cochise), speak straight, 181

Special Interests
(Robert Burnette), 510

Spirits
(Edward Goodbird), all things . . . have souls or spirits . . . these spirits are our gods, 390

Spiritual
(Anonymous AIM leader), spiritual rebirth of our [Indian] nation, 751

Sports teams
(Russell Means), racism . . . attached to sports teams with names like Indians, 630a

Square
(Black Elk), there is no power in a square, 357

Squaws
(Tecumseh), we are not squaws, 60

St. Lawrence
(Mark Maracle), 586

Star-spangled language
(Red Fox), American history . . . in star-spangled language, 430

Starvation
(Red iron), 278

Starve
(Lion Bear), starve like buffaloes in the snow, 162

State responsibility
(Daniel Peaches), 621

Steamboats
(Gall), 288

Stereotypes
(Sherman Alexie), 719
(George Baldwin), 700
(Gaetana DeGennaro), open up people's minds to stereotypes, 721
(Vine Deloria, Jr.), 575; stereotypes of western history, 580
(LaDonna Harris), 552
(Mark Maracle), 585
(Simon Ortiz), 639
(Red Fox), 430
(Don C. Talayesva), 443

Stevens, Isaac
(Seattle), 94, 97

Stone
(Kicking Bird), I am as a stone, 269

Stones
(Delshay), keep my word until the stones melt, 270

Storm
(William McIntosh)m, you are like the mighty storm, 81

Storyteller
(John Stands in Timber), 428

Striving
(Billy Mills), striving to take first and not settle for less, 607

Success
(Quanah Parker), We love the white man, but we fear your success, 312

Sun
(Black Hawk), his sun is setting, 58
(Chief Joseph), from where the sun now stands, I will fight no more forever, 273
(Eagle Wing), whisper our names to the sun that kisses them, 310
("Indians of All Tribes"), as long as the sun shall rise, 727
(Red Cloud), my sun is set, 206
(Sitting Bull), the sun rose and set on their land, 261
(Ten Bears), nothing to break the light of the sun, 113
(Dick Washakie), The sun is a gift from God, 372
(Wovoka), when the sun died, 336

Sun Dance
(Mary Brave Bird), 716

Sunday School Picnic
(Clyde Warrior), whose reactions to social ills will seem like a Sunday School picnic, 491

Superiority
(Big Eagle), 158

Supreme Court
(Vine Deloria, Jr.), 579
(John Echohawk), 658
(Severt Young Bear), p. 159 (bio)

Surgery
   (Lori Cupp), 507–508
Surrender
   (Black Hawk), 58
   (Chief Joseph), 273, 275
   (William Weatherford), 82–86
Survival of American Indians Associ-
   ation
   (Henry Adams), p. 177 (bio)
   (Janet McCloud), p. 147 (bio)
Survivor
   (Ishi), p. 101 (bio)
Swindle
   (Standing Bear), if a white man had
   land, and someone should swindle
   him, 237
Syllabary
   (Sequoya), 70
Symbol
   (Richard A. Hayward), symbol of
   understanding, education and toler-
   ance, 679
   ("Indians of All Tribes"), symbol of
   great lands once ruled by free and
   noble Indians, 729

Talk
   (Satank), tired of the much talk, 168
Talkers
   (Black Hawk), all talkers and no
   workers, 55
Talking
   (Dan Katchongva), sweet way of
   talking, 397
Talking leaves
   (Wilma Mankiller), 661
   (Sequoya), 70
Talladega
   (William Weatherford), 83
Tallaschatchee
   (William Weatherford), 83
Teapot Dome
   (Ruth Muskrat Bronson), 450
Technology
   (George Baldwin), 700–701
Tecumseh
   (Chiksika), p. 30 (bio)
   (Pushmataha), 44

Temperance lesson
   (Simon Pokagon), 255–258
Tenoshtitlan
   (Ben Nighthorse Campbell), 563
Tepee
   (Sioux Proverb), 791. See also Tipi
Themes
   (Michael Dorris), presume or even
   dare to speak for or write about
   themes . . . important for people
   from other . . . tribal backgrounds,
   669
Thieves
   (Baptiste Good), chief of all thieves,
   377
Thorpe, Jim
   (Grace Thorpe), p. 138 (bio)
Threat
   (Standing Elk), 371
Time
   (Mary Brave Bird), Indian time and
   white man's time, 713; not even a
   word for time in our language, 714
   (Spotted Tail), there is a time ap-
   pointed to all things, 214
Tipi
   (Flying Hawk), 322
Tlingit
   (Ruth Muskrat Bronson), 451
Tohopeka
   (William Weatherford), 83
Tomahawk
   (Black Hawk), dug up the toma-
   hawk, 56
Tomb
   (Gertrude Simmons Bonnin), in my
   tomb, I was destitute, 409
Tongue
   (Wild Cat), his tongue was forked,
   164
Tonto
   (Sherman Alexie), 719
   (Vine Deloria, Jr.), 574–575
Traders
   (Big Eagle), 157
   (Palaneapope), 283
   (Ely Parker), abolishment of the
   system of Indian traders, 227

Tradition
  (Lorraine Canoe), 558
  (John Castillo), 717
  (Michael Dorris), within the tradi-
  tion of a particular tribe, 668
  (LaDonna Harris), bringing tradi-
  tion along with us into the future,
  556
Trail of Tears
  (William Shorey Coodey), p. 44
  (bio)
  (Wilma Mankiller), 660
  (John Ross), p. 27 (bio)
Trails
  (Great Plains Indians), may our
  trails lie straight and level, 789
Traitor
  (Big Eagle), shoot me as a traitor,
  160
Translation
  (Francis LaFlesche), 333
  (Alexander Posey), 404, 406
Travel
  (Little Raven), travel the same road
  as the white man, 195
Travestied
  (Francis LaFlesche), thoughts have
  frequently been travestied, 333
Treaties
  (Henry Adams, 653
  (Lewis Downing), security afforded
  by our treaties, 218
  (Oochalata), 344–345
  (Satank), 167
Treaty
  (Delshay), 270–271
  (Dragging-Canoe), usurpations
  sanctioned by . . . treaty, 26
  (Osceola), only treaty I will make,
  141
  (Pushmataha), 46
  (John Ridge), 145, 148
  (Major Ridge), p. 21 (bio), 74–75
  (John Ross), p. 27 (bio)
  (Sitting Bull), 261, 263
Treaty negotiation
  (Black Kettle), 139
Treaty of 1868

(Iron Shell), 349
  (Red Cloud), p. 56 (bio)
  (Roxanne Dunbar Ortiz), p. 166
  (bio)
Treaty of Greenville
  (Little Turtle), 35
Treaty of New Echota
  (Major Ridge), 75
Treaty of Traverse Des Sioux
  (Big Eagle), 156
Treaty-making
  (King Philip), 7
Tree
  (Charles A. Eastman), ever growing
  tree an object of reverence, 338
  (Red Jacket), I am an aged tree, 42;
  you have grown to be a mighty
  tree, 37
  (William McIntosh), we are like the
  . . . bending tree, 81
Trees
  (Anonymous Wintu), 781–782
Tribal
  (Joy Harjo), create a film with a
  truly tribal vision, 699
Trouble
  (Geronimo), trouble has come from
  the agents and interpreters, 242
Truman, Harry
  (Opothleyoholo), p. 33 (bio)
  (Thomas Pegg), p. 96 (bio)
  (John Ross), p. 27 (bio), 105–107

Union Pacific Railroad
  (Luther Standing Bear), 384
  (Roman Nose), p. 70 (bio), 254
United Nations
  (Oren R. Lyons), p. 150 (bio), 537
Unity
  (Herbert Blatchford), 536
  (Peter MacDonald), 521
  (Tecumseh), 61–62
  (Teedyuscung), 10
University of Arizona
  (Leslie Silko), p. 185 (bio)
University of California at Los Ange-
  les
  (Paula Gunn Allen), p. 167 (bio)

University of Chicago
(Inter-Tribal Meeting), p. 191 (bio)
Uranium
(Russell Means), 623–624
Ussen
(Kaywaykla), meaning of Ussen is
Creator of Life, 426
Utterances
(Francis LaFlesche), utterances belit-
tled when put into English, 333

Values
(Dennis Banks), 600
(Larry Echohawk), I was raised
with Indian values, 697
(Allan Houser), 479
(Little Turtle), 36
(Old Tassel), 15
(Simon Ortiz), 637
(Harriett Pierce), 474
(Sitting Bull), 265–266
(Smohalla), 183–186
(David C. Warren), 665
(Elizabeth A. Wells), 631
(Shirley Black Stone Weston), 636
Vengeance
(Tecumseh), 62
Victims
(LaDonna Harris), Indians have
been the victims of fine rhetoric, 551
Victory songs
(Luther Standing Bear), 388
Vietnam War
(Henry Adams), p. 177 (bio)
Violence
(James Kaywaykla), that people
died except by violence, 422
(Clyde Warrior), volcanic eruption
of violence, 495
Virgin Mary
(Cochise), 182
Vision
(Edward Goodbird), a kind of
dream while yet awake we called
. . . a vision, 392
(N. Scott Momaday), the native vi-
sion . . . is a matter of extrasensory
as well as sensory perception, 594

Voice
(Captain Jack), the voice of my people, 286

Wagon Box Fight
(Red Cloud), p. 56 (bio)
Waponahki Museum
(Joseph Nicholas), p. 140 (bio)
War
(Edward Goodbird), 393
(Wilson Keedah, Sr.), went to war
because . . . no jobs, 524
(Shabonee), 77
(Spotted Tail), war brought upon
us by the children of the Great Fa-
ther who came to take our land,
213
(Tahajadoris), to begin a war with-
out just provocation, 9
(Washakie), a war with the Great
Father would be disastrous, 150
War causes
(Big Eagle), 156–159
War cry
(Red Cloud), 199
(Tecumseh), 62
War Department
(Ely Parker), transfer . . . the Indian
bureau . . . back to the War Depart-
ment, 222
War of 1812
(William McIntosh), 78
(John Ross), p. 27 (bio)
(Tecumseh), p. 19 (bio)
War on poverty
(Wilbur Riegert), p. 149 (bio)
Warning
(Powhatan), 6
Warpath
(Pushmataha), we do not take up
the warpath without a just cause,
46
Warrior
(Yellow Wolf), power . . . given the
warrior, 327
Warriors
(Tecumseh), made women of our
warriors, 62

Wars
  (Janet McCloud), the last Indian
  wars, 530
Washakie
  (Dick Washakie), p. 105 (bio)
Washington, D.C.
  (L. David Jacobs), 647
Washington Redskins
  (Sherman Alexie), 719
Washington State
  (Herbert Blatchford), p. 149 (bio)
  (Janet McCloud), 530
Waterman, Thomas
  (Ishi), p. 101 (bio), 356
Water rights
  (Peter MacDonald), 519
Wayne, Anthony
  (Little Turtle), 33–34
Welfare
  (Harriett Starleaf Gumbs), 459
Wessells, Captain
  (Dull Knife), 173
Whiskey
  (Wooden Leg), I spent my scout
  pay for whiskey, 351
"Whiskey eggs"
  (Simon Pokagon), 255
White Antelope
  (George Bent), 299
White man
  (Captain Jack), live like a white
  man, 285
  (Dan Katchongva), 396–398
  (Little Raven), think I will look like
  a white man, 192; the white man
  has taken away everything, 196
White people
  (Spotted Tail), white people are all
  thieves and liars, 216
Whites
  (Gall), the whites run our country,
  288
Whitman, Lieutenant
  (Anonymous Apache), 752
Wife
  (Anonymous Winnebago), do not
  make an idol of your wife, 772
Wild

(Oren R. Lyons), no such work as
  wild, 549
Wild Man
  (Ishi), p. 101 (bio)
"Wild West"
  (Luther Standing Bear), 385
Wild West shows
  (Red Fox), p. 119 (bio)
Wilderness
  (Luther Standing Bear), Only to the
  white man was nature a "wilder-
  ness," 385
William and Mary College
  (Conassatego), p. 7 (bio)
Wind
  (Ten Bears), where the wind blew
  tree, 113
Wisdom
  (Vernon Cooper), Wisdom is of the
  future, 466
Wisest
  (Thomas Pegg), our wisest men
  knew not what to do, 343
Wolf
  (Wild Cat), could not shoot him as
  I could a wolf, 164
Wolf's bark
  (Black Kettle), we have not come
  with a little wolf's bark, 135
Wolf-Power
  (Yellow Wolf), 328
Wolves
  (The Four Bears), wolves will
  shrink with horror, 125
Woman
  (Anonymous Winnebago), not good
  to be enslaved by a woman, 774
Woman beating
  (Black Hawk), cry like a woman, 57
  (Mary Brave Bird), woman beating
  is part of everyday life, 711
Women
  (Cheyenne Proverb), a nation is not
  conquered until the hearts of its
  women are on the ground, 790
  (Linda Hogan), tribal women have
  the lowest wages, 675
  (Annie Wauneka), women must be-

come more active in politics, 476;
women . . . second-class citizens, 475
Word
(Alexander Posey), gorgeous word
pictures, 405
Words
(Dan Katchongva), an inventor of
many words, 397
(Chief Joseph), good words will not
get my people a home where they
can live in peace, 276
(Seattle), my words are like stars
that never set, 87
Work
(Smohalla), men who work cannot
dream, 183
World War II
(Eugene Crawford), p. 83 (bio)
(Ella Deloria), p. 121 (bio)
(Peter Dillon), p. 148 (bio)
(Teddy Draper, Sr.), p. 146 (bio)
(Jim Earthboy), p. 147 (bio)
(Wilson Keedah, Sr.), p. 145 (bio)
(Peter MacDonald), p. 144 (bio)
(Joseph Nicholas), p. 140 (bio)
Wounded Knee Massacre
(American Horse), p. 81 (bio), 289–
292

(Louis W. Ballard), p. 153 (bio)
(Dennis Banks), p. 164 (bio)
(Black Elk), p. 101 (bio), 359–360
(Charles A. Eastman), p. 94 (bio),
340–341
(Russell Means), p. 169–170 (bio)
(Roxanne Dunbar Ortiz), p. 166
(bio)
(Wovoka), p. 93 (bio)
Wounded Knee Occupation
(Dennis Banks), p. 164 (bio), 600
(Mary Brave Bird), p. 189–190
(bio)   (Leonard Crow Dog), p. 152
(bio)
(Russell Means), p. 169–170 (bio),
628
Wovoka
(Kicking Bear), p. 99 (bio)
WPA
(Jim Barnes), 561
Writing
(Four Guns), the Indian needs no
writing, 420

YMCA
(Charles A. Eastman), p. 94 (bio)

Tribe Index

All numbers refer to quote numbers.

Acoma Pueblo, 637–642
Akagchemem, 482–483
"All Tribes," 723–729
Apache, 189–191, 484, 648–650, 717, 752–753
Arapaho, 192–196, 643–645
Assiniboine, 529, 652–654, 754

Blackfeet, 197, 457, 632–635
Brule Sioux, 211–217, 349, 455

Cherokee, 14–17, 25–29, 69–70, 71–75, 99–109, 127–130, 131–133, 145–149, 153, 154, 218–219, 221, 239–240, 342–343, 344–345, 366–370, 412–418, 444, 445–446, 449–451, 473, 557, 594–597, 659–663, 736
Cheyenne, 1–3, 134–140, 169–173, 297–300, 313–319, 351–352, 363–364, 428, 608–610, 643–645, 790–792
Chickasaw, 675–677
Chippewa, 43, 461–465, 526–528, 589, 598–599, 600–606, 702–704

Chiricahua Apache, 178–182, 241–244, 478–481
Choctaw, 44–48, 514–517, 561, 665–666
Coeur d'Alene, 670–674, 719
Comanche, 113–115, 312, 551–556
Cree, 529
Creek, 78–81, 82–86, 122–124, 245–246, 309, 401–406, 698–699, 749
Croatoan. See Lumbee
Crow, 187–188, 320–321, 730, 731
Crow Creek Sioux, 733

Dakota, 161–163, 278–280
Delaware, 10, 738–740

Gros Ventre, 632–635

Hidatsa, 390–395
Hopi, 396–398, 443, 531, 680–682
Hunkpapa Lakota, 259–268, 288

Iroquois, 11–13
Isleta Pueblo, 505

Kaw, 353–355, 700–701
Kiowa, 167–168, 247–252, 269, 594–597
Koyukon Athabascan, 485

Laguna, 612–614, 683–686
Lakota, 550
Lumbee, 466

Mandan, 125–126
Mashantucket Pequot, 678–679
Mescalero Apache, 631
Miami, 32–36
Mingo, 20–24
Miwok, 680–682
Modoc, 284–287, 667–669
Mohawk, 8–9, 467, 558–560, 585–586,
    587–588, 646–647, 741
Montagnais, 735

Navajo, 447–448, 468–472, 475–476,
    486–489, 507–508, 519–522, 523, 524,
    525, 536, 619–621, 648–650
Nez Perce, 155, 272–277, 324–329, 373
Northern Cheyenne, 562–568, 616–618

Oglala Sioux, 198–210, 293–296, 322,
    357–360, 365, 384–389, 420–421,
    590–593, 622–630a, 636, 655
Ojibway, 220, 651, 742–745, 746–748
Oklahoma Creek, 756
Omaha, 76, 323, 330–333, 361–362
Oneida, 486–489
Onondaga, 537–549
Osage, 700–701, 786
Ottawa, 18–19

Paiute, 301–305, 336, 611
Passamaquoddy, 503–504
Pawnee, 656–658, 687–697
Pawnee Loups, 118–121
Pima, 452–454, 499–502, 757
Pine Ridge Sioux, 758–760
Ponca, 231–238, 323, 490–495
Potawatomi, 77
Pottawattami, 255–258
Powhatan, 4–6, 761
Pueblos, 787

Quapaw, 518, 557

Sac, 49–58, 116–117
Sac/Fax, 307–308, 432–433, 496–498
Santee Sioux, 142–144, 156–160, 337–
    341, 732
Seminole, 141, 164–166
Seneca, 30–31, 37–42, 177, 222–230,
    474, 518, 664, 762
Shawnee, 59–67, 110–112
Shinnecock, 458–460
Shoshone, 150–152, 372, 763–767
Sioux, 289–292, 310–311, 350, 371,
    374–376, 377–378, 429–431, 434–437,
    456, 467, 484, 506, 532, 535, 584,
    607, 612–614, 651, 652–654, 705–716,
    750, 788, 791
Sisseton, 334–335
Sisseton-Wahpeton Dakota, 615
67 Tribes, 718
Southern Cheyenne, 253–254
Spokane, 174–175, 176, 719, 768
Standing Rock Sioux, 509–513, 569–
    583
Stoney, 399–400
Suquamish, 87–98

Teton, 769–771
Tlingit, 477
Tohono O'odham, 720–722
Tonto Apache, 270–271
Tulalip, 530

Ute, 189–191

Wabanakis, 419
Wailaki, 734
Wampanoag, 7
Wanapum, 183–186
Warm Springs Apache, 422–427
Winnebago, 346–348, 772–780
Wintu, 781–783
Wyandot, 784

Yahi, 356
Yakima, 438–442
Yankton Dakota, 407–411
Yankton Sioux, 281–283
Yavapai, Apache, 379–383

About the Editor

HOWARD J. LANGER is the author of several articles and three books, including *Who Puts the Print on the Page?* (1976) and *Directory of Speakers* (1981). Having worked in publishing as a reporter, editor, and director of publications, he now works as a free-lance writer and college journalism instructor.